ENCOUNTERING PENNYWISE

Bernadette Marie Calafell, Marina Levina,
and Kendall R. Phillips, General Editors

ENCOUNTERING PENNYWISE

Critical Perspectives on Stephen King's *IT*

Edited by Whitney S. May

University Press of Mississippi / Jackson

The University Press of Mississippi is the scholarly publishing agency of
the Mississippi Institutions of Higher Learning: Alcorn State University,
Delta State University, Jackson State University, Mississippi State University,
Mississippi University for Women, Mississippi Valley State University,
University of Mississippi, and University of Southern Mississippi.

www.upress.state.ms.us

The University Press of Mississippi is a member
of the Association of University Presses.

First printing 2022

∞

Library of Congress Control Number: 2022941007
Hardback ISBN 978-1-4968-4222-0
Trade paperback ISBN 978-1-4968-4223-7
Epub single ISBN 978-1-4968-4224-4
Epub institutional ISBN 978-1-4968-4225-1
PDF single ISBN 978-1-4968-4226-8
PDF institutional ISBN 978-1-4968-4227-5

British Library Cataloging-in-Publication Data available

CONTENTS

Section III: Counterclaims

Section IV: Counterfeits

ACKNOWLEDGMENTS

As someone who works so dedicatedly with circuses, I like to think of my time as well spent leaping between three tremendously vibrant rings. In the first are my friends and colleagues at the department of English at Texas State University, including Katie Kapurch, Kate McClancy, Vicki Smith, Rob Tally, Julie McCormick Weng, Nancy and Steve Wilson, Jon Marc Smith, and Chad Hammett, as well as Scott Christensen and the Women Who Write: Shannon Shaw, Amanda Scott, Ali Salzmann, and Meg Griffitts. Thank you all for your unprecedented support when I said I wanted to Do A Thing.

In the second ring are my professors and friends at the University of Texas. My thanks go to the entire American Studies department, particularly to Alex Beasley, Randy Lewis, Lauren Gutterman, and Cary Cordova for their unwavering belief in this project. Thank you to Janet Davis for her unprecedented ringmaster-ing when I most needed guidance, and to my classmates in her spring, 2020 AMS 386, who cheered me on in this work—over Zoom in the end! Thank you to all of my AMS friends, but especially to those who lifted me up when I entered "Charlie Conspiracy" meme territory: my cohort Hartlyn Haynes, Coyote Shook, Kameron Dunn, and Cooper Weissman, as well as Taylor Johnson Karahan, Kristen Wilson, and Holly Genovese.

And to my third, center ring: my gratitude goes as always to my mother April, and to my sister Aspen and brother-in-law Jordan, for the seemingly endless wellspring of their particular brand of frank encouragement. Thank you Trista and David, whose excitement reminded *me* to be excited. And thank you to my partner Bahar Tahamtani, who inspires me to see the leafling and flower.

Finally, none of this would have been possible without the rigor and vigor of every single affiliate of the Horror and Monstrosity Studies Series and each contributor in these pages. Thank you for all of your hard work and tireless optimism.

ENCOUNTERING PENNYWISE

COUNTERPUNCH

IT as Modern Punch and Judy Show

WHITNEY S. MAY

The "King of Horror" has confided on his official website that the inspiration for his twenty-second novel *IT* struck, rather unexpectedly (if appropriately), while he crossed a bridge. As his worn boots "trip-trapped" against the wooden planks, reminding him of "The Three Billy-Goats Gruff," Stephen King toyed with thoughts of trolls and bridges, monsters and crossings, cities, adulthood, and what lurks beneath it all. He found himself unable to shake these connections, mulling them over for three years before committing to the project. Reflecting on the book's persistent haunting of his thoughts, King reasons: "A good idea is like a yo-yo. It may go to the end of its string, but it doesn't die there; it only sleeps. Eventually it rolls back up into your palm."[1]

When King's idea respooled and *IT* debuted in 1986, featuring a monster whose preferred form was a murderous clown rather than a troll, it forever changed the legacy of the literary clown. Then, in 1990, the *IT* TV miniseries visually and heartily cemented this alteration forevermore into the pop-cultural consciousness before retreating into the periphery to enjoy a cult status among horror fans. Twenty-seven years later, *IT* returned for a sensational two-part film reboot (2017, 2019). Not only is this reappearance curiously in keeping with Pennywise's twenty-seven-year hibernation cycle in the novel, but it also trends alongside a fascinating resurgence of the "evil" clown figure in popular culture. From John Watts's *Clown* (2014) to two seasons of *American Horror Story* (*Freak Show*, from 2014–15, and *Cult*, in 2017), from *Joker* (2019) to the clown-laden political imagery surrounding the 2016 US presidential election and its subsequent administration, Pennywise's reemergence seems peculiarly and unnervingly timely. One must wonder if, like King's yo-yo illustration, the "evil" clown only ever *appears* to lie dormant before returning, continually—perhaps uncomfortably—close at hand.

Although he admits that his original configuration of the novel's antagonist might have been a bridge troll, King's choice to deploy (primarily) a
nightmarish clown to haunt the children of Derry both literally and figu-
ratively confirms the long history of the clown as a figure of subversive
potential. As Beryl Hugill remarks of the most antiquated clowns, "The court
jester was a fool licensed to speak his mind only in the disguise of non-
sense."[2] Benjamin Radford, arguably the definitive expert on "bad clowns,"
updates the parameters of this program to include modern manifestations
of the same impulse: despite de rigueur loyalty to their employers, be these
medieval kings or modern ringmasters, clowns "would often mock those
they served; a jester might gently (and safely) rib a king about his weight
or wealth, for example, while a circus clown might make a joke about how
expensive the cotton candy sold at the concession stand is."[3] It is out of
this dynamic understanding of the clown as cultural interlocutor that this
volume has emerged.

Drawing upon existing scholarship on *IT*, which, if it examines the novel
at all, tends to prioritize the televisual[4] and cinematic[5] adaptations,[6] this
collection considers the pronounced cultural fluctuations of *IT*'s legacies by
centering the novel within the theoretical frameworks that animate it and
ensure its literary (and pop-cultural) persistence. One of the key interests
of this volume is an exploration of the ways the novel, so like its antagonist, replicates (or disavows) the icons of various canons and categories in
order to accomplish specific psychological and cultural work. Each chapter
herein attends to the myriad ways that *IT*, through its various adaptations
and its haunting villain Pennywise, actively subverts the dominant codes of
the eras under which the monstrous It operates in order to speak to these
codes' atemporal longevity and undeniable plasticity. If, as Mark Dery so
succinctly predicts, "[i]n our postmodern media culture, where the carnival
never ends, the reign of the evil clown is permanent,"[7] then this volume
explores the contours of this permanence as a means to interrogate our
unwavering attachment to our best-known evil clown. Much like the novel's
infamous Ritual of Chüd, the circuitous, psychically charged battle of wills
between the band of protagonists in the novel and Pennywise, this collection
recognizes that the key to *IT*'s longevity lies in its symbiotic relationship with
the audience that interpellates it. In this volume, we read the protagonists'
constellations of countermoves against Pennywise as productive outlines
of critique effectuated by the richness of the clown's reflective power. The
essays in this volume are therefore thematically arranged into a series of four
categories of "counters," where each supplies a specific critical lens through
which to view Pennywise's disruptions of both culture and cultural critique.

Naturally, then, this collection begins by seeking to place *IT* within the wider contexts of post-World War II American history in which the novel was incubated. Section I, "Countercurrents," considers the flexible temporalities of *IT*. These offer especially fertile terrain because of the very narrative structure that animates the novel, which flits fluidly between decades as its protagonists—the seven members of the Losers' Club—are hunted first as children in the 1950s and then as adults in the 1980s by a creature wearing the guise of Pennywise the Dancing Clown. Although King's 1986 novel and the 1990 miniseries share this timeline, the recent theatrical adaptations adjust it considerably, effectively advancing it another full generation by resituating the children's scenes in the 1980s and entering the adult Losers into their second and final battle with Pennywise at the time of the films' releases. The first essay in this section maintains that these authorial/directorial decisions make space for nuanced discussions, especially, of the moral panics that inform each cycle. Focusing specifically on the satanic panic of the 1980s and its complicated relationship with various child sexual-abuse scandals through recovered-memory therapy, Fernando Gabriel Pagnoni Berns points to the different ways that King's novel and its television adaptation were informed by the moral panics of the decade. As horror fiction taps into real concerns, anxieties, and fears of its time, Berns determines, Pennywise is the perfect embodiment of the abstract horrors that framed each tumultuous era.

In the second essay, Erin Giannini interrogates the adjusted temporalities of *IT*'s various adaptations to get a clearer picture of the intergenerational traumas reverberating between them all. While she finds that the thematics of the novel remain fairly intact, the 1980s setting allows for differences in both the social matrix in which the characters operate and elements of their characterization, emphasizing some elements while downplaying others. She expertly concludes that while the theatrical decision to reconceptualize *IT* as a Generation X story for the recent films rather than leaving it a Baby Boomer narrative is significant in its own right, it also worryingly suggests that, like Pennywise itself, the socioeconomic and interpersonal dynamics of King's text, particularly where legacies of abuse are concerned, transcend such categorical distinctions.

The focus of the third chapter shifts from time to form. The central question of Diganta Roy's essay is whether and to what extent the perspective of the children in *IT* interrogates and subverts the adult worldview and logic in order to discover new possibilities of interacting with our everyday reality. Roy attends to the narratological perspective of the children in *IT* in conjunction with other horror texts like Robert McCammon's *Boy's Life* (1991) and the hit television series *Stranger Things* (2016–) in order to understand not only issues of child abuse and violence but also to gain a clearer picture of how the child confronts and resolves such issues, psychologically and emotionally.

Section II, "Countercultures," follows form into its antithesis, including essays that analyze alterity and abjection as these appear in and animate King's novel. Margaret J. Yankovich's essay draws from a host of critical perspectives to define and interpret modes of body horror within the text, including queer theory, the emergent field of monster theory, and fat studies. Looking at *IT* within the contexts of body horror and abjection, Yankovich susses out the extent to which unruly, revolting bodies *in revolt* are mobilized by the narrative. Ultimately, her essay highlights the ways in which the text reflects and perpetuates the predominant cultural attitudes toward unruly bodies that are marked by a pronounced fear of corporeal transgression.

Amylou Ahava's essay locates intriguing parallels between *IT* and King's other works, namely, *Carrie* (1974), *The Shining* (1977), and *Cujo* (1981), in their presentations of disability. Although she indicates that disability studies scholarship tends to center on the novel's more-prevalent bully Henry Bowers, a violent boy whose crimes include carving part of his name into the stomach of one of the Losers and murdering his own father, Ahava re-centers Henry's lackey Patrick Hockstetter in this conversation, concluding that a character study on Patrick allows for a better understanding of the character's importance in King's oeuvre. Shifting the lens from Henry to the lesser-discussed sociopath, she argues, offers not only a different analysis of disability in King's text, but also presents further insight into Pennywise as a galvanizing force behind abjection within the novel—and one rivaled only by more realistic impulses toward violence.

Triangulating *IT* through critical theorist Georges Bataille's (1897–1962) work on violence, eroticism, and sacred experience, Keith Currie examines the townsfolk of Derry, especially their complicity regarding the town's periodic child-murder sprees. This complicity, Currie argues by way of Bataille, is manifested in sacred and sacrificial spectacles, festivals, and sporting events, and in the darker examples of human industry such as the mass slaughter of livestock or even the destruction of the natural environment. Departing from Bataille's format, Currie concludes, King's novel offers an escape vector from such a relationship, albeit one that dooms the town to the slow demise experienced by any number of American towns and cities in the post-industrial era.

Section III, "Counterclaims," presents studies of memory, and more specifically, the terms at which the effacement of individual memory sets the stage for broader discussions of responsibility. Penny Crofts's prescient essay considers *IT* as a meditation on the significance of context in the tolerance of, and failure to prevent, evil. Crofts highlights the ways in which the inaction of bystanders through theories of organizational in/action and structured irresponsibility mirror one another across real and fictional bounds. Taking as its case study the framework of *IT* and the Larry Nassar sexual assault scandal, Crofts's chapter reads the spaces between both in order to chart the monstrous capabilities of culpability and complicity in real and imagined spaces. While details of these harms arouse cries of horror and "Never again!" Crofts reflects that it seems, as with the characters of *IT*, we are subject to a form of amnesia, reflected and reinforced by the law, whereby the systems which facilitate, encourage, or tolerate these harms are able to continue across time and place.

Jeff Ambrose reads memories as monstrous when they are not responsibly attended to. His essay traces a key moment for each of the Losers in how their memories become monsters. Ambrose shows that it is only through the Losers' Club itself, their form of group therapy and confrontation, that the Losers are finally able to defeat Pennywise. In remembering together and facing their traumas, they win. However, the fact that the novel ends with the remaining Losers and the townspeople forgetting all about "It" begs the question: why would Pennywise and the resulting horrors, their biggest possible traumas, be so easily forgotten? Considering hierarchies of memory at play in the novel, Ambrose suggests that it might be our more personal traumas, the intimate ones that often happen behind closed doors, that stick in our memory and morph into monsters.

While Ambrose's essay demonstrates the monstrous potential of forgetting, Daniel P. Compora considers the dangers of longing to remember. *IT* characterizes toxic nostalgia at its most rampant, Compora determines, in that the novel and film versions of *IT* use the landscape decade of the 1980s differently to convey the dark side of nostalgia. His essay determines that where both iterations illustrate that regardless of which era holds the nostalgic value for the characters, it is a burden they carry with them, so that nostalgia itself is as much an obstacle to overcome as Pennywise the clown. This means that their defeat of Pennywise is a symbolic victory over the nostalgic curse from which they suffer.

If the previous section investigated the potentiality and pervasiveness of memory, this volume's final segment, Section IV, "Counterfeits," follows this line of inquiry into the way the past is remembered collectively, especially where individual and cultural memories are effaced in the interest of maintaining the historical status quo. Hannah Lina Schneeberger and Maria Wiegel read Pennywise and the "Killer Clown" John Wayne Gacy as a refraction of the American Dream and its ideological import. A significant symptom of this dynamic, Wiegel and Schneeberger maintain, is visible in the sudden increase in American production of documentaries and movies on serial killers. Though Gacy and Pennywise share many characteristics, not in the least their function as a symptom of the toxicity of the American Dream, they must also be distinguished from one another. Their essay, therefore, interprets Pennywise with regard to his function as a fictional character, which is, as they argue, an even more coherent reflection on society than its real life equivalent.

Finally, Shannon S. Shaw reads Pennywise as a nightmarish outline in which the colonial reign of terror is embodied and through which the trauma of colonial destruction seeks retribution. Although King situates this revenge in a nostalgic Norman Rockwell setting and uses a classic emblem of childhood fancy to represent the ruse that was the Rockwellian image, Shaw determines that under the surface of this picturesque Americana, the truths of colonialism boil, and Pennywise consumes the archetype of American idealism: willful innocence. Ultimately, Shaw finds that the performativity of the ideal that is the American Dream functions as a veil under which to hide its very real terrors. It is, as it seems, altogether fitting that the curse of the town of Derry manifests itself as a clown, representing the absurdity at the heart of the American zeitgeist.

Although Pennywise's classificatory aesthetic lies formally within the grotesque whiteface clown category, this volume understands Pennywise's saturnalian function as something more akin to a Mr. Punch, the antiquated clown figure at the heart of Punch and Judy shows historically known for the magnitudes of his brutality that both chafed against and exacerbated the comedic dimensions of his performances, his vicious slapstick often punctuated by his signature tagline: "*That's* the way to do it!" Mr. Punch's theatrical template resonates remarkably well with King's similarly homicidal clown character. Take, for example, two of Pennywise's balloon gaffes in the novel: after hunting down Eddie Kaspbrak, a hypochondriac (seemingly) asthmatic, Pennywise comically taunts him with a balloon bearing the bulletin "ASTHMA MEDICINE CAUSES LUNG CANCER!"[8] After tuning into Beverly's miserable thoughts about her father's incestuous attentions imbricated with concern that she and her friends can never hope to be free of the clown haunting them, Pennywise dispatches another cartoonish balloon her direction bearing the heartlessly humorous affirmative: "THAT'S WIGHT, WABBIT."[9] Both encounters rely upon Pennywise's intimate knowledge of each character's specific fears, which the clown then affirms with a cruelty that is magnified by the seemingly farcical nature of its delivery. Pennywise's ability to comedically externalize the private fears of It's targeted characters demonstrates the clown's capacity to invade and invert the ontological frameworks that organize their interior lives—so that every encounter with Pennywise constitutes, eventually, a parodic exhumation of secret, perhaps otherwise unacknowledged vulnerabilities made available for anyone's—*everyone's*—perusal.

Viewing Pennywise in the light of Mr. Punch, whose "appeal lies in his hyperbolic everyman reaction to common abuses we can all relate to,"[10] opens up the critical possibilities of King's novel as both a lens and mirror through which to understand the culture that collectively and continually reimagines it. As I've written elsewhere, the clown, broadly speaking, functions as a mirror: "It at once regards, and is regarded by, the audience it encounters, unsettling the delineations between audience and performer, subject and object, by way of an otherworldly association that recalls the uncanny."[11] What we bring to and take from encounters with our clowns affords us rich terrain for questioning what we interpret as satire, and what we do not—and cannot—misunderstand as such.

In the adjustments to the scary clown figure that have occurred since Ronald Reagan's presidency (and *IT*'s publication), Scott Poole reads fervid tensions in the ways in which American citizens understand and organize their sociopolitical lives. "The figure of the homicidal clown," he concludes, "lethal, and unpredictable–has become, since the 1980s, the psychotic circus atmosphere that embodies the things so inarguably true about the contradictions, the insanity, of American violence."[12] These tensions have particularly left our contemporary political climate, naturally and yet still disturbingly, mired in a certain brand of "anarchic conservatism"[13] within which the clown figure thrives. It is, perhaps, not especially surprising that Pennywise should reappear during the Morning in America and then again, twenty-seven years later, during whatever it is that we call our "now." On the *IT* reboots as perfectly attuned to the politics of their time, Theresa L. Geller notes that *IT* enters Pennywise's rebirths into to a timeline that coincides reliably with moments of political demonization only to favor those who *do* the demonizing with Pennywise's apparent agreement and complicity. She argues that the novel's "revisionist backstory exempts Derry's (Euro-American) townspeople from collective responsibility for enacting the inevitable violence that is the logical endpoint of political demonology, aided by an alien influence that affects mass historical forgetting, and with it a tamping down of affect, particularly sympathy for others"[14]—a fraught relationship that the films, incubated in their contemporary political climate, only illustrate in sharper relief.

Between these two eras—between Reagan and now, between the period of Morning in America and this strange Mourning Period in America—lies a landscape of fear appropriately peopled (or monstered) by clowns. In the disruptive yet generative spirit of the clown, King's antagonist in particular both invokes violence and illuminates; mocks, and out of this ridicule, reveals the buried truth of the matter. This is the spirit of this volume, which understands *IT* and its antagonist as a source of profound exposure and potential for rebirth. Indeed, after over thirty years, our relationship with Pennywise remains in as much circuitous, sublime disarray as it does renewal. The heady result of this relationship, as the chapters here understand, is that all encounters with Pennywise are always-already counters, too, be these countercurrents, countercultures, counterclaims, or counterfeits.

All of the essays in this volume are nuanced and multidimensional, tracing the literary lineages of *IT* using theoretical constructions of gender, (dis)ability, race, sexuality, and class to answer broader questions about what makes this story of a ragtag group of children facing off against a demonic clown so rigorously lasting across three decades and counting. The essays herein can be read in harmony or piecemeal, but taken together, they present a composite sketch of the subversive power of King's most frightening antagonist. What's more, they constitute a keen self-reflection in the hopes of mining and miming usable—albeit stark—truth from the depths of horror.

In one of the many scenes in the novel wherein Pennywise inflicts pain while wearing a toothy grin, It soberly intones: "Before removing the mote from thy neighbor's eye, attend the beam in thine own."[15] In this volume, we take the clown's advice, and invite you to do the same.

Notes

1. Stephen King, "*IT*: Inspiration," *StephenKing.com: The Official Website*, https://stephenking.com/library/novel/it_inspiration.html, accessed May 11, 2020.

2. Beryl Hugill. *Bring On the Clowns* (Secaucus, NJ: Chartwell Books, 1980), 14.

3. Benjamin Radford, *Bad Clowns* (Albuquerque, New Mexico: University of New Mexico Press, 2016), 9.

4. Mark Browning, *Stephen King on the Small Screen* (Bristol, UK: Intellect Books, 2011).

5. Mark Browning, *Stephen King on the Big Screen* (Bristol, UK: Intellect Books, 2009).

6. Although impressively expansive and informative, neither of Sharon A. Russel's edited collections (*Stephen King: A Critical Companion* nor *Revisiting Stephen King: A Critical Companion*, both from Greenwood Press and published in 1996 and 2002, respectively) address *IT* at all. Likewise, Marcia Amidon Lüsted's *How to Analyze the Works of Stephen King* (ABDO Publishing, 2011) follows this same track.

7. Mark Dery, *The Pyrotechnic Insanitarium: American Culture on the Brink* (New York: Grove Press, 1999), 85.

8. Stephen King, *IT* (New York: Scribner, 2019), 569.

9. King, *IT*, 582.

10. Radford, 17.

11. Whitney S. May, "Spectrality and Spectatorship: Heterotopic Doubling in Cinematic Circuses," in *The Big Top on the Big Screen: Explorations of Circus in Film*, ed. Teresa Cutler-Broyles, 37 (Jefferson, NC: McFarland & Company, 2020).

12. Scott Poole, "'Let's Put a Smile on That Face': Trump, the Psychotic Clown, and the History of American Violence," in *Make America Hate Again: Trump-Era Horror and the Politics of Fear*, ed. Victoria McCollum (Routledge, 2019), 30.

13. Poole.

14. Theresa L. Geller, "Shilling Pennywise: Chump Change in Trump's (trans)America," in *Make America Hate Again: Trump-Era Horror and the Politics of Fear*, ed. Victoria McCollum (Routledge, 2019), 42.

15. King, *IT*, 598.

References

Browning, Mark. *Stephen King on the Big Screen*. Bristol, UK: Intellect Books, 2009.

Browning, Mark. *Stephen King on the Small Screen*. Bristol, UK: Intellect Books, 2011.

Dery, Mark. *The Pyrotechnic Insanitarium: American Culture on the Brink*. New York: Grove Press, 1999.

Geller, Theresa L. "Shilling Pennywise: Chump Change in Trump's (trans)America." In *Make America Hate Again: Trump-Era Horror and the Politics of Fear*, edited by Victoria McCollum, 32–53. Abingdon-on-Thames, UK: Routledge, 2019.

Hugill, Beryl. *Bring On the Clowns*. Secaucus, NJ: Chartwell Books, 1980.

King, Stephen. *IT*. New York: Viking Press, 1986; reprint, New York: Scribner, 2019. All citations from reprint.

King, Stephen. "*IT*: Inspiration." *StephenKing.com: The Official Website*. https://stephenk ing.com/library/novel/it_inspiration.html, accessed May 11, 2020.

Lüsted, Marcia Amidon. *How to Analyze the Works of Stephen King. Essential Critiques*. Edina, MN: ABDO Publishing, 2011.

May, Whitney S. "Spectrality and Spectatorship: Heterotopic Doubling in Cinematic Circuses." In *The Big Top on the Big Screen: Explorations of the Circus in Film*, edited by Teresa Cutler-Broyles, 31–46. Jefferson, NC: McFarland & Company, 2020.

Poole, Scott. "'Let's Put a Smile on That Face': Trump, the Psychotic Clown, and the History of American Violence." In *Make America Hate Again: Trump-Era Horror and the Politics of Fear*, edited by Victoria McCollum, 19–31. Abingdon-on-Thames, UK: Routledge, 2019.

Radford, Benjamin. *Bad Clowns*. Albuquerque, NM: University of New Mexico Press, 2016.

Russell, Sharon A. *Stephen King: A Critical Companion*. Critical Companions to Popular Contemporary Writers. Santa Barbara, CA: Greenwood Press, 1996.

Section I

Countercurrents

Chapter 1

REMEMBERING HALF-FORGOTTEN MEMORIES OF DERRY

The Moral Panics of the 1980s

FERNANDO GABRIEL PAGNONI BERNS

One of the most baffling aspects of Stephen King's *IT* (1986) is that all but one of the novel's main characters—Ben Hanscom, Richie Tozier, Bill Denbrough, Beverly Marsh, Stan Uris, and Eddie Kaspbrak—have forgotten all about the horrors they faced as children in the small town of Derry, and it takes a fateful series of phone calls from Mike Hanlon, the only one whose memory remains, to summon the others back to Derry. There, as kids, all seven battled It, a supernatural presence that exploits the fears of its victims. Many years later, the entity returns to begin its murder spree anew and Mike, the only one of the Losers' Club to remain in Derry, calls up the six former members of the group and reminds them of their childhood promise to return if the killings start again.

In this chapter, I argue that King's novel was modeled, in part, by the different moral panics sweeping the US through the 1980s, especially those related to recovered memory therapy. Half-buried memories of past traumas and horrors, the supernatural, children's sexuality, and even the presence of murderous killer clowns driving vans and assaulting children were part of living through the first half of the 1980s. As horror fiction taps into real concerns, anxieties, and fears of its time, It's guise of Pennywise is the perfect embodiment of a "risk society" that shapes its abstract fears into the form of moral panics.

SIX PHONE CALLS: REMEMBERING THE TRAUMA

The "Six Phone Calls" chapter establishes that most of the surviving children, now adults in 1985, have forgotten all (or most) of the details of the horrible events that happened to them in the 1950s. When Mike makes the titular six calls, his conversation with Richie goes as follows: "'How much do you remember, Rich?' Mike asked him. 'Very little,' Rich said, and then paused. 'Enough, I suppose.'"[1] This "enough" points to traces of anxiety or dread still pervading his life as an adult. Moments later, Mike calls Ben. Drinking at a bar to obliterate the horrors of his now-found evocations, Ben tells the bartender:

> "The matter?" Ben Hanscom laughed. "Why, not too much. I had a call from an old friend tonight. Guy named Mike Hanlon. I'd forgotten all about him, Ricky Lee, but that didn't scare me much. After all, I was just a kid when I knew him, and kids forget things, don't they? Sure they do. You bet your fur. What scared me was getting about halfway over here and realizing that it wasn't just Mike I'd forgotten about—I'd forgotten *everything* about being a kid."[2]

Much as with Ben and Richie, everyone except Mike has forgotten all about Derry and their traumatic encounters with the terrifying Pennywise, even if anxiety has become a companion to their lives. In an earlier scene, Stanley tells his wife: "I wake up from these dreams and think, 'My whole pleasant life has been nothing but the eye of some storm I don't understand.'"[3] Those who return to Derry do so with only the dimmest memories of what had happened decades ago, remembering only half-forgotten horrors and little else.

This narrative device on King's part seems slightly arbitrary and might appear to steal some of the novel's power. After all, the traumatic aspects haunting the kids from Derry would be emphasized if they were able to remember, with clarity, what had happened to all them. Remembering clearly what took place in their lives decades ago would allow them to be haunted by the ghosts of their past throughout their lives, a beloved trope in horror fiction. Forgetting all about the past might seem to add little in terms of narrative weight; however, a closer look at the novel's connection to the era's anxieties reveals the import of King's decision to write characters besieged by childhood traumas they can't seem to name.

The now-adult Losers are, indeed, haunted by trauma, even if they remember little of it. Indeed, repressed, not-quite-known trauma is one of the most important aspects of *IT*. The horror the kids faced in their youth is trapped in their subconscious and, once opened, memories flood the mind with indescribable horror. For example, after his phone call with Mike, Richie broods: "Oh Christ, that was nothing he wanted to know, not at this late date, but it didn't seem to matter in the slightest. Something was happening down there in the vaults, down there where Rich Tozier kept his own personal collection of Golden Oldies. Doors were opening."[4] Richie starts vomiting after hearing his former friend's voice, an action that reveals deep-seated anxieties. Trauma, anxiety, and cyclical repetition are all elements present in real accounts of psychological healing.[5] People unable to properly cure their traumatic past experiences are obliged to repeat a never-ending cycle, just as the Losers' Club of Derry do. The repressed trauma nests inside damaged minds that perpetuate the ritual of violence and, as such, it is fitting that the kids, now as adults, return to Derry to stop a new cycle of murder, chaos, and violence. Thus, past trauma and repetition is properly used as a main narrative mechanism within *IT*'s pages.

Therefore, while representing so many of the main characters as *forgetting their traumatic pasts* may appear to rob the story of some of its impact as a metaphor for trauma and PTSD, in truth, remembering trauma can be linked to amnesia, where the patient forgets many aspects of their previous painful experiences. Psychogenic amnesia "is caused by events whose psychological or emotional meaning produces memory loss without damaging the brain"[6] and is "characterized by sudden onset in response to stress, inability to remember precipitating events, loss of personal identity and extensive retrograde amnesia."[7] The phenomenon of amnesia is even hinted at throughout King's novel. For example, after his phone call, Ben agonizes to his bartender: "'I mean I'd forgotten all about it,' he said, and rapped his knuckles lightly on the bar for emphasis. 'Did you ever hear, Ricky Lee, of having an amnesia so complete you didn't even know you had amnesia?'"[8] Yet amnesia and denial are not terms linked solely to psychopathologies and brain damage, but also to the phenomenon of *moral panics*. Certainly, amnesia, denial, and repression of abuse were common terms through the moral panics sweeping the US during the conservative Reagan era.[9]

King took four years to write *IT*, working from 1981 to 1985 to complete the story[10] amidst one of the biggest moral panics America ever faced, one that linked fears about organized child abuse, missing and murdered children, satanism, alleged survivors of ritual abuse and sex rings, and sweeping changes therapeutic history where repressed trauma was concerned.[11] The first half of the 1980s witnessed an apparent explosion of people talking about children in danger and adults having the keys to past traumatic events buried deep down in their memories. Recovered memory therapy rested on both the assumption that horrifying childhoods were psychologically obliterated by adults ignoring traumas they experienced in their youth on one hand as well as the real existence of satanic rings lurking in America on the other. As Richard Beck argues persuasively, recovered memory therapy of the period discarded real facts "and replaced [them] with horror-movie plots,"[12] like the one presented in *IT*.

Written throughout the first half of the 1980s, *IT* eerily taps into the moral panics of the decade. Pennywise the Dancing Clown is the embodiment of forgotten horrors without discernible form that are at the bottom of the subconscious, mixing together children's sexuality, coulrophobia, and domestic abuse.

MORAL PANICS IN THE 1980s: REPRESSED MEMORIES AND KILLER CLOWNS

It all started with the McMartin Preschool. In the summer of 1983, Judy Johnson, the mother of a child who had attended the McMartin Preschool in Manhattan Beach told the police that her two-year-old son had been molested by one of his teachers. A month later, police arrested the accused teacher and charged him with child abuse before alerting parents of McMartin students of the investigation and soliciting their assistance.[13] Warned that their children may have been abused, many parents started to read against the grain and interpreted, in any anomaly in their children's behavior, the mark of sexual abuse. Their reports reached the media and, soon, updates about many abused children dominated TV news and newspapers. A sample of this coverage includes KABC reporter Wayne Satz announcing that children "had been keeping a grotesque secret of being sexually abused and made to appear in pornographic films while in the preschool's care, and of being forced to witness the mutilation and killing of animals to scare the kids into being silent."[14]

The McMartin Preschool was not alone. After the news about child abuse was brought to light, it seemed that many elementary schools were led by "satanists" posing as schoolteachers or directors. Horror stories start to spring up everywhere from Minneapolis, Pennsylvania, or New Jersey to El Paso. It was not a localized geography, but a sickness that invaded the US, and its consequences took root in the minds of Americans, with stories increasing in horrors. Although the reports were at first about children abused by their teachers, the horror escalated, adding the mutilation and killing of animals, the killing and eating of newborn babies, sex rings trafficking children as slaves and for child pornography, and, linking all these disparate threads, satanic cults leading the schools. Behind the façade of any prestigious school, there was a satanic leader passing as an innocent director. Amidst the epidemic of child abuse reports, "day care directors were advising their employees to avoid physical contact with children if at all possible."[15]

According to Kenneth Thompson, the phenomenon of a moral panic has five key elements:

1. Something or someone is defined as a threat to values or interests.
2. This threat is depicted in an easily recognizable form by the media.
3. There is a rapid buildup of public concern.
4. There is a response from authorities or opinion-makers.
5. The panic recedes or results in social changes.[16]

The fifth point is especially interesting when analyzing King's *IT*. As the novel unfolds, it is clear that Pennywise, the monstrous killer clown, works as an embodiment of moral panic, resurfacing once and again to scare adults and children alike.[17] As Jason Hughes, Julian Petley, and Chas Critcher recognize, the nature of moral panics is cyclical, "responding to patterns of social reaction."[18] Critcher adds that moral panics are presented as the consequence "of some (hypothetically universal, endlessly cyclical) feature of social life, namely panickyness."[19] Every twenty-seven years, the monstrous entity called It, sometimes in the form of Pennywise, returns. In It's wake, a string of crimes, disappearances, and rumors remain, many of them left in ambiguity. King's novel evokes this state of alarm yet in undefined terms: "In the year 1930, for instance—the year the Black Spot[20] burned—there were better than one hundred and seventy child disappearances in Derry—and you must remember that these are only the disappearances which were reported to the police and thus documented."[21] Children have continuously disappeared in Derry, their exact number left unclear. Later, "during 1958, a hundred and twenty-seven children, ranging in age from three to nineteen, were reported missing in Derry."[22]

Much like with moral panics, there are explanations related to its social and cultural context. The disappearances of children in Derry through 1930 could be motivated by the hunger brought by the Great Depression, for example.[23] Still, as the characters address, this explanation is not enough to explain away all the half-forgotten horror. Also, the exact number of years that bring back Pennywise is left unclear; "Derry is a violent place to live in an ordinary year. But every twenty-seven years—although the cycle has never been perfectly exact—that violence has escalated to a furious peak."[24] Like moral panics, the supernatural entity's returns do not follow a concrete length of years: it merely resurfaces from time to time to produce a new wave of scares.

Why children? Moral panics do not necessarily involve children, but history has recurrently pointed at children and youngsters at the center of the phenomenon, both as victims and victimizers. Thompson explains, "The activities of 'youth' in particular have often been presented as potentially immoral and a threat to the established way of life."[25] Youth independence in the 1950s, for example, led to moral panics about youth crime where independent adolescents were depicted as criminals running around in gangs and doing drugs for the sake of being rebellious. Moral panics about youth lurk at the margins of *IT*, as the novel's timeline straddles the '50s and the '80s. To the parents of Derry, children can be mischievous and spread their bad habits to "normal" kids. For example, Sonia Kaspbrak worries incessantly about how "healthy" her son Eddie's friends are, with "health" becoming shorthand for "good": "Eddie's 'friends,' who were probably teaching him to smoke cigarettes in spite of his asthma, his 'friends' who had such an unhealthy hold over him that they were all he talked about when he came home for the evening, his 'friends' who got his arm broken."[26] In other passages from the novel, children are depicted also as potential victims of moral panics regarding strangers. Ben's mother tells him: "One other thing. I don't want you going around alone. You know enough not to accept candy or rides from strangers—we both agree that you're no fool—and you're big for your age, but a grown man, particularly a crazy one, can overpower a child if he really wants to. When you go to the park or the library, go with one of your friends."[27] Derry itself seems to be trapped into moral panics of its own: when the badly decomposed body of a boy shows up in 1960, police suspect that the kid may be a victim of a "child molester."[28] Child molestation is mentioned later as a possible cause of children's disappearance.[29] All these precautions are part of growing up, but are especially common in times of moral panics.

The Reaganomic 1980s were rife with moral panics. Ronald Reagan's presidency was marked by a strong backlash to the progressive mind of the 1970s (feminism, gay rights, policies of the welfare state, etc.) while family values and the conservative mind were reenthroned. The "Just Say No" campaign, with Nancy Reagan as the visible head, is a ready example, as well as the perceived dangers brought by the empowerment of female sexuality, and a particular attention to the (supposed) deterioration of the nuclear family.[30] The latter, so important to the neoliberal politics of the 1980s, was fertile terrain for the resurfacing of moral panics concerning simplistic divisions between those belonging to Evil forces and those who were Good. King's novel was not indifferent to this slippage between "decent" and indecency." The Falcon, a pub with a clientele consisting of bus riders and truckers becomes, at the first years of the 1980s, a gay bar without the owner even realizing it.[31] It seems there is always a heart of moral "corruption" (at least, for the conservative mind) beating behind the surface of "macho" pubs or noble schools. Soon, rumors (all false) about the Falcon start to circulate, pointing it as a place where men go to get "blow jobs in the bathrooms."[32] Moral panics need "the location of normative boundaries between the respectable and the deviant."[33] Reagan revived moral panics concerning the safety of streets for children, as the outside was supposedly filled with drug sellers, gangs, and other vices presented as the consequence of the moral relaxation of the chaotic 1970s:

> Over the course of the 1970s conservatives made the endangered child into a kind of political and rhetorical abstraction, a way of thinking about the country and its citizens that could help advance a wide range of policy initiatives. They opposed the counterculture on the grounds that rock and roll caused adolescents to lose respect for family life. They promoted the War on Drugs with racially tinged morality tales about addicted inner-city mothers and, crucially, the "superpredator" "crack babies" to whom those mothers supposedly gave birth.[34]

Against this backdrop, it was not by chance that news about sexual abuse on children emerged quickly and then, just as quickly, grew to include satanic rings. Moral panics necessitate that morality at large must be in danger from an obscure, threatening figure. As such, moral panics can pivot to satanism, the superlative form of evil in the western cosmological worldview. Thus, not only does the McMartin Preschool's story end with an epidemic of reports of satanism sweeping across the US, but so do many other moral panics reach their apex at the involvement of supernatural intervention.

The moral panics of the 1980s were not born in a vacuum, but had an important antecedent with the publication of the best-selling *Michelle Remembers*[35] in 1980, a year before King began writing *IT*. The book was co-written by psychiatrist Lawrence Pazder with his patient and eventual wife, Michelle Smith. It was the first book on satanic sexual and ritual abuse and became an important document to the investigations of the satanic panics of the 1980s. Dr. Pazder met Michelle (a pseudonym) in 1973, when she searched for help due to depression after she suffered a miscarriage. For four years, Pazder analyzed Michelle's unhappy childhood (she was a witness of domestic violence) until a key moment occurred: Smith, at the middle of a session, started screaming and only stopped after almost half an hour. After the screaming, Michelle started speaking with the voice of a five-year-old girl. Hypothesizing that something highly traumatic was locked within Michelle's mind, Pazder began using hypnotherapy as a way to unpack the woman's buried secrets. According to Pazder, Michelle started to remember a traumatic childhood wherein she was not only a witness to domestic violence, but a victim as well. Under hypnosis, Michelle allegedly recovered her childhood memory, which consisted of having been forced to attend satanic rituals led by the Church of Satan. She claimed that she was taken to her first ritual at the age of five. Her blocked memories involved torture, being locked in cages, forced to witness several human sacrifices (including infants), and sexual assault. The last ritual took eighty-one days, and involved the invocation of Satan himself, who showed up to take Michelle with him. According to the book, only the intervention of Jesus and the Virgin Mary put an end to the horrifying ritual and forced Satan to retire. Allegedly, Michael the Archangel made Michelle forget all about the horrifying events she suffered as a child, wiping out all her memories. The only things remaining were feelings of anxiety and depression covering up the trauma; much like the case of Stanley in King's novel and his feeling that there is an unnamed terror present in his life. Like the Losers, Michelle forgot her alleged encounters with both abuse and supernatural evil. Only Pazder's hypnotherapy intervention seemed to have the power to bring Michelle's repressed memories to light.

King's novel reproduces this general climate, with characters living, as adults, in a daily stage of anxiety. Adult Eddie Kaspbrak is completely attached to a huge range of medicines and vitamins, as he only can live though his anxieties and fears via drugs. The most delicate of the Losers' Club as a kid, Eddie has been scarred for life to the point of being psychologically tied to the past but, as highlighted by the novel, only through subconscious ways. Every memory comes to his mind as "a balefully fizzing firework"[36] that fills Eddie with "panic."[37] There is trauma and, in consequence, connections with the past, but the links are always "subconscious," a word mentioned over and over through the moral panics of the 1980s. Furthermore, it can be argued that Beverly's attachment to Tom Rogan, her abusive husband, may not only be linked to the reproduction of the cycle of violence the woman suffered with her father, but also to her battle against Pennywise. According to Tom, Beverly is a "vulnerable" woman.[38] She is further described as a woman whose willpower has been fractured to the point of turning her

> weak . . . weak somehow. It was as if she was sending out radio signals which only he could receive. You could point to certain things—how much she smoked (but he had almost cured her of that), the restless way her eyes moved, never quite meeting the eyes of whoever was talking to her, only touching them from time to time and then leaping nimbly away; her habit of lightly rubbing her elbows when she was

nervous; the look of her fingernails, which were kept neat but brutally short. [. . .] *She keeps them short like that because she bites them.*[39]

After hitting Beverly, Tom knows she has secrets hidden within, secrets that even she does not know due to negation and amnesia:

> Her face. What had that third expression been, there for a bare instant and then gone? First the surprise. Then the pain. Then the
> (*nostalgia*)
> look of a memory . . . of some memory. It had only been for a moment. *He didn't think she even knew it had been there, on her face or in her mind.*"[40]

Beverly is Michelle's counterpart, a woman shaped by traumatic encounters with both domestic violence within the household and supernatural encounters outside her home.

Michelle Remembers became the recovered memory movement's indispensable text and, together with other books such as *The Courage to Heal: A Guide for Women Survivors of Child Sexual Abuse* (Ellen Bass and Laura Davis, 1988) made "recovered memory therapy" a well-known term for Americans. Recovered memory therapy's books were aimed at people who did not know they were victims. Any symptom of anxiety, such as those displayed by Beverly, could be read with the help of recovered memory therapy, as traces of forgotten ritual abuse. As Beck argues, "odd revulsions, reluctance to spend time with a certain family member, fear of basements, and similar experiences made it likely that buried memories were waiting to be drawn to the surface."[41] Beverly is the perfect illustration of the results of the "recovered memory," a woman struggling with an imperfect present that must heal from previous abuse so she can take her life to the right track.

The buried demons in King's novel vary, as in "real" life, from domestic abuse to encounters with Satan. This formula follows closely the dynamic of the "moral panics" of the era, when "increasing" was a key term, since each week brought to the surface horrors that surpassed the previous ones, varying from sexual molestation to ritualistic killing and cannibalism. Yet the moral panics of the time exceeded the politics of "recovered memory" to add new sources of anxieties. The role of sexuality in the moral panic calls for close attention. The fears of children's sexuality were elevated, through the 1980s, to the status of "social evil." Amidst the spread of AIDS and stories of sexual abuse, innocent childhood seemed especially prone to be infected by sexuality.[42] King's novel is not just a story framed by childhood's expressions of friendship but, also, of explicit sexuality.

The Losers' Club has defeated Pennywise (or so they believe) at the end of the first segment, but are stuck inside a network of tunnels that they cannot seem to navigate. While the kids ponder how they are going to get out, Beverly decides that the only way out is to bring unity to the group and they must do this through a sex session. One by one, the boys of the Losers' Club have sex with eleven-year-old Beverly. At some point, she is even able to feel pleasure: "Mike comes to her, then Richie, and the act is repeated. Now she feels some pleasure, dim heat in her childish unmatured sex, and she closes her eyes as Stan comes to her and she thinks of the birds."[43] King depicts what many parents feared: that a child may have sex (and, even worse, enjoy it). Furthermore, the surroundings invite analogy with the moral panics of the era: the children having sex do so in an underground environment and after defeating a demonic clown, a situation that parallels many stories from the 1980s like *Michelle Remembers*, in which the battle against Satan takes place in an underground cellar.

The children's sexuality and forgotten memories of traumatic, past encounters with abuse and demonic entities are not the only deep connections between King's *IT* and the moral panics of the first half of the 1980s. Pennywise itself, It's main presentation, may be read as another source of fictional horrors tapping into collective anxieties and cultural fears of the time. Together with sex/satanic rings lurking behind the façade of elementary schools, people were particularly afraid of clowns. This rise of coulrophobia was not born in a vacuum, but rather, was a collective answer to new fears about killer clowns hunting down children through the streets of America during the first half of the 1980s. As described by Robert Schneck in his book on "strange-but true" reports from American history, the first reports came in May 1981 of clowns trying to lure kids into their vans in Brookline, Boston, East Boston, Charlestown, Cambridge, Canton, Randolph, and Rhode Island.[44] Quickly as the news spread, however, the clown scare disappeared, leaving behind little in terms of concrete proof besides mass hysteria.

Schneck argues that the moral panic of clowns scaring, kidnapping, and killing children throughout the US was inextricably linked to moral panics spotlighting both children and their safety.[45] Further, the moral panics about clowns in vans may be related to the "Atlanta Child Murders," a case in which, from July 1979 to June 1981, dozens of Black children and adolescents were murdered in Atlanta. Almost all the victims were male, many were strangled or suffocated, and their bodies were hidden in overgrown areas. Rumors spread and soon people were very mindful of people in vans attempting to abduct children. Another basis for the clown scare was John Wayne Gacy, dubbed the "Killer Clown," whose crimes received extensive coverage in 1979 and 1980. A seemingly respectable man from Chicago, Gacy participated in local politics and entertained at charity events dressed as clowns named either "Pogo" or "Patches." In December, 1978, police discovered that Gacy had also raped, tortured, and murdered more than thirty young men and adolescent boys, burying most of the bodies in a crawl space beneath his suburban ranch house. All these social evils coagulated in the 1980s into a broader scare wherein children's sexuality, supernatural beings, and clowns cohered together to put an end to a child's innocence. Curiously, Schneck notices the many similarities between *IT* and the evil clowns of the 1980s. However, he argues that King's novel inspired part of the clown scare rather than the other way around, even if the novel came out in 1986.[46] He suggests that "[t]hroughout the sporadic bad clown reports, no hard evidence was ever found, and no children were actually abducted. This strongly suggests that some form of social delusion was at play,"[47] revealing that the clown scare, although similar to the satanic panic, was an even less-supported moral panic fueled by a time and context where innocent (i.e., nonsexual) childhood seemed to be permanently in danger. The result was a world wherein children could no longer safely play in the streets with paper boats on rainy days—a world King depicted in his horror novel.

CONCLUSIONS

King's novel taps into this social context of moral panics where children witnessed their innocence being shattered by abuse, allegedly satanic entities, and sex, and turned such a climate into a novel revolving around the same topics that framed most of the US at the time. Further, the novel's emphasis on repressed memories evokes the "recovery memory" therapy that dominated much of the social discourse of the era. In the novel, Bill's wife Audra remarks: "Scars can't come back. They either are or aren't."[48] The scars of trauma, however, are mostly invisible, only perceptible through little symptoms revealing what lurks beneath the surface.

Pennywise is not even a real clown or a monster, but an ancient alien force. Living in Derry for centuries, It's very name—"It"—evokes something ambiguous, without a proper source. It feeds from Derry's fears, much like moral panics do through history. In the novel, It's final form (a Lovecraftian spider-like monster) is intentionally vague. It's clown form is just a shape it assumes to terrorize the children of Derry at a given moment. However, as with real moral panics, Pennywise returns with a different form every number of years to put all the children at risk again. Like the TV and film adaptations of *IT* itself, Pennywise resurfaces from time to time to endanger children's innocence in new historical contexts—raising the question of whether It (and trauma) can ever truly be laid to rest.

Notes

1. Stephen King, *IT* (London: Hodder & Stoughton, 1986), 60.

2. King, *IT*, 79; emphasis in the original.

3. King, *IT*, 52.

4. King, *IT*, 63.

5. Michael Orlans and Terry M. Levy, *Attachment, Trauma, and Healing: Understanding and Treating Attachment Disorder in Children, Families and Adults* (London: Jessica Kingsley, 2014), 237.

6. Richard McNally, *Remembering Trauma* (Cambridge: Harvard University Press, 2005), 186

7. McNally, *Remembering Trauma*, 187

8. King, *IT*, 79.

9. Richard, Beck, *We Believe the Children: A Moral Panic in the 1980s* (New York: PublicAffairs, 2015), 122.

10. Claudio Hernández, *The Beginnings of Stephen King* (Babelcube, 2018), 117.

11. Randall Grometstein, "Wrongful Conviction and Moral Panic: National and International Perspectives on Organized Child Sexual Abuse," in *Wrongful Conviction: International Perspectives on Miscarriages of Justice*, eds. Ronald Huff and Martin Killias (Philadelphia: Temple University Press, 2008), 14.

12. Beck, *We Believe the Children*, 265.

13. Beck, *We Believe the Children*, 9.

14. Beck, *We Believe the Children*, 9.

15. Beck, *We Believe the Children*, 11.

16. Kenneth Thompson, *Moral Panics* (New York: Routledge, 1998), 8.

17. Chas Critcher, *Moral Panics and The Media* (Philadelphia: Open University Press, 2003), 147.

18. Jason Hughes, Julian Petley and Chas Critcher, "Moral Panics in the Contemporary World: Enduring Controversies and Future Directions," in *Moral Panics in the Contemporary World*, eds. Julian Petley, Chas Critcher, Jason Hughes and Amanda Rohloff (New York: Bloomsbury, 2013), 8.

19. Critcher, *Moral Panics*, 147.

20. The Black Spot was a nightclub whose customers were mostly Black soldiers from the nearby Army base. It was burned down by the Maine Legion of White Decency in the fall of 1930. The place is mentioned in King's novels *The Shinning* (1977) and *Insomnia* (1994).

21. King, *IT*, 150.

22. King, *IT*, 150.

23. King, *IT*, 150.

24. King, *IT*, 469.

25. Thompson, *Moral Panics*, 1.

26. King, *IT*, 740.

27. King, *IT*, 171.

28. King, *IT*, 165.

29. King, *IT*, 438.

30. Deborah Chambers, *Representing the Family* (London: SAGE, 2001), 140.

31. King, *IT*, 26.

32. King, *IT*, 27.

33. Stephen Markson, "Claims-making, Quasi-theories, and the Social Construction of the Rock 'n' Roll Menace," in *Marginal Conventions: Popular Culture, Mass Media, and Social Deviance*, ed. Clinton Sanders (Bowling Green, OH: Bowling Green State University Popular Press, 1990), 32.

34. Beck, *We Believe the Children*, 118.

35. Michelle Smith and Lawrence Pazder, *Michelle Remembers* (New York: Congdon and Lattes, 1980).

36. King, *IT*, 69.

37. King, *IT*, 70.

38. King, *IT*, 102.

39. King, *IT*, 103.

40. King, *IT*, 103; my emphasis.

41. Beck, *We Believe the Children*, 180.

42. Charles Krinsky, "Overview," in *The Ashgate Research Companion to Moral Panics*, ed. Charles Krinsky (New York: Routledge, 2016), 228.

43. King, *IT*, 1.002.

44. Rober Schneck, *Mrs. Wakeman vs. the Antichrist* (New York: Jeremy Tarcher, 2014), 106.

45. Schneck, *Mrs. Wakeman vs. the Antichrist*, 106.

46. Schneck, *Mrs. Wakeman vs. the Antichrist*, 109.

47. Robert E. Bartholomew and Benjamin Radford, *The Martians Have Landed!: A History of Media-Driven Panics and Hoaxes* (Jefferson, NC: McFarland & Company, 2011), 107.

48. King, *IT*, 133.

References

Bartholomew, Robert, and Benjamin Radford. *The Martians Have Landed!: A History of Media-Driven Panics and Hoaxes*. Jefferson, NC: McFarland & Company, 2011.

Beck, Richard. *We Believe the Children: A Moral Panic in the 1980s*. New York: PublicAffairs, 2015).

Chambers, Deborah. *Representing the Family*. London: SAGE, 2001.

Critcher, Chas. *Moral Panics and The Media*. Philadelphia: Open University Press, 2003.

Grometstein, Randall. "Wrongful Conviction and Moral Panic: National and International Perspectives on Organized Child Sexual Abuse." In *Wrongful Conviction: International Perspectives on Miscarriages of Justice*, edited by Ronald Huff and Martin Killias, 11–32. Philadelphia: Temple University Press, 2008.

Hernández, Claudio. *The Beginnings of Stephen King*. Babelcube, 2018.

Hughes, Jason, Julian Petley, and Chas Critcher. "Moral Panics in the Contemporary World: Enduring Controversies and Future Directions." In *Moral Panics in the Contemporary World*, edited by Julian Petley, Chas Critcher, Jason Hughes, and Amanda Rohloff, 1–32. New York: Bloomsbury, 2013.

King, Stephen. *IT*. London: Hodder & Stoughton, 1986.

Krinsky, Charles. "Overview." In *The Ashgate Research Companion to Moral Panics*, edited by Charles Krinsky, 227–32. New York: Routledge, 2016.

Markson, Stephen. "Claims-making, Quasi-Theories, and the Social Construction of the Rock 'n' Roll Menace." In *Marginal Conventions: Popular Culture, Mass Media, and Social Deviance*, edited by Clinton Sanders, 29–40. Bowling Green, OH: Bowling Green State University Popular Press, 1990.

McNally, Richard. *Remembering Trauma*. Cambridge: Harvard University Press, 2005.

Orlans, Michael, and Terry M. Levy. *Attachment, Trauma, and Healing: Understanding and Treating Attachment disorder in Children, Families and Adults*. London: Jessica Kingsley, 2014.

Schneck, Robert. *Mrs. Wakeman vs. the Antichrist*. New York: Jeremy Tarcher, 2014.

Smith, Michelle, and Lawrence Pazder, *Michelle Remembers*. New York: Congdon and Lattes, 1980.

Thompson, Kenneth. *Moral Panics*. New York: Routledge, 1998.

Chapter 2

GENERATION GAP?

Time, Character, and Narrative Shifts Between Stephen King's *IT* (1986) and Its Recent Adaptations (2017/2019)

ERIN GIANNINI

From a marketing perspective, the decision to set so much of Andy Muschietti's recent *IT* adaptations in 1989 instead of in 1958 makes sense; not only are those sections of the source novel far enough in the past (sixty years) to be considered "historical," but the primary audience for the horror genre tends to skew towards teens and young adults.[1] However, the resonance of shifting the action twenty-five years forward is neither merely good marketing nor a cosmetic change: While the 1980s frequently used the 1950s as a cultural touchstone in music, film, and television,[2] childhood in those eras had myriad fundamental differences, including economic situations (prosperity vs. recession), the passage of the Civil Rights Act, the number of divorces and single parents, and shifts in family sizes, to name but a few.

At the same time, however, King's original text positions the members of both the Losers' Club and their antagonists not as avatars of the prosperous, "innocent" 1950s seen in other 1980s television and film texts, but frequently as suffering the same neglect, abuse, and challenges that would be applied to the next generation (e.g., the Generation X "latchkey" kids). Their relative freedom to spend time together and lack of adult supervision is not portrayed as trust in their innocence or in the safety of small-town America, but rather as a consequence of adults who turn a blind eye to the reality of the dangers their children face, or worse, assume that is it their children's behavior that is the danger. Both generations are subjected to moral panics around the popular culture they consume—from horror comics in the 1950s to the numerous satanic panics of the 1980s around role-playing games and heavy metal—with the subtext that children are inherently im- or amoral without proper guidance. The fears of the children in King's *IT*, whether "stranger danger" (embodied by Pennywise's many guises) or familial abuse or neglect, are also not tied to any particular era.

Thus, in this chapter, I examine both the correspondences and the differences between King's original text and Muschietti's time-shifted adaptations. While the thematics of the original remain fairly intact, the films' 1980s setting allows for differences in both the social matrix in which the characters operate, and elements of their characterization, emphasizing some elements while downplaying others. This is particularly noticeable in the ways they relate to one another as a group and how they approach defeating the evil that Pennywise (and Derry) represent. Making it a Generation-X story rather than a Baby Boomer story is significant in its own right; however, it also suggests that the socioeconomic and interpersonal dynamics of King's text, like Pennywise himself, can at times transcend such generational distinctions.

PUNCTURING THE MYTH OF THE 1950s:
DERRY AS DARK SIDE

The election of Ronald Reagan in 1980, an actor whose most famous film roles occurred in the 1940s but who then found greater prominence as the host of television's *General Electric Theater* from 1953 to 1962, was in part driven by what Richard Walton referred to in the early months of Reagan's first term as a "politics of nostalgia." This nostalgia was not only for Reagan's "naively optimistic mind set of a 19th-century entrepreneur,"[3] but for the then still-young Baby Boomers who'd come of age during war and recession, a likely nostalgia for a childhood that included a young Reagan as a TV personality invited into their homes week after week. This "politics of nostalgia" was exploited by Reagan throughout his presidency, underscored for example by his 1984 reelection campaign's "Morning in America" advertisement, which is full of traditional images, including farmers on tractors, an older man raising a flag, a young boy delivering papers on his bicycle, and a man and woman getting married in a church ceremony.[4] Unfortunately, this "Morning" featured not a single person of color during its minute-long montage of a so-called "revitalized" America, and while it did refer to "working men and women," the only woman featured in the advertisement was a young bride dressed in white—embarking upon a marriage whose gender roles were visually sanctioned by heteropatriarchy.

This desire for what is viewed as a "simpler" time—but in reality was anything but—extended outward into the broader culture of the 1980s, from films such as the *Back to the Future* trilogy and *Peggy Sue Got Married*, television series like *Happy Days* and revivals of 1950s staples such as *Leave it to Beaver* to popular music, including the Stray Cats, with their Sun Records/rockabilly throwback sound. In his analysis of this revival (which he dates from the mid-1970s), Michael Dwyer suggests it was a way the United States:

> alternately attempted to reckon with and move past a contentious and even frightening period of unrest, self-doubt, and upheaval ("the Sixties") . . . marked by reassessments of Great Society social reforms, pitched battles over the permanency and character of civil rights movements, a renewed emphasis on patriotism and optimism, and fierce debates over American identity and American responsibility.[5]

The concept of "the Fifties," in Dwyer's view, "operates as a key structuring myth of American self-understanding."[6]

The key word, of course, is "myth," particularly around the national character of that time as being "better" than the present, assumptions that King's novel dispenses with immediately. The novel itself opens in the 1950s, on a pleasant domestic scene in which older brother Bill Denbrough helps his younger brother George make a paper boat, while their mother plays Beethoven's "Für Elise" on the piano in the living room.[7] Yet even in this scene, darkness lurks literally beneath in George's fear of and experience in the family basement,[8] and as the rest of the novel elucidates, beneath the entire town of Derry itself. Putting aside the supernatural aspect, however, King's view of 1950s America, through the town of Derry, bears little resemblance to paeans of small-town life such as the suburban-based *Leave It to Beaver* or *The Andy Griffith Show*. As Stephanie Coontz suggests:

> [A]dvertisers favored shows that presented "universal themes" embodied in homogenized families without serious divisions of interest by age, gender, income, or ethnic group. The hope was that everyone could identify with these families and hence with the mass-produced appliances that were always shown in conjunction with the mass-produced sentiments.[9]

Indeed, when television is mentioned in the text, it is never the sitcoms Coontz refers to. Instead, Pennywise is compared to Bozo the Clown and Clarabell from *The Howdy Doody Show*,[10] Ben Hanscom professes admiration for Broderick Crawford in *Highway Patrol*, as well as other cop shows such as *Dragnet*,[11] and each member of the Losers' Club mentions *American Bandstand* throughout the text, as one of the few conduits for new music in a small town. Perhaps such "mass-produced sentiments" of idyllic family life were too far from their reality; instead, in King's 1950s small-town Maine, racism, homophobia, and domestic violence are both rampant and never discussed, with at least four named characters (three of whom play a significant role) being the victims of either racism (Mike Hanlon) or parental abuse (Eddie Corcoran, Beverly Marsh, and Henry Bowers). Eddie Kaspbrak suffers a different type of abuse, with his mother trying to control every aspect of his life, while Bill's parents neglect him to the point that he actively courts death.[12] In stark contrast to the more popular (if not necessarily realistic) views of the era, the violence, corruption, class issues, and societal dynamics within Derry simultaneously puncture the 1980s picture of the 1950s and are applicable beyond the era described.

Indeed, beyond popular culture, the 1950s and 1980s shared other similarities. Both decades featured two-term Republican presidents (Eisenhower and Reagan, respectively) whose policies and personalities defined the era. Both were characterized by significant economic growth, although the 1950s was driven by the postwar boom, an increase in manufacturing, strong unions, and investment in infrastructure, none of which Reagan's administration either attempted or benefitted from. The outward economic prosperity in both eras, however, masked the millions excluded from these benefits and living in poverty, King's own family (in the 1950s) among them.[13] While social safety nets such as unemployment insurance, food stamps, and government-supplied financial aid existed in both eras, so too did the shame of availing oneself of said remedies (witness Reagan's constant, infamous invocation of the "welfare queen" as justification for cutting such programs).[14] In fact, throughout his oeuvre King's characters frequently express primarily negative reactions to government assistance, from Peter Goldsmith's gentle disdain for relying on it in *The Stand*[15] to Jack Torrance's nightmares of unemployment and donated commodities in *The Shining*.[16] In the novel *IT*, such sentiments are expressed by Elfrida Marsh (Beverly's mother): "But at the bottom of everything, below even the gutter, was a time when you might have to go *on the county* and drink the worksweat from the brows of others as a gift" [italics in original].[17]

In Derry, there are few to no protections for the children forced to navigate its supernatural and familial horrors. Decades before the term "latchkey kids" was used to describe a wide swath of Generation X,[18] who have been described as a generation that "went through its all-important, formative years as one of the least parented, least nurtured generations in US history,"[19] the children of Derry were, in essence, left on their own with little parental involvement or protection in similar ways. The Marsh family's poverty means that both Beverly's parents work to a cruel level of excess; Ben's mother is a widow trying to survive on a single salary; and Bill's parents, as stated above, let their grief over the loss of their youngest son lead them to neglect their remaining child. While Richie's parents seem to take something of an interest in his life, his father works long hours as a dentist, and his mother, in a brief aside, expresses fear at her son's behavior and impulses, wishing she'd had a daughter instead.[20] Later, Richie recalls how when an attack by one of the numerous bullies the protagonists contend with throughout the novel caused his glasses to break, his mother blames him rather than listening to his explanation.[21] It is the Hanlons, one of Derry's only African American families, who represent one of the only engaged and understanding sets of parents seen throughout the novel. In the book, if not in the films, Mike's father is shown not only surviving and (eventually) thriving despite the racial injustice he suffers (not limited to Derry), but imparting his son with a sense of integrity, justice, and history absent from any of the child/parent interactions throughout the novel. While the children of the novel are not above creating their own myths—as will be examined below—this is in the service of their attempts to defeat the evil that permeates Derry, rather than as a denial of the circumstances of their lives. What they don't have are illusions about small-town life in the 1950s. As Bill tells the group, "Derry is IT"[22]; it offers no safe place for its children.

"WE CAN GET DERRY ON *UNSOLVED MYSTERIES*": TIME-SHIFTING THE ADAPTATION

In these respects, setting the film in 1988–89 does not require significant updates. Within the novel, the adult Losers note that 1985 Derry has a few more banks, has lost some of its more unique architectural features, and has gained more traffic.[23] However, as the adult Bill notes to himself, "the old Derry was mostly buried under all the new construction . . . but your eye was somehow dragged hopelessly to look at it . . . to look *for* it" (italics in original).[24] Derry's essence, however, remains unchanged, both in the novel and in the films. Although filmed in Port Hope, Ontario, shots of brick courthouses, tree-lined streets, and city parks suggest any number of smaller towns across the United States, offering a timelessness that underscores the thematic focus on an evil whose external features may change, but not its goal. Like Bill's adult journey through his newly recalled childhood home, the film's time shift is in many respects cosmetic: different clothes and hairstyles and updated pop-culture references and music. The external features of Derry remains unchanged in both parts of the adaptation, as do the more internal threats of abuse, neglect, and a lack of any social safety net.

Beyond music and clothes, however, there are narrative and character shifts in the films that can be tied to the shift in decade of the era of the narrative and that it was filmed in. Underscoring her status as a latchkey kid, Beverly (Sophia Lillis) actually wears a key around her neck in the film. But she is far from the only one. With the exception of Bill (Jaeden Martell) and Richie (Finn Wolfhard), each member of the Losers' Club in the film is either raised by a single parent or extended family member. The absence of Elfrida Marsh from the film, who does not play a substantial role in the novel, nevertheless means that the incestuously tinged abuse Beverly suffers at the hands of her father (Stephen Bogaert) is more prevalent both narratively and visually. This is underlined significantly in *IT: Chapter Two*; during the adult Beverly's (Jessica Chastain) return to the apartment where she grew up, a flashback suggests that not only did Beverly look like her mother (she had resembled her father in the novel), but that her mother had committed suicide. The ensuing scene—in which her father blames Beverly for her mother's death, sprays Beverly with her mother's favorite perfume, and proceeds to take her in his arms—makes the connection explicit. Further, the 1980s setting in the film also means that the bullying Beverly receives from other girls, primarily around her poverty and looks in the novel, are more openly sexualized in the adaptation; the gossip and taunts to which she is subjected revolve around the false impression that she is promiscuous because she is poor, something that the novel suggests is at the root of her unpopularity at school but never explicitly states.

Yet it is not only how much more explicit these varying levels of abuse are presented that is highlighted in the adaptation; it is Beverly's own characterization. Given that the film medium does not allow for the same type of interiority as the novel form, the younger Beverly is necessarily more action-oriented in the 2017 adaptation. She uses her (problematic) reputation for lasciviousness unjustly assigned by girls at her school to distract Mr. Keene (Joe Bostick) at the drugstore so that Bill, Richie, and Eddie (Jack Dylan Grazer) can shoplift medical supplies after the Bowers gang attacks and wounds Ben (Jeremy Ray Talyor), and she calls in the group when her bathroom is covered in blood. During the fight with Henry Bowers (Nicholas Hamilton), she is the first to pick up a rock (although Ben throws the first one). When the Losers decide to confront the monster for the first time at the dilapidated house on Neibolt Street that seems to serve as his lair and Bill asks who wants to stay outside, only Beverly doesn't raise her hand. During the confrontation with Pennywise (Bill Skarsgård), it's Beverly who takes action, stabbing him in the head with a rebar as he menaces the rest of the group. Indeed, it is Beverly, rather than Bill, who is positioned as the leader of the group within the first film, representing a significant departure from the novel. In perhaps the biggest shift from the text, during her final confrontation with her father, rather than fighting him only so she could escape,[25] she strikes him down without the attendant guilt that Beverly feels in the novel for only defending herself. While not stated in the film, the characterization of Beverly in the 1980s would certainly be informed by the shifts in (white) women's status following the reforms of second-wave feminism in the 1970s.

Beverly is not the only character who undergoes substantive change in the adaptation; both character and narrative shifts occur with all of them. As Kevin Wetmore argues, shifting the knowledge of Derry's past and position as historian from adult Mike (Isaiah Mustafa) to child Ben in the 2017 film robs Mike of his crucial role within the text on multiple levels. Without that aspect, Mike is given far less to do and say in *IT: Chapter One*, but Wetmore suggests that the problem with this shift is deeper and more troubling. In the novel (and touched upon in the 1990 miniseries), Mike's interest in and knowledge of Derry's past is a legacy from his father and speaks to a deeper element: the Hanlons as one of the only African American families in Derry, and the experience of Black men in America more generally. Making Mike not only the repository for Derry's dark history but also the one who stays in Derry and thus the only one to remember that history makes, for Wetmore, a larger point about how being Black in America means never being "allowed" to forget the nation's history of violence and oppression.[26] Not only does the adaptation remove this characterization, but it also renders Mike an orphan. In the film, his parents died in a house fire, abstractly suggesting the similar fate of Derry's segregated Company E, the majority of whom were killed in the novel during a nightclub fire set by Derry's version of the Ku Klux Klan (the Legion of Decency).[27] The change substitutes the adaptation of the one unproblematic parental relationship for one in which Mike's grandfather (Steven Williams) espouses a much harsher worldview tinged with a disdain for Mike's gentleness. Worse, the first film implies that Mike's parents were addicted to crack cocaine, which led to their deaths; it is only in the second film that it is revealed this was a Pennywise-created lie.

These shifts have an effect on the overall narrative as well. In the film, after the confrontation with Pennywise at the Neibolt Street house, the group fractures, too undone and fearful given their recent experiences to risk another fight. It is only when Beverly is taken by Pennywise that the team reforms for the final battle of the film, understanding that their long-standing isolation—for seemingly all the children in 1989 Derry—is what makes them

vulnerable. In the novel, while supportive adults are few, the 1958 Losers'
Club employs certain structuring myths, turning to brave figures in history,
books, film, and television for inspiration when their courage flags.[28] When
that fails, they, in essence, deify one of their own: Bill becomes "Big Bill," a
magnetic, charismatic figure leading them into a moral battle. Richie mentally
compares him to a "knight in an old movie. [. . .] Strong and good";[29] long
after the events of the summer of 1958, one of his final memories of Bill is
a comparison between Bill and John Kennedy.[30] In analyzing the novel and
miniseries through a generational lens, Susan Love Brown traces how the Baby
Boom generation first attempted to "right the wrongs" of the previous generation (particularly around military action and civil rights) and prized self-
fulfillment over the "giving-getting paradigm" of their parents, before finally
mythologizing their own youthful actions into an "origin story"; in essence,
Baby Boomers cast themselves as superheroes in their generational history.[31]
In the novel, the Losers' eventual forgetfulness of both the childhood and the
adult battle against It, Brown argues, is part of the generation's essential myth
about themselves—i.e., that their actions have forever vanquished the societal
evils against which they protested and thus there is no need to remember.[32]
This recasting of their own youthful actions (for both the Losers and the
Baby Boomer generation they characterize frequently) obscures the reality of
both the events themselves and their lasting consequences.[33] The problematic
nature of this viewpoint continues to resonate in the contemporary American
sociopolitical environment; viewing problems as "solved" by the actions of the
Baby Boomer generation suggests that the battle is over, that racism, poverty,
war, and violence have been defeated and no longer need to be thought about
or addressed. For example, Supreme Court Chief Justice John Roberts (of the
Boomer generation), voted—and wrote the majority opinion—to strike down
a key provision of the 1965 Voting Rights Act that required federal oversight of
voting procedures in particular states that historically curtailed the rights of
Black voters, saying "our country has changed" and therefore such provisions
were no longer necessary (Liptak 2013). (He was almost immediately proven
wrong when states such as Texas implemented voter ID and redistricting
that disenfranchised voters of color [Liptak 2013], as well as the even more
restrictive bills passed and signed by Governor Greg Abbott in Texas [Bradner
2021] and Governor Brian Kemp in Georgia [Axelrod 2021] in 2021 following
their party's losses in the 2020 election.)

Muschietti's adaptation seems to indicate that the Generation X version
of the Losers' Club employs no such hero worship or myth-making. While
each character realizes that something is wrong within Derry, that sense of
empowerment brought on by their collective empathy and intelligence is

missing; the need for collective action and community is passed on neither by their parents nor the town itself. For example, in the Fourth of July parade passing behind the Losers' Club when they are finally reunited, the focus is not on the cheering townspeople or the marching band (of which, in the novel, Mike Hanlon was a part), but on Richie wresting a tuba from one of band members and attempting to play it. As mentioned earlier, the younger Mike's knowledge of the town's history is as absent as his parents; in the novel, it was Will Hanlon's interest in Derry's history—and nurturing of his son's curiosity—that drove Mike's own research. This lack of transmitting the importance of these values from one generation to the next is not limited to the adaptation, although the novel addresses it in a different, and essentially simpler, way: none of the adult Losers have children.[34] While not explicitly stated, it suggests that having children marks the end of childhood and thus would render them incapable of fighting It. They would become like their own parents: blind to the evil that menaces Derry.

This fear may not be unfounded, even in examining King's other work in the 1980s. Charlie McGee in *Firestarter* is used and manipulated by a clandestine branch of the US government; Tad Trenton in *Cujo* dies while hiding from the titular rabid dog; and Gage Creed is killed by a semi truck and then reanimated by a cursed burial ground in *Pet Sematary*. All three are close to or younger than the age of *IT*'s youthful protagonists, meaning that Muschietti's time-shifted adaptation makes McGee, Trenton, and Creed near contemporaries of the Losers. As with the children of Derry, they are also vulnerable specifically because of the action (or non-action) of their parents, regardless of their parents' intentions. Others are more actively toxic. In King and Peter Straub's *The Talisman*, written a few years before *IT*, the character of Morgan Sloat embodies the worst of 1980s excesses—greed, selfishness, lust for power—and denigrates the same virtues Bill is thought to embody in King's *IT* when thinking of his now-deceased partner Philip Sawyer as a man who "never played to win" and was "encumbered by sentimental notions of loyalty and honor, corrupted by the stuff you told kids to get them halfway civilized before you finally tore the blindfold off their eyes."[35] Like the parents of Derry in the novel and both the television and film adaptations who look the other way and thus tacitly endorse the town's evil—and the prosperity it brings as a side effect—Sloat is willing to sacrifice his own son to gain more power.[36] In Muschietti's adaptation, the Losers' Club of 1989, with no parental support and navigating a town built on the death and sacrifice of its young, had either already lost those blindfolds or never had them to begin with. In that respect, Bill's appeals to the need for the Losers' collective action to defeat the monster is met not with commitment to the cause or visualizing themselves as famous heroes, but rather each elucidating why it won't work and going their separate ways. It is only when one of their own is taken that they reconnect to take on Pennywise.

This is the element that exposes the widest divergence between the source text and adaptation. In the novel, when the group meets as adults and Ben shares the story of how he lost weight and dealt with a bullying gym teacher, Bill replies with: "[T]he writer in me wonders if any kid ever really talked like that."[37] They are idealized versions within the novel; that is, they aren't "real kids, they're the kids we all wish we could have been."[38] While the 1950s themselves are not mythologized within the text, the children of the 1958 Losers' Club *are* in a way that the 2017 adaptation dispenses with entirely. The novel itself suggests that each of the 1958 Losers were, in some respects, chosen for their strong imaginative gifts and particular talents, ones they parlay into successful careers as adults. This element is present in neither *IT: Chapter One* nor *IT: Chapter Two*. The members of the Losers' Club of 1989—and 2019—are framed not as heroes, only survivors.

CONCLUSION: GONE, BUT NOT FORGOTTEN

More so than the first film, *IT: Chapter Two* fundamentally shifts the overall theme of the novel on a particularly generational level. That it will do so is suggested in a scene with the adult Bill on the set of a film adaptation of his work. Both the director, Peter (amusingly, he's played by film director Peter Bogdanovich), and Bill's wife, Audra (Jess Weixler), who is playing the lead in his film, take him to task for his "endings," which, unlike King's, are always dark and hopeless. The novel closes on Bill briefly remembering, upon waking, his final moments in Derry and the "friends with whom he shared it,"[39] implying that this is as close as any of them come to remembering the events of the novel or one another.[40] This "forgetting" is framed as both essential to a healthy mental state and a sign that "this time it's really over."[41] The film, on the other hand, frames the initial "forgetting" of childhood that afflicts the adult Losers as more actively toxic; that is, as Beverly explains to them, if they don't recall the past and decide to leave without fighting, it (and It) will destroy them anyway. In essence, they are not allowed the comfort of either myth or ignorance; they have to remember the pains of their pasts and fight the evil of their hometown despite them. Nor are they given the comfort of nostalgia, as are their novel counterparts. In the film, the Ritual of Chüd is reconceived as a destruction of the mementos of childhood—an anonymous love poem, a yearbook page, a game token—that will create a darkness to blot out the "deadlights" that It represents. In an analysis of toxic nostalgia through the lens of neuroscience, Jane M. writes that "[n]ostalgia is always a fleeting feeling which can return to us over and over—and this is how it is defined as unhealthy—when it keeps coming back to us in a post-trauma like fashion,"[42] a link that *IT: Chapter Two* embraces. It ends up being defeated not through one person's cleverness, or by a higher power, but by making It "small." Yet the film seems to suggest that the Losers must first make their troubled pasts—including neglect and abuse— "small" as well, with childhood trauma emerging as a part of their experience rather than the defining element.

The film starts with an adult Mike musing on himself and his friends being, rather than "what they choose to remember," in reality, "what [they] wish [they] could forget." This wish for blissful ignorance of the past is not granted the film's Losers' Club, as it is in the novel. Instead, the film closes on a letter Stan (Andy Bean) writes to each of them before taking his own life at the start of the film, borrowing from the novel's ending for a portion of it (in italics): "See, the thing about being a loser is that you don't have anything to lose. *So, be true. Be brave. Stand.* Believe, and don't ever forget we're losers and we always will be." The town of Derry is not destroyed, and the Losers do not forget either It or one another. In his analysis of the novel, Toby Magistrale succinctly defines the forged communities and relationships in much of King's early work, culminating in *IT*: "Abandoned by governmental bureaucracies and the nuclear family itself, King's small, non-traditional alliances represent the light in the darkness of his social landscape."[43] This holds true for the film adaptation as well, with the Losers of 2017 maintaining their memories and thus their connections to one another despite the lack of divine intervention or a structuring myth to guide them. Yet, while the ways in which the Losers' Club deals with the intricacies of small-town life, childhood trauma, and evil are essentially different in the book and its film adaptation, the importance of both a supportive community of friends and an unromantic view of the reality of their experiences and themselves transcend the generational divide.

Notes

1. Rebecca Rubin, "Diverse Audiences Are Driving the Horror Box Office Boom," *Variety*, October 25, 2018, https://variety.com/2018/film/box-office/horror-movies-study-1202994407/.

2. Dwyer, *Back to the Fifties: Nostalgia, Hollywood Film, and Popular Music of the Seventies and Eighties* (London: Oxford University Press, 2015).

3. Richard J. Walton, "Ronald Reagan and the Politics of Nostalgia," *Washington Post*, May 3, 1981.

4. New York Historical Society Channel, "Presidential Ad: 'It's Morning Again in America . . .,'" YouTube, June 8, 2020. Indeed, the advertisement spends several seconds on this white, heterosexual church wedding, with the voiceover at pains to point out that "6500 men and women will get married this year." While the ad goes on to indicate that said couples can look forward to a bright future of low interest rates, the choice to focus so intently on this moment speaks to the (still) ongoing right-wing focus on social changes they find disagreeable at best and immoral at worst.

5. Dwyer, *Back to the Fifties*, 4–5.

6. Dwyer, *Back to the Fifties*, 6.

7. Stephen King, *IT* (London: Penguin, 1986), 3–11.

8. King, *IT*, 6–8.

9. Stephanie Coontz, *The Way We Never Were: American Families and the Nostalgia Trap* (New York: Basic Books, 2000), 175.

10. King, *IT*, 12.

11. King, *IT*, 169.

12. King, *IT*, 220.

13. Stephen King, *On Writing: A Memoir of the Craft* (New York: Simon and Schuster, 2000), 36–37.

14. Jeremy Lybarger, "The Price You Pay . . . On the Life and Times of the Woman Known as the Welfare Queen," *The Nation*, July 2, 2019, https://www.thenation.com/article/archive/josh-levin-the-queen-book-review/

15. Stephen King, *The Stand* (New York: Anchor Books, 2011), 63–64.

16. Stephen King, *The Shining* (New York: Simon and Schuster, 1977), 403–5.

17. King, *IT*, 385

18. While the term "latchkey kid" became widespread during the 1980s, its origins as a descriptor actually date back to the 1940s, when it was used describe children whose fathers were fighting in World War II and mothers who had to work to support the family.

19. Erin E. Clack, "Study Probes Generation Gap: An Industry Update," *Children's Business*, May 1, 2004.

20. King, *IT*, 351. In the novel, Stan Uris seems to have a good relationship with his father as a child; most notably in their shared interest in bird-watching (King, 400–401). However, narrative from Stan's perspective remains limited, due to his suicide at the start of the novel (55–56).

21. King, *IT*, 630–31.

22. King, *IT*, 931

23. King, *IT*, 456–61.

24. King, *IT*, 460.

25. King, *IT*, 865–76.

26. Kevin Wetmore, "Changing Mike, Changing History: Erasing African-America in *IT* (2017), in *The Many Lives of "IT": Essays on the Stephen King Horror Franchise*, ed. Ron Riekki (Jefferson, NC: McFarland & Company, 2020), 72–74.

27. King, *IT*, 431–49.

28. This is not limited to *IT*'s characters; for example, Danny Torrance in *The Shining* invokes Secret Agent Man's Patrick McGoohan (King, 436–37), and Jack Sawyer in *The Talisman*, Nick Fury and his Howling Commandos (King, 18) when they are scared. Only Charlie in *Firestarter* seems to resist this urge, which offers a point about the scarcity of portrayals of powerful or independent women even in early 1980s popular culture.

29. King, *IT*, 347. It should be noted that in the text, Bill seems to resist the mythologizing, questioning his motives for engaging his friends on this quest on behalf of his dead brother and somewhat resentful of his leadership role. Indeed, he wonders if he isn't "a selfish little shit waving a tin sword and trying to make himself look like King Arthur" (King, 698).

30. King, *IT*, 347.

31. Susan Love Brown, "Babyboomer Mythology and Stephen King's It: An American Cultural Analysis," *Americana: The Journal of American Popular Culture* 7, no. 1 (Spring 2008), https://www.americanpopularculture.com/journal/articles/spring_2008/brown.htm.

32. Brown, "Babyboomer Mythology."

33. Bruce Cannon Gibney, *A Generation of Sociopaths: How the Baby Boomers Betrayed America* (New York: Hachette, 2017), 52–70.

34. For at least two members of the group—Bill (493–94) and Stan (47–49)—the text indicates they were trying, and failing, to conceive, even though they were medically fertile; Richie, single, discovered his earlier vasectomy had spontaneously reversed (497–99), suggesting a more mystical reason for their childlessness. While this is also the case in the adaptation, it does not receive the kind of focus it gets in the novel.

35. Stephen King and Peter Straub. *The Talisman* (New York: Simon and Schuster, 1984), 101.

36. King and Straub, *The Talisman*, 786–87.

37. King, *IT*, 474.

38. Grady Hendrix, "The Great Stephen King Reread: It," *Tor*, September 25, 2013, https://www.tor.com/2013/09/25/the-great-stephen-king-reread-it/.

39. King, *IT*, 1090.

40. The exception, this coda points out, would be Beverly and Ben, who leave together, presumably to pursue a relationship. It is suggested, however, that they too will forget the others (1071–72).

41. King, *IT*, 1074.

42. Jane M., "Nostalgia Can be Toxic to Our Minds. Here's Why: There's Neuroscience Behind the Pitfalls of Nostalgia and Sentimentalism—So Don't Fall for the Trap," *Medium*, June 11, 2020, https://medium.com/@newrealities/nostalgia-can-be-toxic-to-our-minds-heres-why-3a9f5a1065e4.

43. Toby Magistrale, *Landscape of Fear: Stephen King's American Gothic* (Madison, WI: Popular Press, 1988), 121.

References

Axelrod, Tal. "Kemp: Voting Law 'Worth the Boycotts as well as the Lawsuits.'" *The Hill*, April 3, 2021. https://thehill.com/homenews/state-watch/546320-kemp-voting-law-worth-the-boycotts-as-well-as-the-lawsuits.

Bradner, Eric. "Texas Governor Signs Voting Restrictions Bill into Law." *CNN*, September 7, 2021. https://www.cnn.com/2021/09/07/politics/texas-greg-abbott-voting-bill/index.html.

Brown, Susan Love. "Babyboomer Mythology and *Stephen King's "IT"*: An American Cultural Analysis." *Americana: The Journal of American Popular Culture* 7, no. 1 (Spring 2008). https://www.americanpopularculture.com/journal/articles/spring_2008/brown.htm.

Clack, Erin E. "Study Probes Generation Gap: An Industry Update." *Children's Business*. May 1, 2004.

Coontz, Stephanie. *The Way We Never Were: American Families and the Nostalgia Trap*. New York: Basic Books, 2000.

Dwyer, Michael D. *Back to the Fifties: Nostalgia, Hollywood Film, and Popular Music of the Seventies and Eighties*. London: Oxford University Press, 2015.

Gibney, Bruce Cannon. *A Generation of Sociopaths: How the Baby Boomers Betrayed America*. New York: Hachette, 2017.

Hendrix, Grady. "The Great Stephen King Reread: *IT*." *Tor*, September 25, 2013. https://www.tor.com/2013/09/25/the-great-stephen-king-reread-it/.

King, Stephen. *IT*. London: Penguin, 1986.

King, Stephen. *On Writing: A Memoir of the Craft*. New York: Simon and Schuster, 2000.

King, Stephen. *The Shining*. New York: Simon and Schuster, 1977.

King, Stephen. *The Stand*. New York: Anchor Books, 2011.

King, Stephen, and Peter Straub. *The Talisman*. New York: Simon and Schuster, 1984.

Liptak, Adam. "Supreme Court Invalidates Key Part of Voting Rights Act." *New York Times*, June 25, 2013. https://www.nytimes.com/2013/06/26/us/supreme-court-ruling.html.

Lybarger, Jeremy. "The Price You Pay: On the Life and Times of the Woman Known as the Welfare Queen." *The Nation*, July 2, 2019. https://www.thenation.com/article/archive/josh-levin-the-queen-book-review/.

M, Jane. "Nostalgia Can be Toxic to Our Minds. Here's Why: There's Neuroscience behind the Pitfalls of Nostalgia and Sentimentalism—So Don't Fall for the Trap." *Medium*, June 11, 2020. https://medium.com/@newrealities/nostalgia-can-be-toxic-to-our-minds-heres-why-3a9f5a1065e4.

Magistrale, Tony. *Landscape of Fear: Stephen King's American Gothic*. Madison, WI: Popular Press, 1988.

New York Historical Society Channel. "'Presidential Ad: 'It's Morning Again in America' Ronald Reagan v Walter Mondale [1984-PRIDE]." *YouTube*, June 8, 2020. https://www.youtube.com/watch?v=pUMqic2IcWA.

Rubin, Rebecca. "Diverse Audiences Are Driving the Horror Box Office Boom." *Variety*, October 25, 2018. https://variety.com/2018/film/box-office/horror-movies-study-1202994407/.

Walton, Richard J. "Ronald Reagan and the Politics of Nostalgia." *Washington Post*, May 3, 1981. https://www.washingtonpost.com/archive/entertainment/books/1981/05/03/ronald-reagan-and-the-politics-of-nostalgia/cf2078d1-2861-425b-b1e9-bca2a37e9d7d/.

Wetmore, Kevin. "Changing Mike, Changing History: Erasing African-America in *IT* (2017)." In *The Many Lives of "IT": Essays on the Stephen King Horror Franchise*, edited by Ron Riekki, 71–83. Jefferson, NC: McFarland & Company, 2020.

Chapter 3

FLOATING FEARS

Understanding Childhood Traumascapes in Stephen King's *IT*

DIGANTA ROY

Children in horror fiction often accentuate the feeling of dread and help-lessness when faced with a mysterious, unknown force. In numerous horror movies, the eerie laughter of a kid or the hurried footsteps of children running have been used to add to the atmospheric detail of the story. However, in the 1900s as the "century of the child" was ushered in, the appearance of child characters had a new critical meaning in both the social and literary landscape of horror literature. The emotional and psychological vulnerabilities of the child not only became an important component of the plot but also inflected the tone and mode of storytelling in horror fiction. *Nightmare on Elm Street*, for example, uses the nightmare as a narrative structure through which it portrays the traumatic past of sexual abuse that the characters suffered as children. In the twentieth century, the space of horror literature is used to understand and actively contest ideas about the child's identity and role in society. Movies such as *A Nightmare on Elm Street* also expose the institutional and systemic victimization of children and use horror as a psychological outlet for the internal trauma. The increase in the number of debates on the urgent need for child protection plans and attention to children's mental hygiene is, however, a recent development. Prior to this, there was a serious lack of discussion on the abuse—physical, mental, or sexual—suffered by children and the ways in which they cope with it. Against this background, this chapter studies Stephen King's seminal horror novel *IT*, arguing that King's monster not only forces us to stare at the ugly face of systemic violence against children but also makes his young characters resilient in a way that challenges the stereotype of the "weak" child that came before the novel. In doing so, King shatters the false sense of power that the perpetrators of violence possess over their child victims, and subverts the myth of adult supremacy.

This chapter will be structured into three thematically related sections. The first considers how King carefully builds the site of trauma, and situates the psychological state of the children within the disturbed space of the traumascape. The second section analyzes how the children respond to this trauma, ultimately emerging as heroic figures who convert their make-believe playground adventures into real-world escapades that have serious, universal consequences. Finally, the chapter establishes a continuity between childhood and adulthood, arguing that through the novel's constant shift between the perspective of the Losers' Club as children and their perspective as adults, *IT* demonstrates the existence of a mutual exchange between these two stages of life, as well as the importance of acknowledging this link for a healthy mental development.

MAPPING THE MONSTER

King's depiction of Derry, just like his depiction of Castle Rock and Jerusalem's Lot in other novels, is psycho-geographic. Guy Debord's definition of psycho-geography allows us to chart the "specific effects of the geographical environment, consciously organized or not, on the emotions and behavior of individuals."[1] On the surface, Derry is just the feeding ground of the monster It, just as Jerusalem's Lot is the lair of Kurt Barlow and the vampires in *'Salem's Lot* (1975).[2] What makes Derry in *IT* stand out is that the predator-prey dynamic configures the quaint little town into spaces that feel safe and spaces that are areas of potential danger. According to John Sears, the idea of place in King's worlds often constitutes an expression of otherness,[3] which, in Derry's case, includes both the monstrous Other, Pennywise, and the social Others, the Losers' Club. As the interlude on the Black Spot shows, the places situated in Derry are politically charged zones which have the power to grant, or ruthlessly take away, one's individual freedom.[4] Therefore, the seemingly random rampage of Pennywise is coupled with the deliberate and calculated victimization of the Other in different parts of the town.

It is important to understand the pattern of movement followed by the Losers' Club to escape the bullies in order to understand how certain parts of the town become sites of victimization. For Ben Hanscom, for example, the children's library, along with the glass corridor that connected it to the adult library, forms a fascinating space of wonder where he immerses himself in the world of books and scribbles a haiku for Beverly. But just outside this space of safety is the world of the criminally dangerous Henry Bowers, who assaults Ben and tries to carve his name into his belly.[5] For Beverly Marsh, unfortunately, the home itself becomes a place of threat because of her abusive father Al, just as for Eddie Kaspbrak, the house on 29 Neibolt Street, where he encounters the leper with a mangled nose, is a zone of danger. But although each of the characters has a different space of vulnerability, they share a common sense of comfort in their underground clubhouse in the Barrens. After Beverly Marsh narrowly escapes being chased by her father, she automatically walks towards the Barrens thinking about the clubhouse and how she could take a quick nap there.[6] Unlike the park or other places where the Losers are either harassed or simply unwelcome, the Barrens forms a safe haven for them, as they themselves confess to Officer Nell who chides them for playing there.[7] Therefore, within the traumatic world of Derry, the Barrens offers "the path of least resistance which is automatically followed in aimless strolls."[8] Despite being a dirty wasteland, it offers the members of the Losers' Club a space for emotional and psychological release. The depiction of Derry, through the eyes of the persecuted children, is thus less cartographic and more atmospheric. As John Sears observes, in King's Gothic model there is a "deliberate confusion of internal, character-psychological or group-dynamic features with external, spatial/topographical features."[9]

What is noteworthy about Derry is that King creates a parallel reality for the children that is free of adult control and thus subverts "adult logic." Here in the clubhouse, or in the Barrens more broadly, Eddie's toxically health-obsessed mother cannot curb his instincts; here, Beverley's abusive father cannot harm her; here, Bill does not feel the cold unresponsiveness of his parents after George's death; here, Richie Tozier is not punished for his impulsive voice impersonations. As the narrator reveals, Ben "understood instinctively, as most kids did, that they lived below the sightlines, and hence the thought-lines, of most adults. [. . .] It was like adults thought that real life only started when a person was five feet tall."[10] King cleverly uses this adult derision of the child's perspective to create two planes of visibility—one for the children, and one for the adults. Beverly's father does not see the blood,[11] splattered across the bathroom floor, that Beverly and the other Losers do; the monster It is also visible only to the children; and only Bill and Richie, and later the other members of the Losers' Club, see the photograph moving in George's album,[12] once again highlighting the heightened perceptivity of children.

The lack of communication between the two worlds leads to the creation of a third plane inhabited by the child, seen there as the monstrous Other. This is the plane where George Denbrough and the other murdered children "float" with Pennywise, as a threat to the "normal" world. But Beverly's father does not hear the voices coming from the sink, nor do Bill's parents hear George's ghost threatening Bill, because the chain of communication between the children and the adults has been permanently broken. In King's *The Shining* (1977), when Danny asks his mother why his father Jack Torrance lost his job, his mother thinks to herself that "to children adult motives and actions must seem as bulking and ominous as dangerous animals seen in the shadows of a dark forest."[13] If the adult world seems like a threat to children due to a lack of connection, so, too, does the instinctive and raw energy of children appear as something monstrous to grownups. The two planes of visibility thus form two parallel narratives in this landscape of terror, the narrative of adulthood and the narrative of childhood, both of which fuse together at the end of the novel when the members of the Losers' Club reunite as adults.

However, the third plane of visibility, inhabited by children as the murderous Other demands a close analysis. When Bill tries to initiate a conversation with his parents after George's death, he is met with silence and neglect. Sitting between his parents, Bill feels their cold indifference: "It was cold because he wasn't *really* the only book between those two ends; Georgie was still there, only now it was a Georgie he couldn't see, a Georgie who never demanded the popcorn or hollered that Bill was pinching."[14] Bill, therefore, not only suffers from the unprocessed trauma of the death of his brother but is also plagued by the guilt of not being able to save his brother. This psychological progression from the trauma of a dear one's death to the guilt of being responsible for it, is reflected in Bill's perception of George as a monstrous figure, threatening to kill him in subsequent chapters. In Beverly's case, the bathroom scene where she sees blood spewing out of the drain is often interpreted as a symbolic representation of menstruation and of Beverly's coming of age. However, her father refuses to acknowledge her sexual awakening, threatening her with physical abuse when he comes to know about the boys she hangs out with.[15] For Beverly the world of It where she hears the voice of several girls calling her to join them is an outcome of the sexual guilt that she has internalized. Thus, the distorted perception of children as monsters in the third plane is essentially a reflection of the guilt that the children suffer from. Because of the cold unresponsiveness of Bill's parents after George's death, or because of her father's denigration of Beverly's sexuality, both Beverly and Bill begin to believe that they will be pulled down into the dirty, unwanted, evil world of the sewers.

Stephen King's *IT* works by creating psychological associations between places in Derry in the minds of the children. The ruins of the Kitchener Ironworks where Mike is attacked by the giant bird,[16] the city center where

Richie Tozier is attacked by the Paul Bunyan statue,[17] and the sewers where the Losers finally fight It in the form of a mammoth spider-like creature[18] thus form "traumascapes," which, according to Maria M. Tumarkin, "are a distinctive category of place, transformed physically or psychically by suffering. [. . .] They are places that compel memories, crystallize identities and meanings, and exude power and enchantment."[19] It is interesting to note that the monstrosity of the spider or the statue or the bird is expressed in terms of their size. Although gigantic creatures are common in many monster tales, this distortion in the scale of objects in *IT* becomes symbolic of the perspective of children, who endow everyday things with a greater value and thus see these figures as "bigger" than they actually are.

In many ways, the people that the members of the Losers' Club grow into are shaped by their experiences in Derry. Bill's career as a novelist, for example, is solely dependent on the horrific visions of the past subliminally making their way into his writing. In fact, it is Mike's belief in the power of the traumascape of Derry which leads him to suggest that they follow their instinct and stroll around the city, so that they can remember the events of 1958 and decide upon the path which they should follow next.[20] The traumascape of Derry is thus a complex mixture of both geographical and psychological elements. Mike says, "Only It's not a matter of outside geography . . . It's . . . inside."[21] But if It is in the mind of the children, the trauma of It is triggered in them by the landscape of Derry. The killing of It is therefore followed by a disastrous storm that destroys everything including the Standpipe—which used to be one of It's haunts—and the glass corridor connecting the two libraries that Ben admired so much.[22] The annihilation of the psychological monster reconfigures the physical landscape of Derry, erasing the markers of fear that the traumascape housed.

HEROES IN LIMBO: FIGHTING TRAUMA, SAVING WORLDS

In order to understand how the children in *IT* process their trauma and emerge as heroes, it is essential to understand the genres in which King dabbles within this novel. Analyzing the reference to the Norwegian tale of "Three Billy Goats Gruff," and comparing Beverly and the boys to Snow White and the seven dwarfs, Heidi Strengell critiques *IT* as a blend of myth, fairy tale, horror, and the realist fiction genre.[23] At the base of *IT* is the classic element of suspense, "the eternal fascination of the fairy tale: would the monster be bested . . . or would it feed?"[24] This apparently simple format of the children's adventure tale, where the quest to kill the monster ends in an ultimate feat of victory, is, however, quickly subverted. King's mythologically rich horror narrative of the cosmic evil It and its good counterpart the Turtle is interwoven with a social narrative of the struggle of children, growing up in a world of abuse and emotional trauma. Consequently, the superficial killing of the tangible monster does not define the telos of King's storytelling.

Jesse Nash acknowledges the fact that King's treatment of the supernatural raises significant questions about the American family structure, and privileges the discourse of its adolescents, who are often misunderstood by the adults.[25] However, he argues that the mythologically exaggerated worlds demand so much attention in such novels, that the world of myth becomes a problem in itself to be solved rather than the sociological issues that created the world in the first place.[26] Nash's argument falls short in two ways. If we analyze the monster of *IT*, for example, the quasi-mythic world of Derry is a symptom of the corruption that Derry suffers, and is thus a manifestation of the same. In fact, as Samantha Figliola maintains, King arguably sees both the vulnerability and the resilience of the children in the face of danger as having a mythic importance of their own.[27] The monster and its social habitat do not form disjointed parts but are instead complementary. By way of their function as a social mirror, both It and Derry reflect back the sinister hatred and psychotic rage of people like Henry Bowers and, once he arrives in Derry, Beverly's husband, Tom. The way to fight the monster does not lead through an alternative fantasy world; it does not distract the readers from the psychological and physical abuse suffered by Beverly at the hands of her father, or the violent bullying endured by Ben, Eddie, and the others at the hands of Henry Bowers, who assaults them on a regular basis. Instead, the path to It's lair cuts through the minds of children, who are compelled to confront their fears and deal with their mental struggles without any help from the adults. Moreover, despite being taunted by It about their inability to face the monster as adults, and their own apprehensions regarding the same, they successfully kill It once and for all by strengthening their former belief systems. King therefore upholds the importance of adults retaining the imaginative power and the open-mindedness of children rather than valuing one developmental stage over the other. The imaginative perspective of the children becomes an epistemological framework in itself, through which a complex knowledge about the cosmic and the social world is attained.

IT transforms a simple children's tale into a twisted tale of horror, wherein the members of the Losers' Club have to defend themselves from the monster without any outside help, and at the risk of losing their lives or even their existence in the deadlights. Tracing the presence of certain fairy tale motifs in *IT*, Strengell observes how King weaves in thematic elements from "Snow

White and the Seven Dwarfs," "Hansel and Gretel," "Jack and the Beanstalk," and other children's tales, only to reveal the deeper implications of horror embedded in them. For example, he likens Beverly's encounter with It to the encounter of Snow White with the witch, highlighting the underlying issue of parental abuse in both cases.[28] The format of the children's tale with gigantic monsters and trolls does not downplay the issue of childhood abuse but rather magnifies the voice of the child victims, by offering them a mode of storytelling conducive to their imagination. That is probably why the cosmic monster It appears as a clown, familiar to the kids, rather than in its original form. Instead of the oft-used trope of the fear of the unknown, King uses the fear of the familiar in order to uncover the ugly truth of child victimization. He subverts the adult worldview, which casually disregards the possibility that children can be a part of serious social discourse, too. When adult Richie calls his radio-host manager Steve Covall to tell him that he would have to go away for a while to keep a promise, the latter replies, "Kids don't make serious promises when they're eleven, for Christ's sake!"[29] This social exclusion of children from matters of "adult" importance is what King challenges in his novel.

In this context, he deviates from two significant trends of representing childhood prevalent in the twentieth-century popular horror. The first is the idea of the demonic child, or as Sabine Büssing calls them, the "evil innocent" who "is a perfectly amiable and tender creature which is driven to do evil things by forces beyond its control."[30] David Seltzer's *The Omen* (1976), William Peter Blatty's *The Exorcist* (1973), and Ira Levin's *Rosemary's Baby* (1968) all feature children who act as vessels for evil by default. On the other hand is the Victorian trope of the sexually innocent child who acts as a sacrificial victim, as seen in Ray Russell's *The Case Against Satan* or Robin Hardy's film *The Wicker Man*—a trope already challenged by Henry James's *The Turn of the Screw* (1898)[31] and which King totally subverts in the orgy scene in the sewers.[32] Both as victims and victimizers, however, most children in twentieth-century horror fiction seem to lack a conscious moral choice. According to Karen J. Renner, in evil-child narratives, evil becomes an effect of a demonic influence rather than a cause originating within the subject; the child is envisioned as inherently corrupted rather than being credited for the wrong actions they commit.[33] They are either wired to do evil because of demonic possession or typecast into vulnerable victims unable to defend themselves. But in *IT*, as in many other works by King, the evil child cannot just be exorcised or returned to the category of the Child,[34] thereby being absolved of all guilt. Rather, their actions as an individual, or as a group, have long-term and widespread repercussions both in their own lives and in the society in which they live, and which demand accountability.

It is interesting to note that King's treatment of the evil child motif offers a much more layered psychological understanding than many other texts mentioned above because of his acknowledgment of the serious social trauma that many children have to face on a daily basis. For example, the transformation of *Carrie*'s titular protagonist from a friendless girl to a violent teenager bent on exacting revenge is fueled by her social exclusion from peer groups. The act of doing "evil" becomes an act of social deviancy much more than an act of moral deviancy in King's novels. Henry Bowers, then, is as much of a victim as the Losers because the physical abuse he suffers at the hands of his father turns him into a criminally minded teenager who is hurried on to the path of his own destruction. The equation of trauma and evil is best understood in the episode in Juniper Hill where Henry Bowers hears the voice of It hollering at him and ordering him to kill the Losers: "Henry went down like a ton of bricks, the voice of the clown following him down into that terrible whirlpool of darkness, chanting over and over again: *Kill them all, Henry, kill them all, kill them all, kill them all.*"[35] The trauma that Bowers had suffered has not only caused him to inflict the same kind of physical and emotional pain on other children but it has forever altered his core, almost enslaving him to a culture of violence. The voice of It which follows and traumatizes him is the voice of his own abusive personality which he developed as a response to familial trauma. Sándor Ferenczi in his study on the traumatic relationship with an adult refers to this defense mechanism in children as the "identification with the aggressor" wherein the victim is compelled "to subordinate themselves like automata to the will of the aggressor, to divine each one of his desires and to gratify these."[36] Bowers listens to the voice of It from the "ghost-moon" asking him to kill because he has already identified himself with the abusive traits of his father from childhood.

King, however, does not engineer moral weakness or moral superiority into the makeup of his child characters. Unlike the "hero" in fairy tales, Bill, Ben, Beverly, and the others are not considered to be always morally correct by default; just as Bowers is not assumed to be "evil" by default. Rather, they are given a space to make ethical choices, depending upon which, they either become good or evil. Jonathan P. Davis argues that although the productive imagination of the children triumphs over the imaginative atrophy of the adults, and is the only means of combating evil in King's world, they are ultimately dependent upon these adults who claim superiority over them. As a result, the corruption of innocence often leads these vulnerable children to absorb the adult impressions of society that involve violence, greed, and hostility.[37] However, the most dramatic moments in the novel are also those in which the children break free from this corrupting adult influence and establish their individuality by making independent moral choices. Both Beverly and Bowers, for example, have fathers who regularly subject them to physical abuse. Beverly overcomes this physical trauma by resisting her father's violation of her body,[38] and by actively fighting against the monster. Bowers, on the other hand, internalizes this culture of violence and abuse, taking out his frustration on Ben and the others, just as his father takes out his frustration on him. Faced with a similar moral situation, Beverly and Bowers take two different courses, and thus have two different ethical personalities.

The reaction of Bowers towards parental abuse—which ultimately leads him to murder his father—is echoed even in King's *The Shining*, and later in *Doctor Sleep* (2013). The murderous rage of Jack Torrance can be attributed to the abuse he suffered at the hands of his own father.[39] Similarly, his son Danny, who had his arm broken by his father for spilling beer on his papers, becomes an alcoholic with anger issues.[40] Both the Bowers family and the Torrance family are therefore trapped in the cycle of an intergenerational transmission of violence, where, as per the study conducted by Woollett and Thomson, children growing up in abusive environments learn that violence is normal, appropriate, and inescapable in intimate relationships.[41] This is why Beverly continues to live with Tom, who assaults her physically; for Beverly, violence and abuse have been normalized as part of her relationships. As opposed to this quiet acceptance of intimate partner violence (IPV), Bowers displays symptoms of displaced aggression. His failure to escape or oppose his father's mistreatment when he fails his exams causes him to divert his anger towards Ben.

However, King does not justify or excuse their behavior as deterministic and inevitable. While Bowers perpetuates the cycle of abuse, the Losers' Club builds a community that provides them the security and the sense of belongingness absent in many of their families, helping them to break the chain of violence. Similarly, in the sequel to *The Shining*, Dan gradually recovers from alcoholism and channels his psychic powers to help dying people, becoming the eponymous "Doctor Sleep." Thus, King provides his child protagonists with alternatives and opportunities to escape the inter-generational cycle of abuse, making them the agents of their own morality. In fact, it is the memory of the Losers' Club, and specifically of Bill, that helps Beverly break free from Tom's clutches. Before remembering her time with the Losers, when Tom catches Beverly smoking, he slaps her and threatens to beat her. Sitting in the car quietly acquiescing to Tom's dictates she real-izes that "[h]e had regressed her. He was in this car with a child."[42] Beverly's response to the aggressor has not only incapacitated her from taking any action against him but has made her equate childhood with powerlessness, thus silencing her history of resistance and struggle as a child. Mike's phone call brings back to her the memory of her past and gives her the strength to fight back against Tom for the first time. The memory of their childhood is therefore not just a source of repressed trauma for the Losers; it is a story of their victory against the forces of oppression, it is a story of hope, no matter how perverted and painful.

Throughout their crusade against It, Bill questions whether he has done the right thing by dragging others into his mission of avenging George's death. This reveals that the ethical choices made in this novel are not unchallengeable actions taken from a moral high ground. The fact that Bill and the others are able to question, assess, and make their own decisions proves that a significant shift has occurred not only in the way that children are represented in fiction, but in the way they are perceived in the society. One of the landmarks in the history of child-rights acts was signed at the United Nations Convention on the Rights of the Child held in November of 1989 in New York. Of the various rights granted to children, including the right to protection from abuse and the right to provisions for basic survival, the right to participation is of special importance. Article 12 of the UNCRC's resulting human rights treaty grants children the right to express their views freely and to be heard in matters of judicial and administrative proceedings relating to that child. Although King's novel slightly precedes the passing of this right to participation, we can already detect the change in the position of children within the social discourse.

One of the obvious visual tropes King employs in order to emphasize the unique perspectives and preoccupations of the children in *IT* is that of the absent parents, wherein, Cary R. Goehring observes, the parents' focus is blurred or the children are removed from their gaze.[43] For example, the coldness of Bill's parents towards him after George's death is in one respect a way to remove Bill from the focused attention of his parents, so that he can carry out the task of killing the monster, without arousing suspicion in them. However, in order to situate Bill and the others at the center of the social discourse, it is essential that they are visible in adult social spaces and not just in an alternative world of their own. King successfully achieves this by showing us the overlapping contact zones between the world of children and the world of adults, giving the children an opportunity to make their presence felt. When Ben's mother sits him down and warns him about the dangers lurking in Derry, asking him if he has seen anything suspicious recently, Ben stops short of telling her about his encounter with Penny-wise under the canal because he feels a responsibility towards her; there is almost a sense that he is trying to protect her from this horrific knowledge and trying to put her mind at ease: "Even children may intuit love's more complex responsibilities from time to time . . ."[44] Therefore, the equation of the protector and the protected is deliberately reversed, so as to alter Ben's position from a passive victim to that of an active survivor and guardian.

As I'll discuss further in the final section, *IT* is as much about childhood as it is about the passing of childhood. The children in King's world, according to Tony Magistrale, "are caught between states of being: Not quite adults, yet forced to experience the complex emotions that push them toward a maturation that remains as terrifying as it is desirable."[45] This rite of passage from childhood to adolescence and then to adulthood requires a ritualistic shattering of the boundaries of protection within which the child is placed. Each of the members of the Losers' Club has their own decisive moment during which s/he breaks through these boundaries of protection. For Bill, this moment occurs after the death of his brother which leads him to take up the dangerous responsibility of killing It. Despite all of the pain he goes through, Bill's trauma doesn't cripple him psychologically. To the contrary, he is forced to assume leadership in the group where everyone looks up to him for advice and guidance. As the narrator says, "And in some odd way they all sensed something comfortingly adult about Bill—perhaps it was accountability, a feeling that Bill would take the responsibility if responsibility needed to be taken."[46] Surprisingly the trauma of his brother's death is what creates this sense of accountability in Bill. Similarly, when Beverly runs away from her father realizing that It was working through him, she not only saves herself from the monster It but liberates herself from the tyranny of Al Marsh and establishes a defining moment for her passage into adulthood by taking control of her sexuality.[47] Eddie too ironically breaks through the restrictions on his movement and actions placed on him by his health-obsessed mother. When Bowers breaks his arm, he muses: "I think it was the first real pain I ever felt in my life. [. . .] it gave me a basis for comparison, finding out you could still exist inside the pain, in spite of the pain."[48] It is after this incident that Eddie learns to resist the dominating influence of his overly protective mother.

The symbolic defeat of Pennywise, who planned to trap Bill in the dead-lights, thus has a dual significance when seen in the context of this child-adult dynamic. On the one hand, it establishes the Losers as child heroes who challenge the adult discourse of protection that is cunningly designed to monitor and delimit their lives. On the other hand, it acts as a mental catalyst, helping them to gradually cross over to adulthood. The intervention of Pennywise in the lives of the Losers' Club does not lead to an "aborted childhood,"[49] as Magistrale believes, because they are forced to confront the dark underbelly

of Derry too early in life. Rather, Pennywise itself is a kind of coping mechanism, which helps the otherwise marginalized children of the Losers' Club
achieve a feeling of social belongingness. Ostracized because of their stutter,
or weight, or race, or gender, they try to reclaim their social status by choosing to defeat the monster and taking on the mantle of the "hero."

REVISITING THE LAIR: ESTABLISHING A CONTINUITY

Most studies of King's treatment of children envision his child heroes as
Wordsworthian ideals of moral goodness pitted against a corrupt world.
According to Magistrale, they are "perfect victims" who have to fight the
prevailing values of their society by the supernatural and imaginative abilities with which they are endowed.[50] Marina Warner, similarly, argues that the
child and the soul are somehow interchangeable, which makes children "the
keepers and the guarantors of humanity's reputation."[51] King himself believes
that the imagination of children acts like "a marvelous third eye that floats
free" that helps them to see with a clarity that adults lack.[52] At the same time,
as Warner says, the idea of a separate sphere of childhood implies that they
are somehow not entirely a part of human society, and are not incorporated
into history.[53] However, I establish in this section that King does not picture
childhood and adulthood as mutually exclusive developmental stages, but as
parts of a continuum with overlapping worldviews. This leads King to raise
one of the most significant questions in works like *IT* or *'Salem's Lot*: can
childhood and its traumas be repressed, forgotten, and swept back into the
dark mental recesses of the past, or is it necessary to acknowledge their persistent impact on one's behavior, personality, and life choices even as an adult?

   IT dramatizes the fear of growing up as much as it focuses on the struggles
of childhood. One of the primary concerns of the members of the Losers'
Club is that the events of the summer of 1958 would bring about their sudden
transformation, ending their spate of childhood adventures and innocence.
King frames this transformation as a shift from the instinctive behavior of
children to the cold reason of adulthood. When Ben, for example, carefully
designs a plan to dodge Henry Bowers at school, he realizes that "the cold-
bloodedness of his calculations, the careful and pragmatic counting of the
cost, with its intimations of onrushing adulthood" scares Ben more than
Henry scares him because, "Henry he might be able to dodge. Adulthood,
where he would probably think in such a way almost all the time, would
get him in the end."[54] Apparently, then, there is a discontinuity between the
cognitive mechanism of childhood and that of the adults. The fear of Ben,

Bill, and the others that they would be unable to defeat Pennywise as adults is arguably, then, the fear that their adult rationality has taken over their childhood personas once and for all.

The anxiety of transforming into an adult is also marked by changes in one's physical appearance. When Bill is about to reunite with the members of the Losers' Club, he becomes conscious of how Mike looks so different with his wrinkles and graying hair, just as he becomes conscious of his own age, which frightens him.[55] This physical transformation into adulthood is symbolized in *IT* by Bill's discarded bicycle Silver, which he finds in a secondhand shop in Derry when he returns as an adult. The bicycle in King's novels is often used as a symbol of the regenerative powers of childhood as opposed to the degenerative and destructive world of adults symbolized by cars. The act of abandoning the bicycle, according to Don Tresca, is therefore a symptom of the encroachment of worldly evil upon the innocence of childhood.[56] When Bill once again rides his bicycle with his wife Audra, she is magically restored from her state of coma induced by It.[57] What brings about this magic, however, is not Silver per se, but rather Bill's fresh perception of his body, brought about by his conversation with the kid riding the skateboard. Thus, Bill's "desire to *be* the boy"[58] when he sees the kid riding his skateboard like he used to ride Silver reconnects him to his own childhood.

The ability of Bill to bring back Audra from coma by riding Silver once again is King's final statement on the importance of bridging "the difference between world and want—the difference between being an adult who counted the cost and a child who just got on it and went, for instance."[59] Silver merely serves as a medium through which Bill is able to overcome his anxieties about his changed physical state, and to reignite the confidence he had as a child. Silver also psychologically connects him to two of the most significant moments of his childhood. The first moment is when he races across the town to get Eddie's aspirator and save his life, and the second is when he and Richie ride on Silver and escape the clutches of It running after them in the shape of a werewolf. While the first episode strengthens the bond between Eddie, Bill, and Ben, the second deals with their bold, impulsive decision to go after Pennywise with a slingshot, pistol, and sneezing powder. Although Bill's oversized biked symbolically hints that the Losers have taken up a task too serious and dangerous for their age, it also represents everything Bill stands for: friendship, loyalty, courage, and determination in the face of trouble. The manipulative plotting of Pennywise that brings Bill back to Derry also reconnects him to his former persona through Silver, just as it helps Beverly to regain her former mental strength and break free from Tom's tyranny. Pennywise is therefore neither just a cosmic monster, nor an amalgamation of Derry's social evils; instead, It symbolizes the raw, untamed, instinctive, and unnamable force of childhood—a childhood whose memories the Losers' Club have securely packed and stowed away from their adult lives. In forcing them to return to their childhood memories, It reawakens in them their childhood eccentricities and emotions so that it can be accommodated and integrated into their adult personas.

CONCLUSION

The philosophy behind *IT* is not just based on the Romantic notion of childhood as a period of pure innocence and simplicity. Nor does it ignore the adult anxieties and experiences as insignificant to its mode of storytelling. Rather, the subversive power of King's novel lies in its ability to simultaneously identify the parallel existence of the world of children and the world of adults, and to establish a meaningful connection between the two. This transition and transformation, which is fraught with danger and deception, requires both the impulsive insight of childhood and the careful foresight of adulthood, so that the individual can develop a healthy psychological space. Thus, Pennywise is more than the troll under the bridge who scares Ben on his way back home; he is the gatekeeper of the bridge between childhood and adulthood, who unconsciously trains them to face the hurdles of growing up. Consequently, a return to one's hometown becomes more than a matter of nostalgia in *IT*. As the members of the Losers' Club return to Derry one by one, the clown with the balloon lies in wait to remind them of the vast undercurrent of unprocessed trauma and childhood experiences which need urgent attention, before they clog and flood the Losers minds like Ben's dam on the Kenduskeag clogs the city's sewer system. The recurrent image of the clogged sewers is also a metaphorical indicator of the way in which the trauma of childhood has lodged itself in the minds of Bill, Ben, and others, so much so that they are unable to access their past memories without disrupting their adult lives. King shows us the importance of unclogging these channels of memories, so that the adult and the child persona can interact and overlap with each other, and annihilate any psychological monster that may have been created in the transitionary space between childhood and adulthood.

Notes

1. Guy Debord, "Introduction to a Critique of Urban Geography," in *Situationist International Anthology*, ed. and trans. Ken Knabb (Berkeley: Bureau of Public Secrets, 2006), 8.

2. Stephen King, *'Salem's Lot* (London: Hodder & Stoughton, 2006).

3. John Sears, *Stephen King's Gothic* (Cardiff: University of Wales Press, 2011), 156.

4. The Black Spot was a club created by the Black soldiers of the army base of Derry when they were asked to stay away from the NCO club by the Town Council, solely because of the racial prejudice they held against them. In 1930, the place was burned down by the Legion of White Decency with the people still inside. The interlude of the Black Spot shows us that Mike situates the history of the town at the confluence of myth, memory, and magic, and thus cautions us against singularly interpreting it as the lair of Pennywise.

5. King, *IT*, 236–37.

6. King, *IT*, 1105.

7. King, *IT*, 391–92.

8. Debord, "Introduction to a Critique of Urban Geography," 10.

9. Sears, *Stephen King's Gothic*, 156.

10. King, *IT*, 1137–38.

11. King, *IT*, 476–77.

12. King, *IT*, 406–8.

13. Stephen King, *The Shining* (London: Hodder & Stoughton, 2011), 14.

14. King, *IT*, 291.

15. King, *IT*, 1092–94.

16. King, *IT*, 333–35.

17. King, *IT*, 703–5.

18. King, *IT*, 1269–70.

19. Maria Tumarkin, *Traumascapes: The Power and Fate of Places Transformed by Tragedy* (Carlton: Melbourne University Press, 2005), 13–14.

20. King, *IT*, 633.

21. King, *IT*, 604.

22. King, *IT*, 1317–20.

23. Heidi Strengell, *Dissecting Stephen King: From the Gothic to Literary Naturalism* (Madison: University of Wisconsin Press, 2005), 168–85.

24. King, *IT*, 213.

25. Jesse W. Nash, "Postmodern Gothic: Stephen King's Pet Sematary," *Journal of Popular Culture* 30, no. 4 (2004): 154–55.

26. Nash, "Postmodern Gothic: Stephen King's Pet Sematary," 158.

27. Samantha Figliola, "The Thousand Faces of Danny Torrance," in *Discovering Stephen King's The Shining: Essays on the Bestselling Novel by America's Premier Horror Writer*, ed. Tony Magistrale (Cabin John: Wildside Press, 2006), 55.

28. Strengell, *Dissecting Stephen King*, 175–77.

29. King, *IT*, 79.

30. Sabine Büssing, *Aliens in the Home: The Child in Horror Fiction* (New York: Greenwood Press, 1987), xviii.

31. Sara Martín Alegre, "Nightmares of Childhood: The Child and the Monster in Four Novels by Stephen King," *Atlantis* 23, no. 1 (2001): 106.

32. King, *IT*, 1309–15.

33. Karen J. Renner, *Evil Children in the Popular Imagination* (New York: Palgrave Macmillan, 2016), 7–8.

34. Renner, *Evil Children in the Popular Imagination*, 8.

35. King, IT, 744.

36. Sándor Ferenczi, "Confusion of the Tongues Between the Adults and the Child—(The Language of Tenderness and of Passion)," *International Journal of Psychoanalysis*, no. 30 (1949): 227.

37. Jonathan P. Davis, *Stephen King's America* (Bowling Green, OH: Bowling Green State University Popular Press, 1994), 49–50.

38. King, *IT*, 1097–98.

39. King, *The Shining*.

40. Stephen King, *Doctor Sleep* (London: Hodder & Stoughton, 2014).

41. Nataly Woollett and Kristen Thomson, "Understanding the Intergenerational Transmission of Violence," *South African Medical* 106, no. 11 (November 2016) :1068.

42. King, *IT*, 130.

43. Cary R. Goehring, "Seven Children and It: Stephen King's *IT* as Children's Story," in *The Many Lives of IT: Essays on the Stephen King Horror Franchise*, ed. Ron Riekki (Jefferson, NC: McFarland & Company, 2020), 20.

44. King, *IT*, 222.

45. Tony Magistrale, *Hollywood's Stephen King* (New York: Palgrave Macmillan, 2003), 45.

46. King, *IT*, 381.

47. King, *IT*, 1095.

48. King, *IT*, 948.

49. Magistrale, *Hollywood's Stephen King*, 34.

50. Magistrale, *Hollywood's Stephen King*, 22–23.

51. Marina Warner, *Managing Monsters: Six Myths of Our Time—The 1994 Reith Lectures* (London: Vintage, 1994), 35.

52. Stephen King, *Danse Macabre* (New York: Gallery Books, 2010), 434.

53. Marina Warner, *Six Myths of Our Time: Little Angels, Little Monsters, Beautiful Beasts, and More* (London: Vintage Books, 1995), 47.

54. King, *IT*, 205.

55. King, *IT*, 582.

56. Don Tresca, "'Hi-Yo, Silver'—The Bicycle in the Fiction of Stephen King," in *Culture on Two Wheels: The Bicycle in Literature and Film*, eds. Jeremy Withers and Daniel P. Shea (Lincoln: University of Nebraska Press, 2016), 172.

57. King, *IT*, 1373.

58. King, *IT*, 720.

59. King, *IT*, 1369–70.

References

Alegre, Sara Martín. "Nightmares of Childhood: The Child and the Monster in Four Novels by Stephen King." *Atlantis* 23, no. 1 (2001): 105–14.

Davis, Jonathan P. *Stephen King's America*. Bowling Green, OH: Bowling Green State University Popular Press, 1994.

Debord, Guy. "Introduction to a Critique of Urban Geography." In *Situationist International Anthology*, edited and translated by Ken Knabb, 8. Berkeley: Bureau of Public Secrets, 2006.

Ferenczi, Sándor. "Confusion of the Tongues Between the Adults and the Child—(The Language of Tenderness and of Passion)." *International Journal of Psychoanalysis*, no. 30 (1949): 225–30.

Figliola, Samantha. "The Thousand Faces of Danny Torrance." In *Discovering Stephen King's "The Shining": Essays on the Bestselling Novel by America's Premier Horror Writer*, edited by Tony Magistrale, 54–73. Cabin John: Wildside Press, 2006.

Goehring, Cary R. "Seven Children and It: Stephen King's *IT* as Children's Story." In *The Many Lives of "IT": Essays on the Stephen King Horror Franchise*, edited by Ron Riekki, 18–31. Jefferson: McFarland & Company, 2020.

King, Stephen. *Carrie*. 1974; reprint, London: Hodder & Stoughton, 2011.

King, Stephen. *Danse Macabre*. 1981; reprint, New York: Gallery Books, 2010.

King, Stephen. *Doctor Sleep*. 2013; reprint, London: Hodder & Stoughton, 2014.

King, Stephen. *IT*. Great Britain: Hodder & Stoughton, 1986.

King, Stephen. *'Salem's Lot*. 1975; reprint, London: Hodder & Stoughton, 2006.

King, Stephen. *The Shining*. 1977; reprint, London: Hodder & Stoughton, 2011.

Magistrale, Tony. *Hollywood's Stephen King*. New York: Palgrave Macmillan, 2003.

Nash, Jesse W. "Postmodern Gothic: Stephen King's Pet Sematary." *Journal of Popular Culture* 30, no. 4 (2004): 151–60.

Renner, Karen J. *Evil Children in the Popular Imagination*. New York: Palgrave Macmillan, 2016.

Sears, John. *Stephen King's Gothic*. Cardiff: University of Wales Press, 2011.

Tresca, Don. "'Hi-Yo, Silver'—The Bicycle in the Fiction of Stephen King." In *Culture on Two Wheels: The Bicycle in Literature and Film*, edited by Jeremy Withers and Daniel P. Shea. Lincoln: University of Nebraska Press, 2016.

Tumarkin, Maria. *Traumascapes: The Power and Fate of Places Transformed by Tragedy*. Carlton: Melbourne University Press, 2005.

Warner, Maria. *Managing Monsters: Six Myths of Our Time—The 1994 Reith Lectures*. London: Vintage, 1994.

Warner, Maria. *Six Myths of Our Time: Little Angels, Little Monsters, Beautiful Beasts, and More*. London: Vintage Books, 1995.

Woollett, Nataly, and Kristen Thomson. "Understanding the Intergenerational Transmission of Violence." *South African Medical* 106, no. 11 (November 2016): 1068–1107.

Countercultures

Chapter 4

"A SUDDEN UPHEAVAL
OF BEAUTY OR TERROR"

Body Horror and Abjection in Stephen King's *IT*

MARGARET J. YANKOVICH

"Description," writes Stephen King in *On Writing*, "is what makes the reader a sensory participant in the story. [. . .] It's not just a question of *how-to*, you see; it's also a question of *how much to*."[1] In *IT*, King deploys profuse descriptions of bodily excess, transformation, and horror to overwhelm the reader with the abject. Indeed, *IT* is a novel full of descriptions of unruly, transgressive bodies—diseased bodies, queer bodies, alien bodies—and it is the corporeal descriptions of these bodies within the text, and their fixation on the warping of human and inhuman forms, from which the narrative derives its visceral power to horrify.

IT is preoccupied with abjection and body horror, which reveals a deep insecurity about the lack of control over our innately unruly bodies. The novel is shaped by repulsive bodies: Eddie Kaspbrak's obsession with disease, made manifest in the leper; Patrick Hockstetter as the ultimate abject child, hypersexualized, violent, and queer; and Pennywise/It as the embodiment of that most primal form of the monstrous-feminine, the "archaic mother."[2] The repulsion the reader inevitably feels toward these chaotic bodies in transgression exposes larger, collective fears surrounding decay, disintegration, and death.

In order to engage with a reading of *IT* in the context of body horror and abjection, these terms must first be defined. Body horror, according to Paul Wells, is "the explicit display of the decay, dissolution or destruction of the body."[3] Wells's emphasis in his definition is on bodily disintegration and transformation: the body horror subgenre is built upon fear of a lack of bodily control and autonomy, and often involves the radical transformation of bodies by supernatural means. In *IT*, the body horror motif is exemplified by the ways in which disease, queerness, and alien monstrosity are mobilized to subject the reader to what Julia Kristeva calls "corporeality,"[4] or an uncanny stretching of the imagination wherein one is left to face images of bodily transgression, and necessitates the collapse of the wall which fundamentally separates the Self and the Other.[5]

"There looms, within abjection," Kristeva puts forth in *Powers of Horror: An Essay on Abjection*, "one of those violent, dark revolts of being, directed against a threat that seems to emanate from an exorbitant outside or inside, ejected beyond the scope of the possible, the tolerable, the thinkable."[6] Horror is derived from that inexplicable moment when excess, waste, and uncleanliness we disdain and compartmentalize as Other, can no longer be separated from a clean, submissive body. It is at this point of crisis or uncanny transgression, when one can no longer separate the filth and disease from oneself, that we are truly horrified by our own bodies in a state of assimilation with the Other. *IT* propels the reader headlong into this moment of crisis, forcing them to confront the mayhem of abject bodies, left unchecked in their excesses. The novel highlights a pervasive social fear of bodies that disrupt normality, that refuse to fit in arbitrarily defined categories of normalcy. In this way, the text reflects and perpetuates the predominant cultural attitude toward unruly bodies marked by a pronounced anxiety over corporeal transgressions and abjection.

"TERRIBLE RESEMBLANCES":
EDDIE KASPBRAK AND THE LEPER

One of the most repulsive images in a novel full of repulsion, is that of the "the leper"[7] young Eddie Kaspbrak meets at the derelict house on Neibolt Street. As Pennywise takes the shape of whatever its child-victim fears the most, it is only logical that, in Eddie's eyes, the shapeshifting monster manifests itself as the personification of contamination and disease—in other words, total *abjection*, which Eddie fears above all else. It is crucial, however, that Pennywise appears as a leper only after Eddie's encounter with a "hobo" who wanders out from under the porch at 29 Neibolt Street. The man offers to "give Eddie a blowjob for a quarter," and Eddie, sickened, "backed away, his skin like ice, his mouth as dry as lintballs."[8] Eddie sees that "one of the hobo's nostrils had been eaten away. You could look right into the red, scabby channel."[9] Here, Eddie confronts a person who embodies his fears of abjection. The "hobo" who confronts Eddie is presented, by way of his ghastly description, as a kind of reanimated corpse; Kristeva would suggest that it is "seen without God and outside of science" and "is the utmost of abjection. It is death infecting life."[10] For Eddie, the "hobo" is abject for how it "disturbs identity, system, order"[11] by threatening the stability of Eddie's own identity with the "hobo's" bodily capacity to contaminate, destroying those borders that define and separate cleanliness from filth, health from disease.

The "hobo's" bodily abjection is also problematically queer. "'I'll do it for a dime,' the hobo croaked, coming toward him. [. . .] Yellow puke was stiffening across the lap. He unzipped his fly and reached inside."[12] Not only does the "hobo" pose a physical threat to Eddie, but he poses a distinctly sexual one as well. "Monsters," Noël Carroll postulates, "may also trigger certain enduring infantile fears, such as being eaten or dismembered, or sexual fears, concerning rape and incest."[13] The "hobo's" monstrosity is thus also located firmly in his queerness, which is conflated with his rotting, filthy body. Later, Richie and Bill explain to Eddie that the disease which afflicted the "hobo" was not leprosy, but syphilis, a "disease you get from fucking."[14] Thus, abjection and disease are entwined with a monstrous, aberrant sexuality that is troublingly queered within the text. In doing so, the narrative renders the "hobo" an expression of not just bodily horror, but a sexual horror. His very presence threatens to destabilize Eddie's already tenuous grasp on the realities of sickness and disease, which threatens to snap when he is later confronted by Pennywise as the leper. More than this, the queering of the "hobo" in his sexual advances toward Eddie, who was at this point in the novel still a child, is deeply disturbing, for it conflates queerness with sexual predation and pedophilia. Here, the text relies on inaccurate and insidious stereotypes of queerness in order to evoke imagery of absolute abjection.

When Eddie returns to the house at 29 Neibolt Street, it is perhaps prompted by an "unhealthy fascination" and "kind of glow in Eddie's imagination"[15] about his previous encounter with the "hobo." The destabilization between the Self (Eddie) and the Other (the "hobo") has already begun; as the "hobo" represents the ultimate abject, in Eddie's mind, he also represents everything Eddie's overprotective mother restricts him from accessing. Consequently, abjection insidiously works its way into Eddie's mind as an alluring freedom, a temptation to give in to everything he was always taught to fear. Indeed, "the time of abjection is double: a time of oblivion and thunder, of veiled infinity and the moment when revelation bursts forth."[16] The allure of the abject lies in its capacity to liberate Eddie from the ordered, suffocating confines constructed by his mother.

Yet when Eddie crawls under the porch of 29 Neibolt Street, he is at once confronted with a monster more putrid than the "hobo": "His eyes bulged.

His mouth creaked open. It was not the hobo with the flayed nose, but there were resemblances. Terrible resemblances. And yet . . . this thing could not be human. Nothing could be so eaten up and remain alive."[17] In *The Philosophy of Horror: Or, Paradoxes of the Heart*, Noël Carroll indicates that "horrific creatures seem to be regarded not only as inconceivable but also as unclean and disgusting."[18] Eddie cannot conceive how a living human being could be "so eaten up"[19] by disease and infection. He is horrified by the inconceivable notion that a being so consumed by waste and defilement could still live. In the face of such abjection, Eddie is shocked into uncanny corporeality.

The next passage is consumed with vivid descriptions of Pennywise disguised as the leper:

> The skin of his forehead was split open. White bone, coated with a membrane of yellow mucusy stuff, peered through like the lens of a bleary searchlight. The nose was a bridge of raw gristle above two red flaring channels. One eye was a gleeful blue. The other socket was filled with a mass of spongy brown-black tissue. The leper's lower lip sagged like liver. It had no upper lip at all; its teeth poked out in a sneering ring.[20]

This scene reads like a perverse catalogue of everything that can happen to a body through the transformative processes of disease and decay, which, despite all logic, could endure. It is the essence of body horror, which, according to Xavier Aldana Reyes, is "imbued in the transformation and mutation of the body" and "the processes of contagion and subsequent dermatologic or carnal metamorphosis."[21] The language describing the creature is devoid of anything human: any pronouns such as his/him are replaced with it/its. Eddie cannot conceive of the possibility that the thing in front of him, with a human shape, is in any way human. It is solely and completely abject.

Most significantly, Eddie's encounter with Pennywise as the leper affirms Eddie's worst fear: that the abject can contaminate his own body, and by extension, threaten the psychic boundaries that protect the Self. "Its hand reached out again, and in some corner of his panic-maddened, screaming mind, Eddie was suddenly, coldly sure that if that thing touched his bare skin, he would begin to rot too."[22] It is not just the fear of looking at this inhuman embodiment of disease that poses a danger to Eddie's Self; it is also the physical threat of contamination that pushes Eddie to the edge of sanity. Carroll poses that "[e]motionally, these violations of nature are so fulsome and revolting that they frequently produce in characters the conviction that the mere physical contact with them can be lethal."[23] Hence, Eddie has the *conviction* that bare contact between his body and that of the leper will cause him to rot, to fall prey to whatever disease—leprosy, syphilis—is carried by It. His mind threatens to snap under the stress that such contamination will fundamentally destabilize Eddie's Self from that Other: total abjection.

Eddie's initial encounter with the "hobo," and later, Pennywise's profoundly abject imitation thereof, reads as quintessential body horror. Reyes posits that "body horror places the focus on indeterminacy and estrangement from one's own body."[24] Furthermore, it is Eddie's estrangement from his own Self in the face of absolute abjection in the form of the leper, that *IT* locates body horror in the fear of the abject and that which "does not respect borders, positions, rules."[25] In Eddie's limited conceptualization of reality—which has been constrained by his hypochondriac mother—the leper does not "fit" and threatens the stability of his reality. Pennywise threatens to contaminate Eddie's sense of Self as the embodiment of the one thing he has been taught to fear above everything else: sickness. In the face of a being who is all-consumed with disease, Eddie must cope with the abject, or it will consume him as well.

"A SQUIRMY SORT OF REVULSION": THE QUEER AND ABJECT BODY OF PATRICK HOCKSTETTER[26]

Perhaps the only character in the novel who is as repulsive as Pennywise itself is Patrick Hockstetter. The horrors of this strange and sadistic child are not fully realized until chapter 17, "Another One of the Missing: The Death of Patrick Hockstetter."[27] For roughly thirty-four pages, the reader sees little of Pennywise. Instead, they witness the monstrous deeds of the singularly abject Patrick Hockstetter, murderer of his infant brother and torturer of neighborhood pets. Remembering Patrick, the Losers share stories of his strangeness, his madness. Beverly recalls how Patrick would carry a box of dead flies that he would show his unwitting classmates: "'*You'd jerk away and he'd grin and then maybe he'd open his pencil box so you could see the dead flies inside,*' Beverly says. '*And the worst thing—the horrible thing—was the way he'd smile and never say anything.*'"[28] Patrick, here, fits neatly in Andrew Scahill's "Taxonomy of Child Monstrosity," which outlines representations of childhood in its "grotesque form."[29] According to Scahill, "child monstrosity resides in the perceived absorbing quality of children—to learn too much, too fast, and to take the lessons and the expectations too far."[30] There are five figurations in Scahill's "Taxonomy of Child Monstrosity," one of which is "The Watcher," which Scahill posits is the monstrous form of "The Innocent."[31]

Scahill explains that "innocence is a lack of traits, a vague emptiness that has the unfortunate side effect of always being potentially filled up with noninnocent [sic] qualities."[32] Patrick is the embodiment of the Watcher: with his vacant, staring expression and morbid silence, he is the "vacuous child who simultaneously haunts the periphery and seems haunted itself."[33] Patrick lingers in the margins of the Losers' memories, especially those belonging to Beverly, who witnesses his abject queerness in a sexual encounter between Patrick and Henry Bowers.

Beverly recalls stumbling across Henry and his friends with their pants down, igniting each other's flatulence with a lighter. Eventually, the group disperses, leaving Henry and Patrick alone together. Patrick tells Henry "'Let me show you something,'" which turns out to be masturbation: "He had one hand between Henry's thighs and one hand between his own. One hand was flogging Henry's thing gently; with his other hand Patrick was rubbing his own. Except he wasn't exactly rubbing it—he was kind of . . . *squoozing* it, pulling it, letting it flop back down."[34] This sexual encounter, initiated by Patrick, is both abject and horrifying to Beverly, who "had not been this scared since the blood had vomited out of the bathroom drain and splattered all over everything."[35] That is, in this moment, Beverly finds the two boys' sexual encounter just as abjectly terrifying as her first encounter with Pennywise, an inhuman monster. Indeed, the way in which the encounter is described has the effect of Othering Patrick's queerness as simultaneously monstrous and abject. There is an unsettling quality to how Patrick touches Henry's penis, rubbing it, pulling it, "squoozing" it. This passage uses a descriptor that King invented to emphasize the fact that Beverly does not possess the language to describe what, exactly, Patrick is doing to Henry. In this way, the sexual encounter Patrick initiates with Henry is perceived by Beverly and, by extension, the reader, as foreign, alien, and distinctly Other.

Patrick's and Henry's bodies are revoltingly transformed by their sexual encounter. Beverly watches as "Patrick's thing had gotten a little longer, but not much; it still dangled between his legs like a snake with no backbone. Henry's, however, had grown amazingly. It stood up stiff and hard, almost poking his bellybutton. Patrick's hand went up and down . . . sometimes pausing to squeeze, sometimes tickling that odd, heavy sac under Henry's *thing*."[36] Beverly, sexually inexperienced herself, has no point of reference for what she sees biologically happen to Henry's and Patrick's bodies. Thus, their bodies are further rendered inhuman and abject, even animalistic in Beverly's eyes. Patrick's penis becomes a "snake with no backbone," a kind of crawling invertebrate, while Henry's becomes alarmingly "stiff and hard" and so elongated it grazes his stomach. Beverly watches in horror as Patrick and Henry's bodies are repulsively transformed into something inhuman and excessive. Their bodies transgress borders of the human/inhuman, and more significantly, the heterosexual/homosexual. In *The Queer Uncanny: New Perspectives on the Gothic*, Paulina Palmer theorizes that "discussions of monstrosity and the ambivalent response of horror and fascination that it tends to provoke frequently hinge on hybridity and ambiguity, concepts traditionally carrying connotations of the grotesque and the perverse."[37] In this way, the sexual encounter between Patrick and Henry reveals a deeply unsettling ambivalence about queer sexuality within the text. While the other two queer characters seen earlier in the novel—Adrian Mellon and Don Hagarty—evince sympathy and pity from the reader, Patrick's seduction of Henry generates absolute revulsion within the text, and his queerness is subsumed by his psychopathy.

The sexual encounter ends abruptly when Patrick asks Henry if he wants Patrick to fellate him: "'Want me to put it in my mouth?' Patrick asked. His big, livery lips smiled complacently."[38] Patrick's lips are sexualized in the text, large and excessive. Henry snaps out of his stupor, "as if startled from some deep dream,"[39] and physically assaults Patrick. It is as if Patrick hypnotized Henry, and beguiled Henry into letting him trespass the boundaries of his body. Indeed, later in the novel, after Henry experiences a psychotic break, the text refers to the moment Patrick molests him as a pivotal point when the narrow "bridge" that Henry walked over the "mental abyss [. . .] had narrowed to a tightrope."[40] The queer sexual encounter between Patrick and Henry, then, becomes a moment in which Henry is left to face his own abject and queer corporeality, which his tenuous grasp on his own sanity cannot withstand.

When Henry leaves, Beverly is left watching Patrick, who resumes his blank expression: "He seemed hypnotized. A line of blood ran from the corner of his mouth to his chin, and his lips were swelling up on the right side. He seemed not to notice, and once again Beverly felt a squirmy sort of revulsion. Patrick was crazy, all right; she had never in her life wanted so badly to get away from someone."[41] This passage is significant, as the text once again Others Patrick based on his queerness. While Beverly knows about the animals Patrick tortures and kills in the abandoned refrigerator, she does not know he has also killed his infant brother; that is told only to the reader. Beverly's conceptualization of Patrick as abject and Other can be traced directly to the moment she witnesses his sexual encounter with Henry, when it is revealed he is queer. Not only this, but the passage also underscores Patrick as the Watcher. Scahill says that "what separates these children from their more prized [innocent] siblings is that underneath the silence and seeming

unwantingness is the site of a harbored desire or malicious intent."[42] In the
text, Patrick's vacant stare is queered by his sexual encounter with Henry,
and so in a manner similar to what occurs in Eddie's confrontation with the
"hobo," certain troubling and profoundly harmful conclusions are drawn
about queer sexuality. In turn, Beverly sees Patrick's sexuality as so aberrant,
that she fears him above all else including, at that time, Pennywise.

Indeed, the novel's treatment of Patrick Hockstetter as a nascent queer
psychopath has chilling consequences. In his highly influential monograph
Monsters in the Closet: Homosexuality and the Horror Film, Harry M. Benshoff problematizes queer theorists' appropriation of monsters and monstrosity as metaphors for the queer experience. While Patrick's queerness is not
merely metaphor, but is made explicit within the text, it nonetheless reveals
how "the monster queer may be a sexy, alluring, politically progressive figure
to some, while to others, enmeshed in a more traditional model of monsters
and normality, s/he is still a social threat which must be eradicated."[43] Patrick
Hockstetter is not only a "social threat" who kills and maims with impunity,
but he threatens the social order—and both Henry and Beverly's conceptu-
alizations of reality—with his queerness. Yet the social order within the text,
that of Derry, is itself a deeply flawed, intensely homophobic one, not unlike
those that exist in the world outside the novel. The reader sees this explicitly
in the assault and murder of Adrian Mellon earlier in the novel. King based
Adrian Mellon on a young man, Charlie Howard, who was assaulted and
killed in Bangor in 1984, where King was living and writing *IT* at the time.[44]
While this deeply impactful scene speaks to King's keen awareness of the
violently homophobic atmosphere of the 1980s, he nevertheless falls back
on insidious stereotypes of queer villainy in the writing of "the hobo" and
Patrick Hockstetter. In these scenes, queerness is conflated with disease,
pedophilia, and psychopathy; such stereotypes are mobilized to drown the
reader in abjection, to the point of undoing what the text has tried to say
in its empathetic portrayal of Adrian Mellon: that people who are queer
are human. Instead, here, queerness is rendered monstrous, inhuman, and
horrifically abject.

"OH DEAR JESUS IT IS FEMALE":
IT AS THE ARCHAIC MOTHER

It takes the shape of anything that can elicit fear and terror from its victims.
A shapeshifter who is most often perceived by the children it stalks as some
form of "Pennywise the Dancing Clown,"[45] the eponymous monster's true

form is ancient, alien, and is gendered within the text as female, though its femaleness violates the heteronormative notion of the gender binary. In other words, when It is seen without one of It's many disguises—including that of Pennywise—It is revealed to be the embodiment of Kristeva's conception of the "archaic mother," the fear of which, she writes, "turns out to be essentially fear of her generative power."[46] It's primordial and alien origin is discovered in the novel when the Losers have a Smoke-Hole ceremony in their clubhouse, and Mike and Richie have a vision of It as it crashes down in primeval Derry from outer space:

> The clouds in the west lit with a bloom of red fire. It traced its way toward them, widening from an artery to a stream to a river of ominous color; and then, as a burning, falling object broke through the cloud cover, the wind came. It was hot and searing, smoky and suffocating. The thing in the sky was gigantic, a flaming match-head that was nearly too bright to look at. Arcs of electricity bolted from it, blue bullwhips that flashed out from it and left thunder in their wake. *A spaceship!* Richie screamed, falling to his knees and covering his eyes.[47]

The origin of It is significant for two reasons. First, It is rendered as an alien body, invading the earth. It is not from earth, and thus, is inherently Other, infecting and colonizing Derry. Second, It is ancient, arriving in Derry millions of years before the novel takes place, when it is a lush and fertile jungle. As Barbara Creed writes, "The archaic mother is the parthenogenic mother, the mother as primordial abyss, the point of origin and of end."[48] Here, It is established as the "point of origin" of the evil that would haunt Derry every twenty-seven years, and also acts as its terminus. It is a site where fear and pain originate, and also the site of death for It's victims. As It gives life to evil, It also demands the sacrifice of Derry's children.

When It reveals itself, it does so to Bill's wife Audra, who is taken captive by Beverly's abusive husband Tom Rogan, and brought to It toward the end of the novel. Here, the novel takes It's point of view, bringing the reader ever closer to understanding It's truly monstrous and archaic form: "*The writer's woman was now with It, alive yet not alive—her mind had been utterly destroyed by her first sight of It as It really was, with all of Its little masks and glamours thrown aside. [. . .] Now the mind of the writer's wife was with It, in It, beyond the end of the macroverse; in the darkness beyond the Turtle; in the outlands beyond all lands.*"[49] When It's true likeness is revealed to Audra, her consciousness is crushed beneath the terrible weight of It's monstrosity.

Again, It is described as the "primordial abyss, the point of origin and of end"[50] as It exists "beyond the end of the macroverse," beyond time and of human understanding of birth, life, and death.

In her analysis of the film *Alien* (1979), Barbara Creed posits that the female xenomorph in that film "is the abyss, the cannibalizing black hole from which all life comes and to which all life returns" which is the "source of deepest terror"[51] for the viewer. Similarly, It also represents a "cannibalizing black hole" in the source of its energy and its monstrous, archaic power: the deadlights. Made privy to It's final, true form, Audra *"was in Its eye; she was in Its mind. She was in the deadlights."*[52] The deadlights are the origin of It's unspeakable, uncanny power, an energy that, once seen, obliterates consciousness. Audra, seeing the deadlights, can only utter, "OH DEAR JESUS IT IS FEMALE—and then all thoughts ceased."[53] It is significant that the deadlights—and It's essence—are gendered female. Creed argues that "constructed as a negative force" the archaic mother "is represented in her phantasmagoric aspect in many horror texts,"[54] and the deadlights are the phantasmagoric embodiment of this negative force, represented as a blinding and all-consuming light.

After coming into contact with the deadlights, Audra becomes catatonic: "Now Audra Denbrough hung high up in the middle of things, crisscrossed in silk, her head lolling against the socket of her shoulder, her eyes wide and glazed, her toes pointing down."[55] Audra, having seen the unseeable, becomes trapped in her own body, her mind all but destroyed by the presence of the archaic mother. Creed writes that "confronted by the sight of the monstrous, the viewing subject is put into crisis—boundaries, designed to keep the abject at bay, threaten to disintegrate, collapse."[56] The deadlights utterly destroy the boundaries that protected Audra from madness and abjection. Her consciousness is unable to withstand the collapse of these boundaries, and she is trapped within her own cage-like body, the only thing left standing in It's terrible wake.

It's power as the archaic mother resides not just in the deadlights, but also its monstrous womb. When the Losers, now adults, once again face off against It, they see It in the form of a grotesque spider:

> It was perhaps fifteen feet high and as black as a moonless night. Each of Its legs was as thick as a muscle-builder's thigh. Its eyes were bright malevolent rubies, bulging from sockets filled with some dripping chromium-colored fluid. Its jagged mandibles opened and closed, opened and closed, dripping ribbons of foam. Frozen in an ecstasy of horror, tottering on the brink of utter lunacy, Ben observed with an

eye-of-the-storm calm that this foam was alive; it stuck the stinking stone-flagged floor and then began to writhe away into the cracks like protozoa.[57]

This moment marks what Ben sees as the Losers' "common unsought and unfathered vision"[58] of what It truly is: the monstrous-feminine incarnate. The description of It as a huge, dripping, wet, poisonous black widow firmly entrenches It in the realm of the monstrous-feminine, the "merging of all aspects of the maternal figure into one—the horrifying image of woman as archaic mother, phallic woman, castrated body and castrating parent represented as a single figure."[59] It, in its final form as the spider, is an amalgamation of all the most horrifying aspects of the mother made one monstrous creature.

Perhaps most terrifying, however, is that It is pregnant. Ben watches It in horror as it moves toward Bill, and

saw that It was possessed of a stinger long enough to impale a man. A clear fluid dripped from its tip, and Ben saw that this was also alive; like the saliva, the poison writhed away into the cracks of the floor. Its stinger, yes . . . but below that, Its belly bulged grotesquely, almost dragging on the floor as It moved . . . *That's Its egg-sac*, Ben thought, and his mind seemed to shriek at the implication. *Whatever It is beyond what we see, this representation is at least symbolically correct: It's female, and It's pregnant.*[60]

What is truly monstrous about It's pregnancy is that the archaic mother is here merged with the phallic woman, as seen in the stinger, huge and dripping with a venomous, semen-like liquid. Upon seeing the bulging belly, pregnant with gruesome spawn, Ben realizes that the Losers' failure to defeat It during their last encounter stems from their failure to destroy its womb. This description of It reveals the Losers' discomfort and horror facing an alien intersex body, one that is perceived to violate the boundaries of the male/female gender binary.

"That's why we had to come back, no matter what," Ben thinks, "because It is female, It's pregnant with some unimaginable spawn . . ."[61] It is not enough, then, to merely kill the archaic mother; It's horrible offspring must be destroyed as well. Indeed, Creed postulates that "it is the suggested presence of the gestating, all-devouring womb of the archaic mother which generates the horror,"[62] and here, is the locus of the continuation of It's power. If the Losers cannot destroy its womb, its eggs, they cannot defeat It, for its power to generate on its own is what prolongs its monstrous existence.

Here, in the last pages of the text, the Losers—and by extension, the reader—confront the most horrific kind of abject body: the monstrous-feminine. All of the body horrors and abjection they have faced in the past lead to the moment, this gore-stricken, corporeal climax. The gendering of It as female, a female who possesses both male and female traits, is just as troubling as the queering of the "hobo" and Patrick Hockstetter; in this gendering, monstrosity and abject horror are located firmly in a fear of an intersex body that wields some kind of foreign, alien power.[63] It is only when this body is destroyed that order can be restored, the abject banished to the shadows. The consequence of this representation is obvious: The novel asserts that female bodies that disrupt the male/female dichotomy, and have attributes of both sexes, are inherently monstrous and abject. This Othering profoundly alienates those readers whose bodies do not "fit" in the dominant male/female dichotomy, as they are made to see a version of themselves that is cracked and distorted by the abject.

CONCLUSION

The novel's preoccupation with abjection and body horror is perhaps most profoundly felt in the trauma of Stan Uris, the one member of the Losers' Club who breaks his pact with his friends and dies by suicide rather than face Pennywise again. The reason he refuses to return to Derry as an adult and defeat It is glimpsed when Stan is still a child, after his encounter with Pennywise at the Standpipe. There, Pennywise appears to Stan as dead children who haunt the Standpipe, and these apparitions "had done something worse than frighten him: they had *offended* him."[64] The novel extrapolates that it is not the fear of Pennywise/It that Stan cannot live with, but It's utter abjectness, and how it is incompatible with his grasp of reality. "You can live with fear, I think, Stan would have said if he could. Maybe not forever, but for a long, long time. It's *offense* you maybe can't live with, because it opens a crack inside your thinking."[65] This fear of the abject propels Stan into a boundaryless domain where he has to come to terms with his own corporeality, which he cannot survive, consciousness intact.

The crux of the novel, then, is not about fear. Instead, it is about *offense*, and more specifically, it is about bodies that offend and revile with their abjectness. For some—like the remaining members of the Losers' Club—it is possible to overcome the profound horror of abjectness, through their child-like ability of "incorporating the inexplicable into their lives,"[66] something Stan could never do, even as a child himself. Julia Kristeva writes that "the abject shatters the wall of repression and its judgments."[67] Abject bodies do so in this novel, dismantling the borders separating the diseased from the healthy, queer from the heteronormative, and alien from the human. The assimilation of the abject within the everyday in *IT* constitutes "a sudden upheaval of beauty or terror,"[68] a borderless and disorderly space where bodily horrors once unimaginable, become one in the same as moments of the incandescently sublime.

Even so, in making this point about the breakdown of the borders separating terror from the sublime, King has made more than a few questionable choices within the text: queering a would-be child predator (the "hobo") and a young psychopath (Patrick Hockstetter), as well as making a monstrous, alien body intersex. In conflating these bodies with the abject, *IT* seems to confirm our darkest fears, that those we see as Other are as monstrous as we imagine them to be. This is a conservative notion, an insidious through line that runs deep within horror literature. Abjection, here, is mobilized in such a way that the novel evinces horror from the reader at the sight of unruly, excessive bodies wreaking havoc—but not to the extent that we are challenged to question *why* they upset us so, and *what* interlocking systems of oppression these representations serve.

Notes

1. Stephen King, *On Writing: A Memoir of the Craft* (New York: Scribner, 2000), 173, emphasis in original.

2. Barbara Creed, *The Monstrous-Feminine: Film, Feminism, Psychoanalysis* (Abingdon: Routledge, 2007), 24.

3. Paul Wells, *The Horror Genre: From Beelzebub to Blair Witch* (New York: Wallflower Press, 2000).

4. Julia Kristeva, *Powers of Horror: An Essay on Abjection*, trans. Leon S. Roudiez (New York: Columbia University Press, 1982), 120.

5. Elizabeth Gross, "The Body of Signification" in *Abjection, Melancholia and Love: The Work of Julia Kristeva*, eds. John Fletcher and Andrew Benjamin (1990; reprint, London: Routledge, 2012), 80.

6. Kristeva, 1.

7. Stephen King, *IT* (1986; reprint, New York: Scribner, 2016), 308.

8. King, 312.

9. King, 312

10. Kristeva, *Powers of Horror*, 4.

11. Kristeva, 4.

12. King, 312.

13. Noël Carroll, *The Philosophy of Horror: Or, Paradoxes of the Heart* (1990; reprint, New York: Routledge, 2004), 74.

14. King, 313.

15. King, 314.

16. Kristeva, *Powers of Horror*, 9.

17. King, 316.

18. Carroll, 41.

19. King, 316.

20. King, 316.

21. Xavier Aldana Reyes, *Body Gothic: Corporeal Transgression in Contemporary Literature and Horror Film* (Cardiff: University of Wales Press, 2014), 54.

22. King, 317.

23. Carroll, *The Philosophy of Horror*, 43.

24. Reyes, *Body Gothic*, 54.

25. Kristeva, *Powers of Horror*, 4.

26. For the following analysis of queer abjectness in this section of my chapter, I pull theoretical frameworks from queer theory that have been utilized in film studies. While it seems idiosyncratic to use film theory and analysis in an essay about a novel, rather than film, there are compelling arguments in Andrew Scahill and Harry M. Benshoff's critical work with queer film studies that are relevant for literary analysis as well, as I will show below.

27. King, 819.

28. King, 820, emphasis in original.

29. Andrew Scahill, *The Revolting Child in Horror Cinema: Youth Rebellion and Queer Spectatorship* (New York: Palgrave Macmillan, 2015), 15.

30. Scahill, 15.

31. Scahill, 16.

32. Scahill, 16.

33. Scahill, 16.

34. King, 832.

35. King, 832.

36. King, 832.

37. Paulina Palmer, *The Queer Uncanny: New Perspectives on the Gothic* (Cardiff: University of Wales Press, 2012), 152.

38. King, 833.

39. King, 833.

40. King, 928.

41. King, 835.

42. Scahill, 16.

43. Harry M. Benshoff, *Monsters in the Closet: Homosexuality and the Horror Film* (New York: Manchester University Press, 1997), 256.

44. Emily Burnham, "The 1984 Murder of Charlie Howard in Bangor Will Be Dramatized in the 'IT' Sequel," *Bangor Daily News*, September 4, 2019, https://bangor dailynews.com/2019/09/04/news/bangor/the-1984-murder-of-charlie-howard-in-bangor -will-be-dramatized-in-the-it-sequel/.

45. King, 14.

46. Kristeva, *Powers of Horror*, 77.

47. King, 767.

48. Creed, *The Monstrous-Feminine*, 17.

49. King, 1031, emphasis in original.

50. Creed, *The Monstrous-Feminine*, 17.

51. Creed, 25.

52. King, 1032, emphasis in original.

53. King, 1032.

54. Creed, *The Monstrous-Feminine*, 27.

55. King, *IT*, 1032.

56. Creed, *The Monstrous-Feminine*, 29.

57. King, 1064–65.

58. King, 1065.

59. Creed, *The Monstrous-Feminine*, 27.

60. King, 1065.

61. King, 1065.

62. Creed, *The Monstrous-Feminine*, 27.

63. Writer Lois Kennedy has developed a typology of queer representation that spans the breadth of Stephen King's fiction, from his earliest writings to his work today. She argues that queer and queer-coded characters within the King universe generally fall into one of five categories: "the Mannish Lesbian, the Trauma Victim, the Weakling, the Predator, and the Well-Adjusted." While there are no less than three characters in *IT* that fit the mold of the "Predator" type, Kennedy argues that this type of queer representation in his works "died out after the early 90s." Indeed, King has shown growth in terms of queer representation in his stories today, as Kennedy argues he has gone "from insensitive, hateful depictions of gay characters to insightful and positive ones" in his contemporary fiction. Kennedy cites a number of King's contemporary works that feature positive queer representation: *Cell* (2006), "A Very Tight Place" from *Just After Sunset* (2008), and "Mile 81" from *The Bazaar of Bad Dreams* (2015). There is also fan favorite Father Callahan, who first appears in *'Salem's Lot* (1975) and was reintroduced in *The Dark Tower V: Wolves of the Calla* (2003) as queer. Note, however, that all the queer characters in these more recent works are *cisgender* queer characters; there is a dearth of positive representation of trans and gender-nonconforming characters in King's fiction to this day. And so, there is work yet to be done.

64. King, 436.

65. King, 436.

66. King, 542.

67. Kristeva, *Powers of Horror*, 15.

68. King, *IT*, 542.

References

Benshoff, Harry M. *Monsters in the Closet: Homosexuality and the Horror Film*. New York: Manchester University Press, 1997.

Burnham, Emily. "The 1984 Murder of Charlie Howard in Bangor Will Be Dramatized in the 'IT' Sequel." *Bangor Daily News*, September 4, 2019. https://bangordailynews

.com/2019/09/04/news/bangor/the-1984-murder-of-charlie-howard-in-bangor-will-be
-dramatized-in-the-it-sequel/

Carroll, Noël. *The Philosophy of Horror: Or, Paradoxes of the Heart*. 1990; reprint, New York: Routledge, 2004.

Creed, Barbara. *The Monstrous-Feminine: Film, Feminism, Psychoanalysis*. Abingdon: Routledge, 2007.

Gross, Elizabeth. "The Body of Signification." In *Abjection, Melancholia and Love: The Work of Julia Kristeva* edited by John Fletcher and Andrew Benjamin. 1990; reprint, London: Routledge, 2012.

Kennedy, Lois. "'As Gay as Old Dad's Hatband': The Five Kinds of Gay and Bisexual Characters in Stephen King's Writings." Horrornovelreviews.com, Matt Molgaard (in association with Dan Melby's *The Dark Sight of Art*), December 16, 2015.

King, Stephen. *IT*. 1986; reprint, New York: Scribner, 2016.

King, Stephen. *On Writing: A Memoir of the Craft*. New York: Scribner, 2000.

Kristeva, Julia. *Powers of Horror: An Essay on Abjection*. Translated by Leon S. Roudiez. New York: Columbia University Press, 1982.

Reyes, Xavier Aldana. *Body Gothic: Corporeal Transgression in Contemporary Literature and Horror Film*. Cardiff: University of Wales Press, 2014.

Scahill, Andrew. *The Revolting Child in Horror Cinema: Youth Rebellion and Queer Spectatorship*. New York: Palgrave Macmillan, 2015.

Wells, Paul. *The Horror Genre: From Beelzebub to Blair Witch*. New York: Wallflower Press, 2000.

Chapter 5

PATRICK HOCKSTETTER

Natural Madness in Stephen King's *IT*

AMYLOU AHAVA

In *IT*, Patrick Hockstetter represents a rarely seen character type in Stephen King's universe: Although the bully presents with a psychological disability, he does not gain his desire to kill from any outside force. Typically in his works, King combines mental/psychological disabilities with the supernatural to obscure whether the character resorts to violence because of sickness or because of possession. Within the mind of these characters, madness and the supernatural work together or sometimes even galvanize one another. In *Carrie* (1974), for example, the titular character finds her telekinetic and telepathic abilities manifesting in connection with her PTSD from the abuse she experienced at home and school. And while Cujo becomes mentally and physically ill from rabies, the novel (1981) heavily implies that the dog is also possessed by the evil spirit of the serial killer Frank Dodd. Even elsewhere in *IT*, the main bully, Henry Bowers, experiences mental degeneration which earns him the social and medical diagnosis of being "crazy."[1] But it is notably the combination of child abuse and years of conditioning from his father that start Henry on the path to derangement: Pennywise merely finishes the journey for him. However, instead of combining or blurring the lines between disability and supernatural madness as seen in prior texts such as *Carrie*, *The Shining* (1977), and *Cujo*, King supplies in Patrick a character with a biological form of madness which seems to be present from his very birth, leading him to murder as a small child. Yet, in studies of *IT* that dissect the use of insanity within the text, the character of Henry Bowers, the barbarous leader of the Bowers Gang, earns most of the attention while Patrick tends to appear only in texts focusing on queer readings.[2] King further pushes the reader's concept of evil by attributing murderous qualities to Patrick thereby creating a strong juxtaposition with the hero, Bill. And because it is not trauma or neglect that pushes Patrick to kill, but instead inherited madness, the boy resembles more of the characteristics of It than Henry.

With Patrick's powerful madness and premature death, the young character depicts the figure of inherent insanity, and his proneness to murder coupled with a lack of empathy since toddlerhood, propels Patrick beyond the usual depiction of madness in King's universe. Patrick, therefore, represents a break from King's tradition of combining madness with trauma (either real or supernatural), so that Patrick's inherited madness distinguishes him from other character's even within the text of *IT*. In the novel, Patrick does not display the loud, aggressive madness associated with Henry Bowers. The lead bully seeks out smaller children to terrorize, but Patrick finds quiet comfort in his madness. Shifting the lens from the main bully Henry to the lesser discussed sociopath, Patrick, offers not only a different analysis of madness in King's text, but also presents further insight into effectiveness of the innocence of Bill, one of Henry and Patrick's victims, and the evilness of Pennywise, the ostensible villain.

From the other characters in the book, Henry's madness earns him the title of the most "genuinely evil kid" in town, but his madness (like his father's) comes from trauma.[3] On the other hand, Patrick's madness quietly fades to the periphery of acknowledgment. Even though his parents and teachers realize the boy's interests and demeanor categorize him as strange and unsettling, the loud brashness of Henry and the other bullies takes precedence over Patrick's quiet and undetected crimes. Patrick becomes the surviving Hockstetter whom his parents suspect of his brother's murder but ultimately ignore. The teachers recognize Patrick's dangerousness to some extent, but the narrator removes blame from the teachers because Patrick's birth occurred a few decades too early for proper psychiatric evaluation and care. King's inclusion of Patrick in a text already filled with madness and supernatural evil, however, serves as a reflection on "natural order."[4] It exists as an undetectable creature with a proclivity for death, but so, too, does Patrick. And while It exists only in the world of King, Patricks exist outside of literature and walk among us.

Perhaps because of his brief role in *IT*, Patrick does not attract attention from King scholars and critics, this volume notwithstanding. Instead of highlighting Patrick's naturally developed madness, the boy often becomes diminished to simple bully status or does not even garner a mention. In fact, Patrick's appearance usually exists as a part of the Bowers Gang or classified as one of the dead with no acknowledgment to the boy's individuality.[5] And within the text, only Eddie and Beverly truly recognize the dangerous and subversive madness which emanates from Patrick. Perhaps the admittance of a truly psychotic child unsettled the adult critics' mindset. People find the possibility of a mad child unsettling and difficult to believe, in either reality or fiction.

The literary inclusion of Patrick Hockstetter does nothing to propel the main action of the story. Indeed, even though the boy earns an entire chapter dedicated to him, he appears very little outside this chapter and then almost exclusively as a ghost or as a mere memory to Eddie. Yet, even though Patrick never directly interacts with Bill Denbrough, the inclusion of the mad child serves as the antithesis of the head of the Losers. Not until chapter 17, "Another One of the Missing: The Death of Patrick Hockstetter," does the character gain enough of his own voice and agency to tell his own story. Through sporadic nightmares and Eddie's fragmented memories, King pieces together a character who changes the perspective on children and madness. Indeed, exploring the dichotomy of Stuttering Bill and Patrick through the lens of Andrew Scahill's *The Revolting Child* yields better insight into the innocent child prototype familiar in King's universe and in comparison, Beverly (and the reader) witnesses the dangerous and unpredictable mad child.[6]

Instead of viewing evil children as smaller versions of evil adults, Scahill believes the difference between good and monstrousness in children operates on a fulcrum. He indicates that harmless and even appealing characteristics in children can quickly morph into far more sinister traits. In dissecting the minds and behaviors of children, Scahill creates five classifications for children—the Innocent, the Child of Nature, the Dreamer, the Wise Child, and the Trickster—and notes that taking one trait too far results in a monstrous child.[7] For instance, the Child of Nature represents a "connection to the natural world" and even empowerment through their connection to animals or plants (e.g., Harry Potter). Stuttering Bill holds the opposite characteristics of Patrick, as the leader of the Losers embraces nature for the advantage of protection and security rather than as an outlet for cruelty. The Barrens (the lush forest in town) serve as the clubhouse for Bill and his friends. Animals come to Bill's aid as the Turtle (the unseen adversary to It) plays an important role in guiding adolescent Bill. Even the imaginary animal of Silver further establishes Bill as a Child of Nature. The overly large and ramshackle appearance of Bill's bike looks comical or dangerous to the less imaginative adults, but within the mind of the Child, the machine represents a noble steed who brings the rider confidence.

However, on the opposite side of the spectrum sits the Feral Child, a far more ferocious creature who represents the inability to tame nature. Instead of finding companionship in animals, Patrick tortures any creature he can find. The animals bring him pleasure, but no physical nutriment, so Patrick

even goes against nature as his killings do not serve as any goal but entertainment.[8] On the other hand, Patrick's playground consists of a junkyard,
devoid of natural beauty and is instead filled with filth and danger. Scahill
reasons that the switch from Child of Nature to Feral Child occurs based on
the bodily control.[9] Patrick does not possess the ability to recognize pain in
his victims and even more outside his control is his search for sexual desire.
He finds sexual release in killing animals and even cannot resist touching
the penis of another bully when given the chance. Patrick gives into basic
sexual instincts when he molests Henry, not fearing repercussions, only
looking for sexual satisfaction.[10] So, separated from rational thought, Patrick
indulges his desires as long as his impulses fit the "rules" because "his sense
of self-preservation was well developed" and he understands the concept of
being "suspected."[11]

In "Innocence Lost as a Recurring Motif in Stephen King's Horror," Harem
Qadar considers the contradictions of the presentations of innocence in
American society. The children included in King's novels may seem like
easy prey, but when childlike goodness becomes invoked in cultural productions, innocence can be an advantage. Qadar believes using children as
the main focus of *IT* allows King to approach his story in a more "proac-
tive" way because these characters "have no skeptical preconceived notions
to abandon."[12] The juxtaposition between Bill and Patrick allows for King
to demonstrate the ultimate innocence presented in Bill and therefore to
additionally show how Patrick exists as a sick, dangerous, and evil child
devoid of the common qualities adults associate with kids. Returning to *The
Revolting Child*, Scahill distinguishes the horribleness of a child from the
indiscretions of an adult,[13] studying various children villains to determine
that part of their evilness comes from their abandonment of their innocence.
IT, like much of King's fiction, serves as a *Bildungsroman* and/or as a story
about the loss of innocence. As an author whose work is marketed towards
grown readers, King's common audience becomes adults reflecting on their
childhoods. So, the target audience takes an adult perspective of the Losers'
Club and its bullies and therefore places their notions of innocence on the
characters. Patrick's madness prevents the boy from demonstrating the innocence typically seen in child characters, but the adult characters never truly
witness his abandonment from childhood. Only the Losers and the reader
understand Patrick never consciously strayed from his childish innocence.

King's inclusion of a madness, however, is not meant to encourage negative feelings about disability, but to evoke emotional feelings, particularly
abjection by going against our preconceived notions of children. At the center

of Julia Kristeva's exploration of abjection exists the "place where meaning collapses," where the child "defaces clearly demarcated identities in an abject disturbance of symbolic orderliness," and which represents the "in-between" or the uncertain.[14] Jessica Balanzatgui focuses on the child's otherness and their blend of "familiarity and strangeness, victim and victimizer, innocence and threatening indecipherability," especially the ways in which these threaten the adult perception and previously assigned notions of childhood.[15] Examples of abjection could be a clown at midnight or a child playing with a fridge in a junkyard. The thought of a child playing in a dump should make us feel uneasy. Include an intact refrigerator, and unease becomes fear, but not fear in the way Patrick creates. We should fear for Patrick's safety because of all the stories of children accidentally becoming locked inside discarded appliances. However, the fear which should be directed at Patrick's safety instead mutates into anxiety about what Patrick will *do* in the fridge—a dread that is well-placed, as I'll discuss later.

Regarding the journey the Losers follow from learning about It to finally deciding to confront the monster, King relays two, fairly parallel stories that both occur in boys' rooms. Stuttering Bill lovingly constructs a toy boat for his younger brother Georgie. Patrick also engages with his young brother, but the different interactions which occur in the Denbrough and the Hockstetter bedrooms demonstrate the expected actions of childhood innocence and the abjection which occurs when a child breaks from the norm. The cultural and societal role of the child typically demonstrates characteristics of "innocence, nativity, cuteness, and vulnerability," which in turn, serve as the opposite of "grown-up" qualities such as "experienced, knowledgeable, rational, and powerful."[16] The Denbrough brothers share quiet giggles and brotherly love, before Bill unknowingly sends Georgie out to his death when the smaller boy encounters Pennywise in the storm drain. The opening chapter of *IT* shows all the quintessential characteristics of a child with the happy-go-lucky Georgie running down the street. Bill teases his brother and admits the annoying qualities of his younger sibling, but the bond still shows through any of the good-natured sibling rivalry displayed between the brothers. In this brief exchange, the role of innocent child becomes an almost compulsory trope adult readers staunchly hold on to: "the little wonder, the beautiful victim, the cutie-pie rebel whose diminutive insurrections come more as flattery of our power than a challenge to it."[17]

The interactions taking place in Stuttering Bill's bedroom present a familiar and appealing situation for the readers, but Patrick's moment of brotherly contact goes against our natural and societally approved expectations of children. Unlike the wide-eyed, exuberant behavior demonstrated in the six-year-old Georgie Denbrough at the beginning of the novel, Patrick exhibits no childlike wonder or pleasures and instead the first mention of Patrick becomes paired with negative ideas of dislike, inconvenience, and even fear. Even at five, Patrick discerns his role in the world as the only "real" thing. So, with the arrival of Avery, Patrick's interpretation of the social order begins to shift, and he experiences fear for one of the few times in his life. King does not clarify whether this mention of fear refers to the entirety of Patrick's twelve years of life or only to the years leading up to the murder of his brother. However, mentioning that the small boy very rarely experiences fear draws attention to Patrick's psychological make-up. At five, he does not become frightened due to the average childhood fears, such as Georgie's fear of the dark while venturing into the gloomy cellar to retrieve paraffin. Instead, Patrick experiences fear because he only understands himself as "real," and Avery's presence threatens this value system. He marks his origin as being "brought [. . .] home from the hospital," and therefore fears that if Avery holds a similar origin story, then logically the younger sibling must also be "real."[18] While the fear of younger siblings might occur in most children, Patrick's concerns do not stem from feelings of being unloved, but that he will be replaced as the only "real" being not only in the home, but in the world. Unlike Bill, Patrick feels no affection or need to protect his younger sibling and instead looms over his brother and looks down on the infant as an inferior. Although in Patrick's childhood narrative he is one year younger than Georgie, Patrick possess the qualities Balanzategui associates with adults, those of being experienced, knowledgeable, rational, and powerful. Five-year-old Patrick understands the changes brought about by the existence of the baby, so he rationally justifies eliminating Avery from his life. Additionally, his knowledge of the "rules" allows Patrick to calmly kill the infant without getting caught. Taking up Dominic Lennard's analysis of the Child Villain in *Bad Seeds and Holy Terrors*, the villainy of the child stems from the youth "not doing what adults suppose they should be doing," which includes most childhood antics.[19] But what Lennard means is that children not only go against the perfect child image depicted in Scahill's taxonomy, but that child villains also go against "common sense" and "natural behavior of a child."[20] Eliminating common sense or "natural" intentions sends the child to the opposite end of Scahill's spectrum. Similar to Lennard's project, this chapter determines that King's inclusion of Patrick creates a far more disturbing level to the novel as readers react strongly "when [their] definitions of children are contradicted."[21] Patrick rationalizes his decision, even though based on faulty logic which emerges from his diseased psyche. When performing the act of infanticide, the older brother's mind sees the baby as an "it" as he "held *it* down" until "[*i*]*t* eventually became totally still" and Patrick still "held *it* down for another five minutes," and therefore calmly eliminates what causes his fears.[22]

Patrick's behavior towards others (especially his younger brother) and his perception of being the only "real" person works as a human mirror to the main killer in *IT*. In fact, Pennywise and Patrick serve as two sides of the same King trope. Throughout *IT* scholarship, the titular creature serves as a representation of Derry, as the monster shows the deception of innocence and the evils that lurk beneath the surface of the town. Patrick exists as the "raw" sickness and It represents the supernatural components. Not only does It prey on children, but the familiar and even innocent figure of Pennywise inspires an abject terror in the reader. Much like a killer clown, a killer child provokes abject terror, as our preconceived notions of clowns as well as of children, tell us these figures *should* represent innocence and laughter. However, in this novel, true terror occurs when they *don't*.

Frequently It wears the face of a more innocuous or even friendly being, most notably the first (and most recognizable) appearance with Pennywise the Dancing Clown initially observed by Georgie in a storm drain. "It's always been here, since the beginning of time . . . since before there were men *any-where*. [. . .] It was there then, sleeping, maybe, waiting for the ice to melt, waiting for the people to come" (italics in original).[23] The prehistoric and possibly extraterrestrial origin of It suggests that King argues that "evil exists only as a theoretical construct without human beings," and that the "realness" of the evil merges when greedy, irresponsible humans "serve as its hosts."[24] It and Patrick both come from before and are the only "real" entities—at least in their minds. When the Losers face off with It, the monster becomes irritated with the audacity of the group because It "did not want change or surprise. It did not want new things, ever. It wanted only to eat and sleep and dream and eat again."[25]

The first mention of Patrick also occurs in the lead-in for a flashback as Eddie recalls a nightmare wherein he is lost under the streets of Derry. In the dream, Eddie clearly sees the decaying body of Patrick Hockstetter, but the narrator gives no mention of the dead boy's connection to the bullies or any of the child's dangerous behavior. Instead, during the first mention of Patrick, the only description given creates a sense of pity and loss for the reader because he is only known as "a boy who had disappeared" followed with graphic details of the worms eating through the child's face.[26] Further evidence of an innocent nature comes from a cynical interjection of the title of a common childhood paper topic "How I Spent My Summer Vacation" followed with the angry comment of "I spent it dead in a tunnel!"[27] With the introduction of the Bowers Gang in Ben's flashback and the innocent mention of Patrick in Eddie's story, King elicits false sympathy from the reader and waits until later in the book to reveal the psychopathic behavior of the child. The delayed reveal of the character's behavioral disorder pairs with many of the initial encounters with It. The first appearances of both It and Patrick take place in the sewer and both characters initially come off as lost or in need of help. Not until about halfway through the book does Eddie hint at the deception of Patrick and how even though the boy was found in the sewer, perhaps he was more than just a lost little boy.

Derry is not what it seems, but neither is Patrick nor Pennywise. The town and both characters come off as innocent upon first appearance, but all three later reveal themselves to hold sinister intentions. Beneath the iconic, anodyne, small-town image of Derry lurks a "history of persecution of outsiders" that dates back several generations: "the town's children, the gay, and black communities [all] exist outside the social mainstream."[28] Horror typically represents the "unknown, that which cannot be categorized, or of threats to the cultural order."[29] However, King's work goes against this example because his novels stress "threats related to the cultural order itself" and present the "malice, selfishness, and callous lack of foresight" present in society.[30] In an early review of *IT*, Lloyd Rose believes the book fails as a horror novel because "the creature haunting its sewers" is less convincing then Derry itself, which Rose refers to as "Lake Wobegon with dry rot."[31] However, Magistratle disagrees with this comment because It "punishes the city at the same time as it represents it."[32] The creature It is evil, but the monster also represents Derry and reflects the monstrosity of humans due not only to the crimes the people commit, but also the crimes they ignore. The adults ignore the disappearance of children, the high level of child abuse, and the sexual and violent tendencies of Patrick. Within the text, King hints that the blindness to It's actions allows for continued prosperity in the town. Stephenson admits Pennywise's murder sprees are "horrific," but the "*human* acts of violence that are most horrifying" involve hate crimes and child abuse (italics in original).[33] While King credits the evil buried beneath the town which prevents adults from fully comprehending the deadliness of the situation, the town actually represents abject terror and the observers' inability to accept danger in a familiar setting. Similarly, Patrick's age disguises his murderous actions and allows him to hide in plain sight.

Stephenson even acknowledges that "human monsters come in younger forms" as well with the inclusion of Henry Bowers and "psychopathic" Patrick

Hockstetter.[34] Patrick's serial pet murders can also be contributed to the "blindness" the adults of Derry experience when it comes to death. All the other fridges at the dump had their doors removed to prevent a child's accidental death, but Patrick's appliance remains untouched by the owner of the junkyard and the author can only attribute his freedom to kill to the power Patrick possesses, "or perhaps some other force" assisted in.[35] The male members of the Losers' Club announce their realization of the boy's madness because of the fly-box, but Beverly, the sole female perspective, further illuminates the situation when she shares stories of Patrick's wandering hand. No girl was free from Patrick and in class they would "feel his hand" on their side or still-developing breasts.[36] When confronted about the inappropriate touching, Patrick would "smile and never say anything."[37] Despite the girls reporting the unwanted touching, nothing could be done because even the teacher was scared of him.[38] His third- and fifth-grade teachers know about his pencil box filled with dead flies and even understand the "implications" of such behavior, but unfortunately, due to the number of students in the classroom, Patrick benefits from anonymity (especially when sharing a space with louder and more violent characters such as Henry Bowers or Victor Criss). So, instead of addressing the dead insects, the teachers quietly ignored it. And instead of discussing with Patrick or even reporting his inappropriate (and unwanted) touching with his female classmates, the teachers simply organized the classroom to place distance between the girls and the groper. Much like the unexplainable children's deaths and disappearances that occur in Derry, the adults learn to ignore indiscretions and even make any crimes invisible to themselves. Patrick's groping did not stop; instead, the teachers simply removed the act from their view. When discussing Patrick in school, King makes a deliberate comparison between the young killer and It in their shared ability to hide in plain sight. Instead of solving a problem by addressing the source of the issue, the adults find a quick fix that simply removes the issues from their eyesight. The teachers become so preoccupied with bullies that the school resembles a "carnival [. . .] with so many rings that Pennywise himself might have gone unnoticed."[39] Therefore, despite Patrick's unsavory behavior, all his oddities go largely ignored by all the adults in his life, which allows him (much like It), to murder without repercussion. Similar to his teachers, both Patrick's parents suspect their first-born holds darker and potentially dangerous habits, but they allow themselves to brush their worries away. After the murder and before the discovery of the body, Patrick and his mother share a normal enough exchange between parent and child, but despite the nice words and supportive nature, the mother knows "in a part of her so deep she hardly knew it was there" that Patrick is not normal.[40] The "disquieting" darkness and "sameness" to his drawings brought unease to his mother, but not enough for her to associate her son with anything dangerous.[41]

The impulses for death and torture always exist in both Patrick and It, but both the demon and child follow "rules" regarding when and on whom they are allowed to prey. "It's sole purpose is to consume the elements around it and be filled by that which is consumed. For longer than Derry existed, the force had made a home there [. . .] but never Itself [had] experienced either pain or fear."[42] It does not feed on the children exactly, but instead appears to gain nourishment from "their fears and desires," much like Patrick, who finds arousal in torturing other creatures, only to have the pleasant sensations quickly fade once the being dies.[43] So, It must reemerge every twenty-seven years or so, and Patrick must kill every month or so because the urges become too strong.

After murdering Avery, Patrick's world becomes grey once again when "the shot wear[s] off," and the excitement quickly fades.[44] He fulfilled his hunger and did away with the threat, and now Patrick can return to a dormant life within the community. Patrick does not forget the colors and the sensations associated with killing and he finds small ways to reignite the feeling, but his real desire to kill coincidently (or not) reemerges when It does. According to Mike Hanlon, "Derry was Its killing-pen, the people of Derry Its sheep."[45] Fatefully, these sheep are fit for the slaughter by *two* monsters: on the day Georgie Denbrough goes out to play and meets Pennywise the Dancing Clown, Patrick discovers his rusty, yet intact refrigerator in the city dump. The sight of the abandoned appliance sexually arouses Patrick and the strength of the sensation becomes comparable to when he "fixed Avery."[46] Despite Patrick's slow thinking skills, he immediately recognizes the discarded fridge as a source of death. So, as It tortures the adults of Derry by stealing and killing their children, Patrick runs a similar campaign which involves stealing and killing the pets of Derry. Over the next six or eight months, dozens of cats and dogs disappear from their homes, and despite the searches and lost ads, none of the pets are found. Much like It using Derry as a "feeding-pen," Patrick returns again and again to the fridge. Patrick's killing spree compares to It with his selection of victims, only choosing one at a time and never being seen by an adult. After capturing the pets (most likely lured with promises of innocent attention or treats), Patrick takes the animals back to his metal killing room, so like the sewers deep beneath Derry where It lives.

Even the premise of *IT* stems from Stephen King's greatest fears: losing his children. In *Landscape of Fear*, Magistrale prompts King to disclose what "terrifies" him the most. He responds: "Opening the door of my children's bedroom and finding one of them dead."[47] And with all of the child deaths that occur in *IT*, only one plays out as King's fears: the death of Avery Hockstetter. After a nap and a chat with her eldest son, Mrs. Hockstetter goes to her baby's room to find him dead. Even more curiously, King does not make his monstrous creation It the cause of such a nightmare; instead, a five-year-old boy unleashes King's greatest fear. So, in a 1,000-page book with multiple child murders, only once does King create his greatest fear. Patrick exists as our cultural fear of abnormality, specifically undetected mental disorders with no known causes. Patrick also exists as the embodied version of "pure evil." Placing the character in different rules or purposes perpetuates the causation of enfreakment, which forces readers to acknowledge their preconceived notions of the abnormal and the connection to the monstrous. Even though *IT* appears to end with happiness for all the surviving Losers, "monstrousness is not vanquished, so much as temporarily evaded," with at least some hints the evil will return or reemerge in a new form.[48] It existed before time and remained mostly undetected for centuries. Patrick only lived twelve years, but he emerged as the monstrous and carved out a significant amount of murders in those short years. And much like It, nothing prompted his desire to kill. He was born with his proclivity for death, suggesting that it's only a matter of time until another "real" child arrives.

Notes

1. Stephen King, *IT* (New York: Signet, 1997), 749.

2. "The face of Mr. Flip": Homophobia in the Horror of Stephen King" by Douglas Keesey discusses the sexual encounter between Henry and Patrick and the impact the interaction had on Henry. *Stephen King: The Second Decade* by Tony Magistrale mentions Bowers, Hockstetter, and Criss in discussion of bullies in King, but only credits Bowers with madness and claims the head bully's madness represents Derry. "Stephen King's *Misery*: Manic Depression and Creativity" by Carol A. Senf briefly touches on Henry Bowers and Patrick in relation to Madness but does not go past summary. *Stephen King's Literary Companion* by Rocky Wood lists several King characters with mental illness and mentions Henry, but not Patrick.

3. King, 73.

4. King, 491.

5. "The Turtle Can't Help Us": Evil, Enchantment and the Magic of Faith in Stephen King's *IT*" by Gregory Stevenson provides only a one sentence summary of Patrick in

relation to human monsters, but focuses the discussion on Henry Bowers, Tom Rogan, and Bev's father. "'He Hits His Fists against the Post': Stuttering Bill, Trauma and the Protective Power of the Imagination in Stephen King's *IT*" by Hayley Mitchell Haugen lists Henry Bowers, Patrick Hockstetter, and Victor Criss as bullies and representations of the viciousness of American youth, but only describes Henry beyond the label of "bully."

6. Andrew Scahill, *The Revolting Child in Horror Cinema: Youth Rebellion and Queer Spectatorship* (New York: Palgrave Macmillan, 2015) 13.

7. Scahill, 14.

8. Scahill, 17.

9. Scahill, 17.

10. King, 785.

11. King, 793.

12. Harem Qader "Innocence Lost as a Recurring Motif in Stephen King's Horror." *Journal of Literature, Languages, and Linguistics* 15 (2015): 10.

13. Scahill, 15.

14. Julia Kristeva, *Powers of Horror: An Essay on Abjection* (New York: Columbia University Press 1982), 2.

15. Jessica Balanzatgui, *The Uncanny Child in Transnational Cinema: Ghosts of Futurity at the Turn of the Twenty-First Century* (Amsterdam: Amsterdam University Press, 2018), 67.

16. Balanzategui, 9.

17. Dominic Lennard, *Bad Seeds and Holy Terrors: The Child Villains of Horror Film*, (New York: State University of New York Press, 2014), 1.

18. King, 789.

19. Lennard, 3.

20. Scahill, 3.

21. Scahill, 3.

22. King, 790.

23. King, 763.

24. Tony Magistrale, *Stephen King: The Second Decade, Danse Macabre to The Dark Half* (New York: Twayne Publishers, 1992):103.

25. King, 1008.

26. King, 96.

27. King, 96.

28. Magistrale, 103.

29. Melinda Hall, "Horrible Heroes: Liberating Alternative Visions of Disability in Horror" *Disability Studies Quarterly* 36, no. 1 (2016), accessed April 1, 2020. https://dsq-sds.org/article/view/3258/4205.

30. Hall, 9.

31. Lloyd, Rose. "The Triumph of the Nerds." *The Atlantic*, September 1986, 103.

32. Tony Magistrale, *Landscape of Fear: Stephen King's American Gothic* (Ohio: Bowling Green State University, 1988), 112.

33. Gregory Stevenson, "'The Turtle Can't Help Us': Evil, Enchantment and the Magic of Faith in Stephen King's *IT*," in *The Many Lives of IT: Essays on the Stephen King Horror Franchise*, ed. Ron Reikki (Jefferson, NC: McFarland & Company, 2020), 45–56.

34. Stevenson, 59.

35. King, 793.

36. King, 772.

37. King, 772.

38. King, 772.

39. King, 788.

40. King, 790.

41. King, 790.

42. Jennifer Jenkins, "Fantasy in Fiction: The Double-Edged Sword" in *Stephen King's Modern Macabre: Essays on the Later Works,* eds Patrick McAleer and Michael A. Perry (Jefferson, NC: McFarland & Company, 2014), 10–23.

43. Jenkins, 16.

44. King, 790.

45. King, 1023.

46. King, 792.

47. Magistrale, *Landscapes,* 73.

48. Cheyne, 51.

References

Balanzategui, Jessica. *The Uncanny Child in Transnational Cinema: Ghosts of Futurity at the Turn of the Twenty-First Century.* Amsterdam: Amsterdam University Press, 2018.

Cheyne, Ria. *Disability Literature, Genre.* Liverpool: Liverpool University Press, 2019.

Federman, Cary, Dave Holmes, and Jean Daniel Jacob, "Deconstructing the Psychopath: A Critical Discursive Analysis." *Cultural Critique,* no. 72 (Spring 2009).

Hall, Melinda. "Horrible Heroes: Liberating Alternative Visions of Disability in Horror." *Disability Studies Quarterly* 36, no. 1 (2016). https://dsq-sds.org/article/view/3258/4205.

Haugen, Hayley Mitchell. "'He Hits His Fists against the Post': Stuttering Bill, Trauma and the Protective Power of the Imagination in Stephen King's *IT.*" In *The Many Lives of IT: Essays on the Stephen King Horror Franchise,* edited by Ron Riekki, 9–17. Jefferson, NC: McFarland & Company, 2020.

Jenkins, Jennifer. "Fantasy in Fiction: The Double-Edged Sword." In *Stephen King's Modern Macabre: Essays on the Later Works,* edited by Patrick McAleer and Michael A. Perry, 10–23. Jefferson, NC: McFarland & Company, 2014.

King, Stephen. *IT.* New York: Signet, 1997.

Kristeva, Julia. *Powers of Horror: An Essay on Abjection.* New York: Columbia University Press, 1982.

Lennard, Dominic. *Bad Seeds and Holy Terrors: The Child Villains of Horror Film.* New York: State University of New York Press.

Lloyd, Rose. "The Triumph of the Nerds." *The Atlantic,* September 1986.

Magistrale, Tony. *Landscape of Fear: Stephen King's American Gothic.* Bowling Green, OH: Bowling Green State University, 1988.

Magistrale, Tony. *Stephen King: The Second Decade, Danse Macabre to The Dark Half* (New York: Twayne Publishers, 1992).

Qader, Harem. "Innocence Lost as a Recurring Motif in Stephen King's Horror." *Journal of Literature, Languages, and Linguistics* 15, (2015).

Scahill, Andrew *The Revolting Child in Horror Cinema: Youth Rebellion and Queer Spectatorship*. New York: Palgrave Macmillan, 2015.

Stevenson, Gregory, "'The Turtle Can't Help Us': Evil, Enchantment and the Magic of Faith in Stephen King's *IT*." In *The Many Lives of IT: Essays on the Stephen King Horror Franchise*, edited by Ron Reikki, 45–56. Jefferson, NC: McFarland & Company, 2020.

Strengell, Heidi. *Dissecting Stephen King from the Gothic to Literary Naturalism*. Madison: University of Wisconsin Press, 2005.

Chapter 6

NOT FALLING APART IN THE FACE OF HORROR

Abjection and Base Matter in Stephen King's *IT*

KEITH CURRIE

In his influential essay "The Notion of Expenditure" (1933), the French writer Georges Bataille (1897–1962) observed that "humanity acts in a way that allows for the satisfaction of disarmingly savage needs," and "seems able to subsist only at the limits of horror."[1] Bataille, who lived through the most turbulent period of the twentieth century, is a thinker for whom horror can be considered a fundamental concept. Indeed, his entire oeuvre can be regarded as a protracted effort to address the need for, as he put it, "a thinking that does not fall apart in the face of horror," and "a self-consciousness that does not steal away when it is time to explore possibility to the limit."[2] Bataille's death in 1962, as Fred Botting and Scott Wilson have acknowledged, "precluded a rigorous encounter with the massive and rapid transformations of capitalism and global society that began in the post-war period," but it by no means precludes the application of Bataillean concepts and observations to the cultural productions of this period, such as works of literature and genre fiction.[3] Indeed, Bataille's work and thought possess a particular resonance in regard to works of the contemporary horror genre, which regularly engage with the key Bataillean concepts of base matter, eroticism, transgression, and sacrificial violence. Although Bataille did not explicitly engage with either the cinematic or literary modes of the horror genre in his own writings, preferring instead to discuss literature as a whole, he would doubtless have recognized the appetite for the extreme content of horror fiction that propelled the genre's most skilled practitioners to mainstream success and critical acclaim in the final decades of the twentieth century. These practitioners, artists who specialize in depictions of lives subsisting at the limits of horror, are attempting, whether consciously or otherwise, to address contemporary society's urgent need for a thinking that is robust enough to survive an encounter with horror without collapsing.

The horror genre, as the commentator Daryl Jones has noted, is inherently extreme and paradoxical in nature. Horror, he writes, "maintains a dialogic relationship between radicalism (the urge to confront) and conservatism (the desire to control). Horror occupies extreme terrain, it deals in shock and outrage, nausea and abjection, fear and loathing."[4] This complex range of emotional reactions is at least partially recognized by the American novelist Stephen King (1947–present), in a revealing passage from his nonfiction work *Danse Macabre* (1981): "I acknowledge terror as the finest emotion . . . and so I will try to terrorize the reader, but if I find I cannot terrify him/her I will try to horrify, and if I find I cannot horrify, I'll go for the gross-out. I'm not proud."[5] This admission from an acclaimed practitioner of horror demonstrates that the role played by the emotions in the task of reading and responding to a horror text should not be underestimated, for our reactions to the horror text are conditioned as much by social and cultural processes as they are by our individual psychology and experiences. Paul Santilli recognizes this when he writes that the horror genre "is worth looking at in order to learn how our culture envisions its rejected or abjected other."[6] This observation applies not only to horror's numerous monsters, but to the many marginal or marginalized human others that also populate the genre. King, as this critique will demonstrate, is a writer notable for his interest in marginalized characters.

King is the author of a vast corpus that encompasses several modes of fiction, but he remains synonymous with the horror genre in the public consciousness. Many of the novels and short stories of which this corpus is comprised are linked together via a dense web of allusions, shared characters, locations, and mythologies, replete with an array of deities, demons, and monsters. King's readers have designated this intricately interlinked series of worlds his "multiverse."[7] King's 1986 novel *IT* occupies a significant, albeit retroactively assigned position within this multiverse, which would be developed further by the author in the years following the novel's publication. *IT* is notable for its length and narrative complexity, and for its antagonist: a shapeshifting meta-monster able to assume the forms of some of horror's most iconic denizens, a characteristic which gives the work the appearance of a dark love-letter to the genre. This antagonist, which introduces itself as "Pennywise the Dancing Clown," is arguably one of King's most memorable creations. The novel is also significant in regard to its disavowal of the genre's traditional range of stock adult protagonists, focusing instead upon a group of protagonists who appear, through the use of a complex and layered narrative structure, as both successful but flawed adults in their late thirties, and lonely, marginalized eleven-year-olds. *IT* is by no means the first of King's novels to feature child protagonists, but it is the first of them to place a large group of children at the center of the action. This tactic reinforces his assertion in *Danse Macabre* that "[t]he job of the fantasy-horror writer is to make you, for a little while, a child again."[8] This return to childhood, which King considers integral to the genres of fantasy and horror fiction, is also recognized by Bataille as a vital aspect of literature itself.[9]

While not the longest of King's novels, *IT* is nevertheless a lengthy, complex work, featuring an intricately nonlinear narrative structure that blends three distinct story types: a coming-of-age narrative set in the summer of 1958, a homecoming narrative set in the spring of 1985, and a fragmentary journal kept by one of the protagonists throughout 1985, which punctuates the primary narrative in the form of "interludes." These interludes provide the reader with glimpses of the occluded and violent history of the novel's setting, the fictional New England town of Derry. While stylistically and tonally different from one another, the novel's primary narrative strands are nevertheless interconnected. The 1985 narrative initiates the 1958 narrative, which is excavated in accordance with the vicissitudes of the adult protagonists' returning childhood memories as they converge upon Derry. While these narratives are not exact doubles of one another, they nevertheless display a similar pattern of development, which centers upon the protagonists'efforts to form—or in the case of the 1985 narrative to reestablish—a community or fellowship. The child protagonists name this fellowship the Losers' Club, an ironic appellation that acknowledges their marginal status within Derry, and they retain the moniker in 1985 despite their fame and success.

This layered narrative addresses a wide range of contrasting themes: childhood is contrasted with adulthood, solitude with belonging, joy with horror, and the power of good, ultimately, with the power of evil. In addition to these themes, the novel engages dynamically with the theme of individual identity—both within and outside of a social structure—and explores the implications that confrontations with horror and abjection have in regard to the preservation and maintenance of that identity. These three themes—identity, abjection, and horror—are at the heart of my critique, and will be explored with reference to both Bataille and the literary critic and psychoanalyst Julia Kristeva (1941–present), a thinker over whom Bataille's writings exerted a palpable influence. In particular, Bataille's theorizations of horror and base matter pair fruitfully with Kristeva's concept of abjection, despite these theorists' separation along significant epistemological lines: while Bataille chose to operate at the borders of philosophy, sociology, and literature, Kristeva is considered a key figure in poststructuralist thought working from within the discipline of psychoanalysis. Their differences notwithstanding, Bataille and Kristeva share an interest in extreme states of being, and in limit-experiences— literally experiences taking place at the limits of language, consciousness, or being itself. They are similarly united in their conviction that fiction is the best or perhaps the only medium through which such states and experiences can be communicated. This critique will therefore demonstrate that *IT* is a text saturated not only in terror and horror, but in base matter and abjection. Further, it will explore the roles played by these concepts in the development of the narrative, with particular reference to the manner in which they are experienced and confronted by the protagonists.

Bataille's explorations of the concept of horror exerted a considerable influence on Kristeva's treatment of abjection. Bataille regarded horror as a turbulent and paradoxical affect, containing elements of revulsion and desire, and related to the fragility of the various prohibitions surrounding death and sexuality. Bataille also links abjection to these prohibitions, intimating that it "is merely the inability to assume with sufficient strength the imperative act of excluding abject things," an act which "establishes the foundations of collective existence."[10] These "abject things," by virtue of the fascination and revulsion they provoke in us, may also be considered objects of horror. The object of horror par excellence in Bataille's writings is the decomposing human cadaver, which he describes as "a fetid, sticky object without boundaries, which teems with life and yet is the sign of death."[11] Yet this object without boundaries in Bataille is also, paradoxically, an object of desire: "It is hard to imagine that a human individual would not withdraw from such an object in disgust," he observes, "But would he withdraw if he were not tempted? Would the object nauseate if it offered him nothing desirable?"[12] Desire, in Bataille, is usually associated with erotic desire. But Bataille is not stating that objects of horror trigger sexual desire as such. Rather, these objects confirm the presence and authenticity of desire in us, and fascinate us because they confront us with the heterogeneous existence from which we are separated at the moment of our birth, and to which our bodies shall return at the moment of our death. This heterogeneous existence, as Bataille acknowledges, may also be accessed—albeit fleetingly—through the experience of eroticism.

Bataille's objects of horror can also be considered virulent manifestations of his related concept of base matter, a concept which he outlined with reference to the dualistic cosmologies of Gnostic and Manichean religious traditions. These traditions blended a wide range of religious and mythological elements, considered good and evil to be active and oppositional cosmic forces, and created detailed cosmologies, populated with a range of gods, demiurges, demons, and archons. Bataille discerned in Gnosticism a "despotic bestial obsession with outlawed and evil forces," a "sinister love of darkness," and a "monstrous taste for lawless archons."[13] He argues that "it is possible to see as a leitmotif of Gnosticism the conception of matter as an active principle having its own eternal autonomous existence as darkness which would not be simply the absence of light, [. . .] and as evil which would not be the absence of good, but a creative action."[14] Bataille describes this conception of matter imbued with this active principle as base matter, which is matter that "is external and foreign to ideal human aspirations," matter that "refuses to allow itself to be reduced to the great ontological machines resulting from these aspirations."[15] Bataille's borderless object of horror, then, is also an excellent example of base matter, insofar as it challenges our perception of the material order.

While an investigation of the Gnostic, or indeed the myriad other religious and mythological influences upon King's multiverse would be an undertaking in its own right, it is worth noting here that it contains a range of beings who resemble the demiurges and archons of the Gnostics, and that a further defining feature of the multiverse is a dualistic cosmic struggle between the forces of good and evil. Indeed, *IT* itself opens out upon a markedly dualistic cosmology, in which the active principles of good and evil are embodied in two cosmic entities, namely It/Pennywise—who represents evil—and a being called the Turtle, who serves a power which the Losers understand as good, and encourages the Losers in their struggle with Pennywise. Further, *IT* is littered with examples of Bataillean base matter, most of which are associated with the novel's antagonist, a demonic, shapeshifting entity that manipulates matter, space, and even reality itself in the manner of a gnostic archon. It takes the form of mummies, walking corpses, and living bodies in the process of being devoured by disease, and can also animate inanimate objects such as statues and photographs. Further, It is able to manipulate the systems designed to drain, channel, and contain lesser manifestations of base matter in the form of unpleasant waste matter. A sinister emphasis is placed upon Derry's sewer system, and the various storm drains, lavatories, and household drains that connect to it; indeed much of the novel's horror stems from the antagonist's ability to subvert these systems in order to terrorize, and even prey upon its victims. A particularly affecting example of this subversion occurs in the 1958 narrative, when Beverly Marsh witnesses a geyser of blood erupting from the drain of a bathroom washbasin; she is horrified by the blood-spattered bathroom, and her horror deepens when she realizes that her parents don't see the blood at all. She asks some of her friends to look at the bathroom, and they are also able to see the blood. This supernaturally augmented blood, which can only be perceived by the children who will go on to form the Losers' Club, is an excellent example of Bataille's notion of matter animated by an active and evil principle. It also alerts the Losers to the uncomfortable idea that they can expect no help from the adults around them. Their response is to clean the bathroom and wash the bloody rags at a nearby laundry; as they wait for the wash to complete, Beverly's friends share their own stories of encounters with the antagonist. These stories, which are retold each time a new member joins the Losers' Club, take on the appearance of a set of founding mythologies for the nascent fellowship, and in this light the washing away of the base matter that has defiled Beverly's bathroom takes on the appearance of a solemn rite of purification.

The supernatural properties of this blood notwithstanding, its appearance is a moment in which abjection erupts into the narrative. Blood signifies abjection by virtue of its having crossed a corporeal border. The blood in *IT* cannot be attributed to a corporeal source, but it is nonetheless a source of horror because it reminds those who see it of their own corporeality. Abjection, as we shall see, is a concept associated with thresholds, borders, and margins of all kinds. Kristeva's writings address the concept in terms of both social structures and subjective identities. She argues that it constitutes a necessary stage in the process whereby the psychoanalytic subject achieves its individuation and autonomy, and a social or cultural structure establishes itself as such. Kristeva calls abjection a "twisted braid of affects and thoughts," which "does not have, properly speaking, a definable object."[16] The abject, she continues, "is not an ob-ject facing me, which I name or imagine. Nor is it an ob-jest, an otherness ceaselessly fleeing in a systematic quest of desire."[17] The abject, then, is neither a subject nor an object, recalling Bataille's description of the object of horror as an object without borders. Reaffirming the complex nature of the state provoked by the presence of the abject, Kristeva writes that it is "a composite of judgment and affect, of condemnation and yearning, of signs and drives."[18] This description recalls Bataille's account of horror as a turbulent and paradoxical affect combining repulsion and desire. Rather than being synonymous with abjection, however, horror should be understood as a significant element of this composite concept. Kristeva equates it with "dark, violent revolts of being, directed against a threat that seems to emanate from an exorbitant outside or inside, ejected beyond the scope of the possible, the tolerable, the thinkable"; this threat "cannot be assimilated," and must therefore be rejected or "radically excluded."[19] Kristeva attributes the banishment of this threat to the superego, that part of the subject's identity that is shaped by the laws, values, and symbolic structure of it's culture. The relationship between abjection and the superego is expressed by Kristeva in the maxim "to each ego its object, to each superego its abject."[20] The abject, then, is associated with elements of the real, which cannot be assimilated by cultural or symbolic structures. In this sense, abjection can be considered the subject of horror par excellence, for, as Santilli recognizes, "[t]he experience of horror evokes elements of the real that have not been assimilated into a culture and so into normal reality."[21] Abjection therefore constitutes the border "of a reality that, if I acknowledge it, annihilates me. There, abject and abjection are my safe-guards. The primers of my culture."[22]

Kristeva describes the outbreak of abjection as "[a] massive and sudden emergence of uncanniness, which, familiar as it might have been in an opaque and forgotten life, now harries me as radically separate, loathsome. Not me. Not that. But not nothing, either."[23] Her association of abjection with the uncanny is especially significant in regard to *IT*, a work of supernatural horror in which the uncanny plays a vital role. The uncanny—the English translation of the German *unheimlich*—is a concept that can be difficult to pin down, possessing qualities of familiarity and strangeness, openness and secretiveness, homeliness and unhomeliness. Daryl Jones observes that the uncanny "tends to arise out of a sense of uncertainty as to whether we are encountering or experiencing something which is alive or dead, organic or inert, material or supernatural."[24] The uncanny permeates *IT*, and indeed the novel's antagonist's defining feature is its uncanniness, for It often uses the inherently uncanny form of a grotesque clown in order to communicate with It's victims. Derry, too, is an uncanny place whose citizens are often manipulated into violent acts that serve secret and sinister purposes that are not comprehended by their participants. Significantly, abjection, and the uncanny erupt into the protagonists' lives at the same time in the opening chapter of the 1985 narrative. Leonard G. Heldreth has noted the regularity with which, in King's fiction, "an event or person from the past upsets the calm of a character's present existence."[25] We observe the playing out of this disruption when six of the Losers receive a phone call from a half-forgotten friend in their former hometown, who reminds them of a promise they made twenty-seven years ago and asks them to return to Derry. These communications shatter the equilibrium of their adult lives, disinterring memories of a past that they had all but forgotten. These resurfacing memories are so psychically destructive that the accountant Stanley Uris immediately retreats to his bathroom and commits suicide. The surviving Losers experience the return of these memories differently. The disc jockey Richie Tozier feels crypts cracking open inside of him: "The stench he smelled was not decaying bodies but decayed memories, and that was somehow worse."[26]

The horror novelist Bill Denbrough, however, feels "as if a black sack in his mind were bulging, threatening to spew noxious (dreams) images up from his subconscious and into the mental field of vision commanded by his rational waking mind."[27] Later, as he travels back to Derry, the chauffeur Eddie Kaspbrak feels as if he "has been poisoned by his own memories."[28] More than memories of abjection and uncanniness, these memories are themselves uncanny in that they are both alien and horribly familiar, and abject in the sense that they have been radically excluded. This exclusion makes the moment of their return a moment of rupture that disturbs and disrupts the protagonists' identities.

In addition to their evocations of decay and noxious poison, and the implications of contamination they carry with them, these descriptions of the return of dangerous memories signpost a theme that had become a mainstay of King's fiction prior to the publication of *IT*. Behind the many ghosts and monsters that populate King's fiction, as Heldreth has noted, "stands the less dramatic but more relentless horror of the past."[29] Past-time, he continues, "escapes and intrudes into the present, corrupting the current moment with old values, outgrown beliefs, and long-suppressed fears."[30] In *IT*, the theme of a horrifying and radically excluded past is explored at length by the journal entries that punctuate the primary narrative. Their author, the Derry librarian and amateur historian Mike Hanlon, acts as a link between the 1958 and 1985 narratives, placing the calls that summon the other Losers back to Derry. Mike's situation is particularly interesting because, unlike the other Losers, he retains his memories of the 1958 ordeal. Further, he has committed himself to the task of compiling a secret history of Derry, which describes a series of disasters that are barely alluded to in the town's official histories, and barely remembered by the townspeople themselves. He is also, in the manner of a contemporary true-crime enthusiast, collecting every detail he can concerning a series of child murders taking place in Derry, in order to convince the other Losers of Pennywise's return. "On one level of my mind," he writes in the first interlude, "I was and am living with the most grotesque, capering horrors; on another I have continued to live the mundane life of a small city librarian."[31] This quotation appears to advance the idea that it is possible to live at the limits of horror—and indeed to live with the knowledge of terrible memories whose return frightens the other Losers so badly—and still lead a purposeful and even meaningful existence. But the growing agitation and terror that pervade the interludes suggest that such a life would begin to take a toll on one's mental health.

It is through Mike's journal entries that we learn that Derry is a city marked by repeating patterns of child murders and disappearances, culminating in spectacles of sacrificial violence. The child murders are the direct work of Pennywise, but the latter events are either caused by natural or industrial disasters, or by human agents. These latter events are driven by human prejudices stemming from the desire to exclude that Kristeva identifies as a significant element of abjection—homophobia, racism, xenophobia, and other more nebulous prejudices—and directed towards geographical or cultural outsiders. These crimes assume their sacrificial character via the peripheral presence and involvement of the monstrous antagonist, who appears to draw strength and power from the sacrifice. Mike's writings, and the recollections of the townspeople whom he interviews, are haunted as much by this peripheral presence as they are by the crimes it appeared to endorse. These crimes are not sacrifices in the sense that Bataille understood the concept, for they do not involve "a privileged moment of communal unity."[32] Indeed, the extent to which the townspeople participate in these crimes vary from event to event, but an argument could be advanced that the remainder are rendered complicit by virtue of their failure to intervene. The symbiotic relationship between It and the townspeople is reflected upon by the adult incarnation of the protagonist Bill Denbrough in the 1985 narrative strand: "Derryfolk had lived with Pennywise for a long time . . . and maybe, in some mad way they had even come to understand him. To like him, need him. Love him?"[33] Bataille's remark concerning the failure to exclude abject things seems particularly apropos in regard to Derry, which is a community that has failed to exclude its monstrous resident and has instead come to depend upon it, even as it feeds upon them, because it periodically offers them victims to violently exclude instead, and permits them to give vent to impulses that would normally be kept in check. In this sense, these acts can be considered "a convulsive communication of what is ordinarily stifled."[34]

In its role as a monstrous "other" that menaces the Losers, Pennywise can be considered synonymous with the abject in several ways. Monsters trigger abjection because, as Fred Botting has noted, they "make visible in their transgression the limits separating proper from improper, self from other."[35] King himself appears to recognize these properties of the monstrous when he observes that "We love and need the concept of monstrosity because it is a reaffirmation of the order we all crave as human beings. It is not the physical or mental aberration in itself that horrifies us, but rather the lack of order that these aberrations seem to imply."[36] This disruptive property of the monstrous is also, as Kristeva confirms, a significant property of the abject: it is "not lack of health or cleanliness that causes abjection," she writes, "but what disturbs identity, system, order. What does not respect borders, positions, rules. The in-between, the ambiguous, the composite."[37] Pennywise, as we learn from the information scattered piecemeal throughout the novel, is an ambiguous and composite entity which adopts a wide range of monstrous personae that obscure its true shape and form. Further, a sense of the antagonist's innate ambiguity can be perceived in the terms used by the Losers in order to identify it: it is sometimes referred to as "Pennywise" or "the clown," but is most often identified with the single ungendered pronoun "It," which itself becomes a proper noun in the 1985 narrative strand.[38]

Beyond this monstrous ambiguity, It can also be considered abject to the extent that it is synonymous with both perversity and crime. Kristeva considers all crime abject "because it draws attention to the fragility of the law," but "premeditated crime, cunning murder, hypocritical revenge are even more so because they heighten the display of such fragility."[39] The crimes of Pennywise, which involve trickery, temptation, and deception, in addition to extreme violence, certainly fulfill these criteria. Moreover, It appears to delight in corrupting others, or manipulating them into acting upon either their outraged morality or their latent violent or perverse desires, often without the manipulated party realizing that they are being manipulated. "The abject is perverse," Kristeva observes, "because it neither gives up nor assumes a prohibition, a rule, or a law; but turns them aside, misleads, corrupts; uses them, takes advantage of them, the better to get around them."[40] This sense of the perverse taking advantage of rules and laws is most apparent in the interludes, but it is also apparent in the manipulation of the human agents that Pennywise uses against the Losers in the latter stages of both the 1958 and 1985 narrative strands.

If It can be considered synonymous with Kristeva's abject to the extent that It is ambiguous, criminal, and perverse, the Losers can also be considered abject insofar as they disturb and disrupt Derry's status quo. They do this in the 1985 thread by returning to Derry as outsiders with the intention of overthrowing Pennywise, but in the 1958 strand, they are in the process of being marginalized by the townspeople for deviating from the prevailing social norms. Two important questions arise in regard to the early stages of this narrative: To what extent are the Losers experiencing abjection prior to the moment of contact with the antagonist? And how do the Losers confront and, eventually, make use of abjection in their struggle with Pennywise? In order to answer these questions, we need to take a look at Kristeva's account of the subject's response to the threat of abjection.

Kristeva refers to the subject faced with abjection as a "deject," who responds to the threat confronting it by attempting to situate and separate itself, becoming "a tireless builder," and "a devisor of territories."[41] Crucially, while trying to reinstate the borders that have been called into question, the deject loses its bearings, becomes fascinated with the abject, and embarks upon a journey into its personal archaeology that will culminate with its recognition of itself as abject; Kristeva calls this moment "the abjection of self."[42]

In the opening chapters of the 1958 narrative strand, the Losers—who have not yet constituted themselves as such—can be considered dejects to the extent that they are attempting to situate themselves within a community from which they are being slowly marginalized, and are beginning to understand that they are therefore at risk of abuse and violence. They have effectively begun the psychological journey that culminates with the abjection of self, but this ultimate realization is yet to be apprehended. Significantly, it is as they try to navigate the hostile environs of Derry on their own that each of the Losers experiences an encounter with Pennywise. This psychological journey is also mapped out in physical terms, as they attempt to situate themselves within a town whose residents are either apathetic or hostile toward them. They are initially accepting of the identities imposed upon them by their peers, but begin to resist them and, ultimately, to reject them. The identities they reject are informed by aspects of their biology, character, cultural, or social status, which have come to define them in the eyes of their community: Bill Denbrough has a stutter, Ben Hanscom is overweight, Mike Hanlon is an African American in a majority white city, Beverly Marsh comes from a low-income housing district, Stan Uris is Jewish, Richie Tozier wears glasses and is an impulsive mimic, and Eddie Kaspbrak is anxious and asthmatic. On account of these biological, psychological, or cultural traits, they are victimized by the town's bullies, in a series of encounters marked by escalating violence. These encounters drive the Losers to take refuge in an overgrown area of wasteland in the center of town known somewhat misleadingly as the Barrens, which is largely shunned by the townspeople. The protagonists begin to lay claim to this territory, and it is here that the Losers' Club begins to develop. This territory, which is defined by its wildness and shunned status, can be considered a physical representation of the "excluded ground" upon which Kristeva's deject strays in his fascination with the abject.[43] In this sense, we can see the protagonists as characters already caught up in a process whereby they are simultaneously abjecting and being abjected.

Another thing worth noting about these child characters is that they are living in the hinterland between childhood proper and puberty; they sense the onset of the adult world, and are both fascinated and frightened by it. They are particularly unsettled by the world of sex, the language of which is being introjected into their world by their parents and peers. In regard to the child murders happening in the town, the children overhear the adults describing them as the work of a "sexfiend," an association that establishes an uncomfortable link between sexuality, violence, and death, creating a threat that is rendered visible as a shadowy figure haunting the outer margins of the town. Thus, the Losers can be considered beset by abjection prior to, or at least concomitantly with, their encounters with Pennywise.

While the Losers are caught up in the inexorable process of rejecting and being rejected by their local community, their relationship to the wider culture to which they belong—that of 1950s America—is on the whole much more positive. While they recognize that they deviate from its prevailing norms, they are nevertheless sustained by popular culture, and they take their bearings by its most rebellious and subversive elements, namely, comic books, cinematic horror, and the then-burgeoning rock 'n' roll music genre. Richie Tozier in particular perceives "power in that music, a power which seemed to most rightfully belong to all the skinny kids, fat kids, ugly kids—the world's losers."[44] This power notwithstanding, the Losers' culture nevertheless leaves them dangerously exposed to Pennywise because it is a culture rich in depictions of the monstrous. Pennywise, who can read the minds of its victims and extract images of terror and horror from them, therefore transforms itself into a number of cinematic horror's most famous monsters, with embellishments tailored to speak to the Losers' individual fears. Pennywise's ability to analyze the minds of It's victims intersects significantly with Kristeva's assertion that the abject is "a cynic, and a psychoanalyst."[45] Indeed, some of It's manifestations to the Losers directly address their phobias and are extrapolated directly from their personal experiences. An excellent example of a manifestation of this sort can be found in the leper that appears to Eddie Kaspbrak. This leper is extrapolated from an encounter that Eddie has with a syphilitic hobo in the yard of a derelict house near Derry's rail yard, who offers to give him sexual favors in exchange for money. Eddie learns about syphilis after the fact when he confides in his friends, but his immediate thought upon seeing the hobo is: "Oh my god he's got leprosy! If he touches me I'll catch it too!"[46] Compelled some weeks later to return to the derelict house, he begins to imagine himself a hobo, but his thoughts soon turn to disease: "I can feel myself turning bad like an apple that's going soft, I can feel it happening, eating from the inside to the out, eating, eating, eating me."[47] He then encounters Pennywise in the guise of a leper, who repeats the hobo's offer of sexual favors. This manifestation represents the confluence of Eddie's fear of sex—the knowledge of which has been introjected into his mind through his encounter with the hobo and through conversations with his friends—and the fear of disease that has been inculcated in him by his mother. Eddie's leper is the most overtly sexualized manifestation of

Pennywise's appearances in the 1958 strand, but Pennywise will later use Beverly Marsh's father's fear of his daughter's friendship with the male members of the Losers' Club, and indeed his perverse desires towards her, as a means of forcing the final confrontation with the Losers. As her father attacks and attempts to rape her, Beverly realizes that "It was working through him."[48]

Beverly's father's attack on her—which she narrowly escapes—proceeds and precipitates the moment at which the Losers realize that their exclusion from Derry is complete: "They had, at some point between getting up this morning and lunch-time, simply become ghosts."[49] This moment also coincides with the moment at which Bill Denbrough realizes the true extent of the relationship between Derry and It, and understands that the Losers have been marked as sacrificial victims. Struggling desperately against his stutter, he tells the other Losers that "Duh-herry is Ih-Ih-It! Eh-eh-hennyp-p-lace we g-g-go . . . when Ih-Ih-It g-g-g-gets uh-us, they w-w-wuh-hon't suh-suhsee, they fw-w-won't huh-huh-hear, they w-w-won't nuh-nuh-know."[50] This moment of revelation—and indeed the confrontation that follows it—is repeated in the 1985 narrative strand, when the Losers are once again attacked by Pennywise working through human agents.

Accordingly, both narrative strands culminate with the descent of the Losers into the depths of Derry's sewer system, and a dramatic and violent confrontation with Pennywise. These descents into darkness and filth parallel the descent into the self undertaken by the adult Losers at the beginning of the 1985 narrative strand, and can also be read as a physical iteration of the deject's journey into its personal archaeology, which "takes the ego back to its source on the abominable limits from which, in order to be, the ego has broken away."[51] In other words, the Losers are recapitulating the moment at which they violently broke away from their mothers—the moment of their birth—with Pennywise in the role of the mother who, revealed as abject, must in turn be radically excluded by the Losers. This identification of Pennywise with the abject mother is made explicit in the 1985 confrontation, when the Losers make the horrified realization that It is in fact female, and preparing to give birth. This revelation lends the 1985 confrontation a savagely matricidal quality that is absent from its 1958 counterpart. The Losers succeed in destroying not only Pennywise and her offspring, but a large part of Derry itself, which is struck by an extreme weather event. Lavatories and drains explode all over the city in a quite literal return of the repressed, as the monstrous creature that was in effect the mother of Derry is reduced, in the last analysis, to nothing more than "a huge steaming bundle of alien meat," base matter robbed of its active principle and reduced to waste matter to be entombed beneath a dying city.[52]

While the denouement of the 1958 narrative lacks the ultimate destruction of Pennywise, it nevertheless dramatizes the culmination of the process of abjection in which the Losers have been engaged, and in a manner that remains as controversial in the present moment as it was upon publication in 1986. Having severely wounded the monster and endured an experience of horror on the threshold of a reality that threatened their annihilation, the Losers begin to lose their cohesion as they begin to succumb to their individual fears, realizing that they are lost in the labyrinth of tunnels beneath the city. Sensing the group's disintegration, Beverly informs the boys that she knows a way "to bring [them] back together" and then starts undressing.[53] What follows is arguably the novel's most Bataillean scene, as Beverly reunites the Losers through the experience of eroticism. Mounting a defense of this episode is necessarily problematic, even when viewed through the rubric of a theory that recognizes the fundamental kinship of horror and desire, because it strays beyond the bounds of acceptability, and violates a taboo on depictions of children engaging in sexual activity. One violates a taboo as pervasive as this at some considerable risk, and in the hands of a less skilled author and in any other context than that of extreme horror this scene might appear gratuitous, but transgression is necessary in order to reinstate the taboo. Transgression, Bataille observes, "does not deny the taboo but transcends it and completes it."[54] This scene therefore constitutes a crucial moment in the narrative, because desire arrives at the moment when the Losers need it the most. Eroticism, Bataille observes, "is assenting to life up to the point of death."[55] Like abjection, it draws its participants to the very limits of their being, but if abjection takes the subject back to its origins, eroticism is "a state of communication revealing a quest for a possible continuance of being beyond the confines of the self."[56] Bataille's treatment of eroticism generally assigns a passive role to the female partner, but the most extraordinary aspect of this scene is the degree of agency afforded to Beverly, who initiates the quest by taking "the decisive action" of stripping naked.[57] Sex having been violently introjected into her world by her father, who revealed the fragility of the taboo concerning sex by intending to break it himself while pretending to enforce it, Beverly turns her abjection and shame into a source of joy and power: "[t]here was power in this act, alright, a chain-breaking power that was blood-deep."[58] This experience of joy is contrasted with the experience of horror even as their fundamental kinship is acknowledged, when Beverly realizes that, for her peers, "sex must be some unrealized, undefined monster; they referred to the act as It."[59] Yet even as she transcends the taboo, she acknowledges the necessity of its reinstatement, thinking that "it must never be spoken of, not to anyone else, not even to each other."[60]

This scene, which involves the loss of self that accompanies the erotic experience, can be considered the culminating gesture of the process through which the Losers have been journeying throughout the 1958 narrative. Abjection "is a resurrection that has gone through death (of the ego). It is an alchemy that transforms death drive into a start of life."[61] If the alchemy of eroticism reunites the fellowship in the 1958 narrative, the 1985 narrative, which concludes with the final dissolution of the Losers' Club, and the pro-tagonists' gradual forgetting of It, of Derry, and ultimately of one another, is governed by the logic of abjection. Having successfully abjected It, the Losers are now able to finally and decisively abject their former selves.

Leonard Heldreth reaches a similar conclusion, noting that the jettisoning of the former self is a significant motif of King's fiction: "[t]he past must be permanently escaped—even the past self must be escaped—if the future is to achieve realization and the individual is to create, through experience, a new self."[62]

Having demonstrated that *IT* is a text saturated in terror, horror, base matter, and abjection, the final task of this critique is to assess the extent to which the novel succeeds in formulating, in Bataille's words, "a thinking that does not fall apart in the face of horror." Abjection, base matter, and hor-ror are indeed confronted and ultimately overcome by the Losers in their struggle with It, yet in the final analysis they fall back upon the morality instilled in them by their culture, a morality that is outraged by the rapacious nature of Pennywise. It is this sense of outrage that finally allows them to defeat It as well as to purify the abjection infecting Derry. In this respect, their actions bear out Kristeva's assertion that "an unshakable adherence to prohibition and law is necessary if that perverse interspace of abjection is to be hemmed in and thrust aside."[63] Yet the destruction of Pennywise, and the end of its reign over Derry, represents a considerable divergence from Bataille's outlook concerning base matter, a concept that he held to be both eternal and autonomous, making any victory achieved against it only a tem-porary reprieve. The novel can nevertheless be considered a Bataillean text to the extent that it charts the Losers' development of an outlook that Bataille designates a "hypermorality," "a rigorous morality results from complicity with the knowledge of evil, which is the basis of intense communication."[64] This rigorous morality, far from adhering rigidly to prohibition and law, acknowledges that these laws are fragile, and can be bypassed or manipu-lated. Further, it acknowledges that some prohibitions must sometimes be transgressed in order to affirm the necessity of their observance.

If the novel is at its weakest when attempting to represent evil as an objec-tive concept embodied by It, King's work is arguably at its strongest when confronting the many human evils that are manipulated and amplified by It. These evils, acts committed against those who deviate from Derry's prevailing cultural norms, are crimes driven as much by the dark undercurrents of prejudice and hatred roiling beneath the surface of contemporary American culture as they are by Pennywise. Mike Hanlon's effort to keep an account of their eruptions into the open and the deadly consequences that follow can therefore be regarded as the novel's most courageous act, for it expresses the idea that vigilance fortified with knowledge of the horrors of the past can prevent past events from repeating themselves. This knowledge and vigilance, which in *IT* is presented as the task and burden of a single individual who is prepared to probe the origins of a corrupt and violent status quo, is arguably the task of discourse itself. In this sense, abjection is not only the subject *par excellence* of horror, but the central subject of all discourse. Kristeva appears to suggest just such an idea when she asserts that "discourse will seem tenable only if it ceaselessly confronts that otherness, a burden both repellent and repelled, a deep well of memory that is both unapproachable and intimate: the abject."[65] A discourse capable of meeting this challenge could also, finally, fulfill our urgent need for a thinking that does not fall apart in the face of horror.

Notes

1. Georges Bataille, "The Notion of Expenditure," in *Visions of Excess Selected Writings, 1927–1939*, eds. Allan Stoekl, trans. Allan Stoekl, with Carl R. Lovitt and Donald M. Leslie (Minneapolis: University of Minnesota Press, 1985), 117.

2. Georges Bataille, "Preface to the History of Eroticism," trans. Robert Hurley, in *The Bataille Reader*, eds. Fred Botting and Scott Wilson (Oxford: Blackwell, 1997), 238.

3. Fred Botting and Scott Wilson, "From Experience to Economy," introduction to *The Bataille Reader*, eds. Fred Botting and Scott Wilson (Oxford: Blackwell, 1997) 28.

4. Daryl Jones, *Sleeping with the Lights On: The Unsettling History of Horror* (Oxford: Oxford University Press, 2018), 15.

5. Stephen King, *Danse Macabre*, narrated by William Dufris (New York: Hodder and Stoughton, 1981); Audible audio edition, eighteen hours, four minutes, chapter 5, 23:05.

6. Paul Santilli, "Culture, Evil, and Horror," *American Journal of Economics and Sociology* 66, no. 1 (January 2007): 176.

7. For an expansive list of the many connections that bind King's texts, worlds, and mythologies together, see *The Dark Tower: Connections*, https://stephenking.com/darktower/connections/.

8. King, *Danse Macabre*, chapter 17, 51'05.

9. See Georges Bataille, *Literature and Evil*, trans. Alastair Hamilton (London: Penguin, 2012), 3.

10. Georges Bataille and Essais de Sociologie, quoted in Julia Kristeva, *Powers of Horror: An Essay on Abjection*, trans. Leon S. Roudiez (New York: Columbia University Press, 1982), p.56.

11. Georges Bataille, "The Phaedra Complex," trans. Robert Hurley, in *The Bataille Reader*, eds. Fred Botting and Scott Wilson (Oxford: Blackwell, 1997), 253.

12. Bataille, "The Phaedra Complex," 253.

13. Georges Bataille, "Base Materialism and Gnosticism," in *Visions of Excess Selected Writings, 1927–1939*, ed. Allan Stoekl, trans. Allan Stoekl, with Carl R. Lovitt and Donald M. Leslie (Minneapolis: University of Minnesota Press, 1985), 48.

14. Bataille, "Base Materialism and Gnosticism," 47.

15. Bataille, "Base Materialism and Gnosticism," 51.

16. Julia Kristeva, *Powers of Horror: an Essay on Abjection*, trans. Leon S. Roudiez (New York: Columbia University Press, 1982), 1.

17. Kristeva, *Powers of Horror*, 1.

18. Kristeva, *Powers of Horror*, 10.

19. Kristeva, *Powers of Horror*, 1–2.

20. Kristeva, *Powers of Horror*, 2

21. Santilli, "Culture, Horror, and Evil," 174.

22. Kristeva, *Powers of Horror*, 2.

23. Kristeva, *Powers of Horror*, 2.

24. Jones, *Sleeping with the Lights On*, 18

25. Leonard G. Heldreth, "Rising Like Old Corpses: Stephen King and the Horrors of Time-past," *Journal of the Fantastic in the Arts* 2, no. 1 (Spring 1989): 5.

26. King, Stephen, *IT*, read by Steven Weber (New York: Hodder and Stouton); Audible audio edition, 44:53, chapter 3, "Six Phone Calls," 1:05:36.

27. *King, IT*, chapter 3, 3:59:49.

28. *King, IT*, chapter 7, "The Dam in the Barrens," 03:04.

29. Heldreth, "Rising Like Old Corpses," 5.

30. Heldreth, "Rising Like Old Corpses," 5.

31. King, *IT*, "Derry: The First Interlude," 04:22.

32. Georges Bataille, "The Sacred," in *Visions of Excess Selected Writings, 1927–1939*, ed. Allan Stoekl, trans. Allan Stoekl, with Carl R. Lovitt and Donald M. Leslie (Minneapolis: University of Minnesota Press, 1985), 242.

33. King, *IT*, chapter 10, "The Reunion," 07:59.

34. Bataille, "The Sacred," 242.

35. Botting, Fred, *Limits of Horror: Technology, Bodies, Gothic* (Manchester: Manchester University Press, 2008), 8.

36. King, *Danse Macabre*, chapter 5, 1:03.

37. Kristeva, *Powers of Horror*, 4.

38. King, *IT*, chapter 10, 1:35:36

39. Kristeva, *Powers of Horror*, 4.

40. Kristeva, *Powers of Horror*, 15.

41. Kristeva, *Powers of Horror*, 8.

42. Kristeva, *Powers of Horror*, 8.

43. Kristeva, *Powers of Horror*, 5

44. King, *IT*, chapter 11, "Walking Tours," 1:57:07.

45. Kristeva, *Powers of Horror*, 15–16.

46. King, *IT*, chapter 7, 52:08

47. King, *IT*, chapter 7, 1:019.

48. King, *IT*, chapter 19, "In the Watches of the Night," 20:55.

49. King, *IT*, chapter 19, 3:08:56

50. King, *IT*, chapter 19, 3:06:37

51. Kristeva, *Powers of Horror*, 15

52. King, *IT,* chapter 23, "Out," 15:35.

53. King, *IT*, chapter 22, "The Ritual of Chüd," 1:6:39.

54. Georges Bataille, *Eroticism: Death and Sensuality*, trans. Mary Dalwood (San Francisco: City Lights, 1986), 62.

55. Bataille, *Eroticism*, 11.

56. Bataille, *Eroticism*, 17.

57. Bataille, *Eroticism*, 17.

58. King, *IT*, chapter 22, 1:22:53.

59. King, *IT*, chapter 22, 1:30:03.

60. King, *IT*, chapter 22, 1:33:29.

61. Kristeva, *Powers of Horror*, 15.

62. Heldreth, "Rising Like Old Corpses," 6.

63. Kristeva, *Powers of Horror*, 16.

64. Bataille, *Literature and Evil*, 3.

65. Kristeva, *Powers of Horror*, 6.

References

Bataille, Georges. "Base Materialism and Gnosticism." In *The Bataille Reader*, edited by Fred Botting and Scott Wilson, translated by Alan Stoekl, with Carl R. Lovitt and Donald M. Leslie Jr. Oxford: Blackwell, 1997.

Bataille, Georges. *Eroticism: Death and Sensuality*, translated by Mary Dalwood. San Francisco: City Lights, 1986.

Bataille, Georges. *Literature and Evil*, translated by Alastair Hamilton. London: Penguin, 2012.

Bataille, Georges. "Preface to The History of Eroticism," translated by Robert Hurley. In *The Bataille Reader*, edited by Fred Botting and Scott Wilson. Oxford: Blackwell, 1997.

Botting, Fred. *Limits of Horror: Technology, Bodies, Gothic*. Manchester: Manchester University Press, 2008.

Cheyne, Ria. *Disability, Literature, Genre: Representation and Affect in Contemporary Fiction*. Liverpool: Liverpool University Press, 2019.

Clute, John. "Horror." In *The Darkening Garden: A Short Lexicon of Horror*. N.d. Reproduced with permission from www.weirdfictionreview.com.

Heldreth, Leonard G. "Rising Like Old Corpses: Stephen King and the Horrors of Time-Past." *Journal of the Fantastic in the Arts* 2, no. 1 (Spring 1989): 5.

Jones, Daryl. *Sleeping with the Lights On: The Unsettling History of Horror*. Oxford: Oxford University Press, 2018.

King, Stephen. *Danse Macabre*. Narrated by William Dufris. New York: Hodder and Stoughton, 1981. Audible audio edition.

King, Stephen, *IT*. Read by Steven Weber. New York: Hodder and Stoughton, Audible audio edition.

Kristeva, Julia. *Powers of Horror: An Essay on Abjection*. Translated by Leon S. Roudiez. New York: Columbia University Press, 1982.

Martín Alegre, Sara. "Nightmares of Childhood: The Child and the Monster in Four Novels by Stephen King." In *Atlantis* 23, no. 1 (June 2001): 105–14.

Santilli, Paul. "Culture, Evil, and Horror." *American Journal of Economics and Sociology* 66, no. 1 (January 2007): 173–94.

Section III

Counterclaims

Chapter 7

THE TOWNSPEOPLE OF DERRY IN STEPHEN KING'S *IT*

Bystanders and Responsibility for Evil

PENNY CROFTS

While there is some dissent about the parameters of horror, there is agreement among fans and theorists alike that the function of the genre is to (aim to) arouse the *affect* of horror, an emotion which the theorist Noël Carroll had described as a combination of fear and disgust.[1] Frequently, this affect is achieved through inexplicable terrors, such as supernatural monsters.[2] But while these nightmares may be expressed in the manifestation of the monstrous, they are purposefully encoded to express and arouse the anxieties and concerns of the age.[3] These include broader concerns such as the battle between good and evil, fears of losing one's soul or succumbing to evil, and the impossibility of justice and what justice would look like. A common trope in the genre is the failure of authority in response to horrors. Protagonists are frequently confronted with this failure in the form of an inability by characters or institutions in authority to adequately respond, prevent, protect, or believe, or worse, authorities that create, exacerbate, or enable wrongs. This failure in response to supernatural threats expresses and encodes broader anxieties about the failure to respond to real ones. In horror, then, lies exquisite terrain for analyses of complicity—and its monstrous capacities.

Although in Stephen King's *IT*, Pennywise the evil, supernatural monster is the most obvious and fabulous villain, a great deal of the horror of *IT* lies in the representation of the complicity of the townspeople of Derry. *IT* illuminates the ways in which evil flourishes because the bystanders around the perpetrator fail to intervene and therefore are part of a conspiracy of silence. *IT* offers a meditation on the significance of context in the tolerance of, and failure to prevent, evil. Although *IT* is fictional and almost unbelievable in terms of the complicity of the townspeople, this complicity is actually all too common.[4] *IT* offers an opportunity to explore the culpability of bystanders through the representation of the town and townspeople of Derry. The portrayal of bystanders provides an accurate representation of how harm and crimes are sustained within and by large organizations, as revealed by the many international inquiries into the failure to prevent and respond adequately to child sexual abuse within and by organizations.[5] While details of these harms arouse cries of horror and "never again," it seems, like the characters of *IT*, we are subject to a form of amnesia, reflected, and reinforced by the law, whereby the systems which facilitate, encourage, or tolerate these harms are able to continue across time and place. This chapter explores this horror through an analysis and comparison of the bystanders in the novel (and films) *IT*,[6] and the individuals and organizations that surrounded and shielded Larry Nassar while he sexually abused American gymnasts for decades with seeming impunity.

This chapter compares the townspeople and town of Derry with the third parties that disregarded, enabled, and facilitated Nassar's offending. The genre of horror is often perceived as lacking in seriousness,[7] as too visceral and too popular,[8] but it can also be a source of philosophical, social, and legal critique.[9] However, this comparison is valuable because it provides detail and nuance regarding the expectations and culpability of bystanders, the barriers to becoming an upstander, and the significance of organizational context in making these decisions. I focus on three broad categories proposed by Kaufmann in his analysis of bystanders: abstainers—those who did not want to know; engagers—those who knew and did nothing; and finally enablers—those who committed offenses.[10] I argue that the failure to act by individuals and organizations in authority can and should be regarded as culpable and worthy of criminal sanction.

PENNYWISE AND LARRY NASSAR

In *IT*, the monster that presents itself as Pennywise kills and maims across centuries, with the violence coming to a crescendo every twenty-seven years and ending with a "gaudy sacrifice."[11] Pennywise is often ignored, but also frequently joined by townspeople in these acts of violence. The heroes of *IT* are a gang of "losers" who survived a confrontation with Pennywise as children in 1958 and swore to return to defeat Pennywise if their resolution of the monster was incomplete. The historian of the group, Michael Hanlon, states that "the murder rate in Derry is six times the murder rate of any other town in comparable size in New England."[12] He states that "things really are not right here in Derry; things in Derry have *never* been right."[13] Despite this, the violence continues unabated with an absence of any (effective) official reaction.

In the contemporary era of #MeToo, there is increasing awareness and condemnation of rampant sexual crimes committed over long periods of time by perpetrators such as Larry Nassar, Harvey Weinstein, and Jeffrey Epstein. These crimes are not new. What these and other cases show is not only how widespread and unchecked sexual abuse is, but also how many people and organizations around the perpetrator disregard or even enable it.[14] As in *IT*, the harms continue long-term in the absence of official reaction or intervention. Larry Nassar is by no means the worst (or best) of this unfortunate group, but provides a case study for analyzing long-term offending against children within an organizational context.[15] Larry Nassar had an osteopathic medical degree, and served as national medical coordinator for USA Gymnastics for twenty-five years until he "retired" from the role. He also worked at Michigan State University's College of Osteopathic Medicine and was team physician at Twistars Gymnastics Club and for the university.[16] In September 2016, the *IndyStar* published allegations of sexual abuse by Nassar. Since that time, hundreds of people have come forward with allegations of sexual abuse. He was sentenced in 2018 to 175 years in prison after pleading guilty to sexually abusing seven girls.

ABSTAINERS, WILLFUL BLINDNESS, AND AMNESIA

In *IT*, Pennywise is able to continue harm precisely because of the inaction and silence of bystanders. An early and utterly credible example of this is in chapter 2 of the novel and the opening scenes of the second film, which portray the horrific and homophobic killing of Adrian Mellon at the end of the Canal Days Festival. The homicide is "justified" from the perspective of the killer, who is offended by Adrian and his boyfriend Don Hagarty, because the killer's "civic pride had been wounded by seeing a fucking faggot wearing a hat which said I love DERRY."[17]

IT powerfully portrays abstainers, those who passively witness the crime, turn away and/or choose willful blindness. As the character Hanlon says, "In Derry, people have a way of looking the other way."[18] Adrian's murder represents this powerfully. Three guys punch Adrian in the face, tripping him, booting him in the stomach, and knocking him into the roadway. "A car passed. Hagarty rose to his knees and screamed at it. It didn't slow. The driver, . . . never even looked around."[19] It is arguable that the driver was not aware of what was going on, but the novel suggests that this is a form of willful blindness specific to Derry, wherein its townspeople actively choose not to see or hear the violence that occurs there so frequently. This is shown particularly when Hagarty starts screaming for help:

> *"Help!"* Hagarty shrieked. *"Help! Help! They're killing him! Help!"*
>   The buildings of Main Street loomed dark and secret. No one came to help—not even from the one white island of light which marked the bus station, and Hagarty did not see how that could be: there were people in there. He had seen them when he and Ade walked past. Would none of them come to help? None at all?
>   *"HELP! HELP! THEY'RE KILLING HIM, HELP, PLEASE, FOR GOD'S SAKE."*[20]

In the novel, it is not just the actions of Pennywise that are horrific; it is this failure to witness, that is, to see or to hear, and thus to abstain from intervention that evokes horror.

This failure to witness has parallels with the bystanders around Nassar. A common defense by people surrounding Nassar was that of ignorance, including by the coaches Martha and Bela Karolyi. This was despite numerous claims of abuse from multiple victims being made across time and place.[21] For example, a parent raised concerns about Nassar's behavior at Twistars; a small number of female athletes at Michigan State complained to no avail about inappropriate examinations in 1997.[22] In 2014, a university investigation of another complaint cleared Dr. Nassar of misconduct, but imposed conditions (which were never enforced) that he was required to have a third person present when treatment involved sensitive areas of the body and to wear gloves.

This assertion of ignorance about Pennywise and Nassar is enabled by an amnesia enforced by official silence and silencing. Amnesia and abstaining from action are not always culpable. For example, victims may themselves have a form of amnesia (an indicator of trauma) which leads them to abstain from acting.[23] In *IT*, the gang of "losers" who had survived their confrontation with Pennywise in 1958 have forgotten everything—including Derry and each other. One of the characters comments that "It's like having a case of amnesia so bad you don't know you've got it."[24] This repression or amnesia was also reported by Nassar's victim/survivors; for example, one of his victims commented "I think I've blocked out a lot of what he did to me."[25] In law, the majority of statutes criminalizing the failure to report a crime exempt victims from the offense, in deference to the victims, to protect the victim's privacy, to promote a culture where victims feel comfortable to confide in others, and to avoid the invidious and unjust result of punishing a victim.[26]

Although it is common to point to the silence around offenders, it is more accurate to instead emphasize that this silence is a result of action; it is due to a silencing. There is an element of silence that goes beyond individuals and is a cultural or organizational silencing—an official or preferred policy of forgetting. The cognitive sociologist Zerubavel has explored the ways in which collective silence has a social or cultural aspect—that what we notice and do not notice, is largely socially patterned, and this can be shaped by power.[27] This is shown when the historian of the gang of losers, Hanlon, attempts to remind Derry of some of its gaudy sacrifices, with a display in the Canal Days Museum. The sponsors of the museum, the Derry Ladies' Society:

> [V]etoed some of Hanlon's proposed exhibits (such as the notorious tramp chair from the 1930s) and photographs (such as those of the Bradley Gang after the notorious shoot-out). But all agreed it was a great success, and no one really wanted to see those old gory things anyway. It was so much better to accentuate the positive and eliminate the negative, as the old song said.[28]

Likewise, there was an official silencing of Nassar's offenses which enabled him to continue offending.[29] This official quiet was shown in a series of non-disclosure agreements imposed on complainants.[30] Additionally, parents of victims were told to be quiet:

> Gina Nichols, Maggie's mother, recalled telling Steve Penny, then the president of USA Gymnastics, that the police had to be called immediately. But he insisted that she not tell anyone, she said. The organization would take care of alerting law enforcement . . . "We're working on this. Keep it quiet."[31]

These quotations demonstrate preferences by the USA Gymnastics Association and the Derry Ladies' Society for what can and will be spoken about and officially remembered, and what is to be silenced and preferably forgotten through techniques of informal and formal organizational silencing. The absence of reporting and recording procedures by the USA Gymnastics Association, Michigan State University, and American Olympic Committee might mean that upper management could well have been broadly unaware of complaints as there was no way to link information and no effort to do so. But it is this lack of knowledge or belief that child abuse was occurring that is the problem and is itself culpable.[32] As a consequence of this policy of silence, USA Gymnastics repeatedly failed to forward allegations of sexual abuse to police or to the other places at which Nassar worked. Even after finally contacting the FBI, the AGA did not inform the other places where Nassar worked that a potential molester was in their midst, allowing him to abuse an estimated fifty more victims while the FBI investigation took place. This is an organizational failure that reflects a form of willful blindness, a preference or policy to not know within the organization. As the character Hanlon observes in *IT*, "something's going on here but it's private."[33] The effect of the official policy of silence, despite individuals speaking out, is that the offender is able to continue offending. There is a malignancy to the silence and silencing of bystanders. In contrast, *IT* portrays the necessity and power of the "losers" remembering and speaking to each other in 1985 of the harms committed by Pennywise in 1958, and how they combined together to defeat Pennywise. In Nassar's case, the power of speaking out and publicizing allegations is demonstrated by the snowball effect of the reporting in the *IndyStar* of abuse allegations by two of Nassar's victims, which led to many more victims coming forward.

ENGAGERS AND THE CONTEXTS OF HARM

An additional category of bystanders are engagers, those who actively engage in unhelpful but not illegal conduct, such as mocking the victim.[34] In *IT*, Pennywise is able to operate so effectively because the children upon whom the monster preys live in a context of cruelty and violence. For example, the homophobic homicide takes place in the context of casual homophobia expressed in graffiti described as "coolly logical anti-gay statements such as KILL ALL QUEERS and AIDS FROM GO YOU HELLBOUND HOMOS!!"[35] Even the police officer responding to Hagarty's grief and pain at the murder of his partner finds "it impossible to take seriously. This man—if you want to call him a man—was wearing lipstick and satin pants so tight you could almost read the wrinkles in his cock. Grief or no grief, pain or no pain, he was, after all, just a queer. Like his friend, the late Adrian Mellon."[36] Pennywise capitalizes on a culture of homophobia and racism.

I do not wish to suggest that Larry Nassar was a monster, as this accords him extreme powers and suggests that only extreme measures can possibly defeat him.[37] Instead, his offending was situational, enabled, and facilitated by a criminogenic organization.[38] But in addition to the horror of the harms caused by Nassar, there are parallels with Pennywise. Pennywise was dressed as a clown, ostensibly the friend of children, a figure of fun. Pennywise briefly offered kindness as a way of seducing children to come closer, offering balloons to George, before killing him.[39] Like Pennywise, Nassar was able to operate so effectively because he offered kindness in contexts of cruelty and abuse. Nassar offered medical services at the elite level of gymnastics where the line between coaching and abuse was blurred. He became a person the kids trusted because he listened to them, brought them food when the coaches were worried about their weight. He smuggled candy to gymnasts during grueling practice sessions and loaned them his cell phone when theirs were prohibited.[40] Nassar was described in clown-like terms, as "goofy but maybe a bit too attentive."[41] His actions were clearly grooming, but like Pennywise, they were so effective because he offered kindness and care in a context of cruelty.

Both Pennywise and Nassar are recorded at major events. In Pennywise's case, these are scenes of gaudy sacrifice. In Nassar's case, these tend to be regarded as scenes of triumph, but can also be characterized as scenes of pain and cruelty. For example, one of the former gymnasts on the Netflix documentary *Athlete A* comments on the celebration of the gymnast Kerri Strug, who persevered despite a broken ankle in the 1996 Olympics so that America would attain its first team gold medal. The former gymnast says, "Why are we celebrating this? Don't pretend she had a choice." This scene of triumph is also, or instead, a scene of sacrifice and cruelty, explicitly valuing and celebrating medals over the safety and wellbeing of the young girls on the team. And this is applauded not only by people within the organization but the audience. In *Athlete A*, a gymnast asserts that emotional and physical abuse of elite gymnasts was the norm, and Bela and Martha Karoli validated this cruelty through medals. This cruelty is not limited to American gymnasts but has been recognized as a problem in high level sports generally.[42] As Beverly comments in the novel this culture of cruelty enabled Pennywise: "It might only have used the tools that had been there just lying around, waiting to be picked up."[43]

INDIVIDUAL AND ORGANIZATIONAL ENABLERS

In his analysis of bystanders, Kaufmann has argued that the most culpable are those who engage in harmful conduct.[44] This is informed by a positive, individualistic model of wickedness, privileging intentional wrongdoing as the most culpable.[45] There are a disturbing number of people around Nassar and Pennywise who actively engage in harmful conduct. Many townspeople in *IT* join in massacres and gaudy sacrifices.[46] Some enablers around Nassar have since been charged with criminal offenses. For example, the president and CEO of USA Gymnastics Steve Penny was arrested in 2018 on a felony charge of evidence tampering. He was accused of ordering the removal of documents from a national team center at Karolyi Ranch, Texas, after learning of an investigation into Nassar's behavior there. He has pleaded not guilty.[47] The documents he ordered destroyed have not been recovered.

This category of enablers needs to be expanded to include the people or organizations in authority who fail to fulfill their duty to act. While the dominant model of culpability in society and law focuses on individuals intentionally doing the wrong thing,[48] philosophers of wickedness have pointed to a classic, negative model of wickedness of evil as lack or dearth of goodness, of failure.[49] The advantage of this model is that it incorporates not only individual failure to act but organizational failure to act. Large organizations have a great capacity to inflict systemic harm, and yet the larger they are, the less likely they are to be held liable in criminal law, particularly as the size and diffusion of authority in large organizations frequently precludes identifying a responsible individual.[50] Both *IT* and Nassar's bystanders show that the failure to act, to speak up, is integral to enabling the perpetrator to continue offending. This includes a failure to fulfill a legal duty to report child sexual abuse. For example, the Michigan State coach Kathie Klages reportedly told a teenager that she couldn't believe claims of Nassar's abuse because "that was somebody she trusted and knew for years" and told another gymnast to "not talk about this anymore."[51] Klages not only did not report the offending but shut down complainants. Klages has since been found guilty of lying to police about her knowledge about Nassar's offending.[52] This failure to fulfill a legal duty to report enabled Nassar to continue offending for decades. Likewise, Penny, the USA Gymnastics CEO, did not alert authorities of complaints against Nassar, claiming that "to the best of my knowledge, there's no duty to report if you are—if you are a third party to some allegation."[53] USA Gymnastics failed to fulfill its legal duty of supervising Nassar, allowing him to examine girls in private in violation of best practices and the organizations' current standards of conduct.[54] These omissions or failures all created an environment which enabled Nassar to offend with impunity.

The failure extended to a failure to investigate by people and organizations in authority. In *IT*, Hanlon states, "Here in Derry children disappear unexplained and unfound at the rate of forty to sixty a year. Most are teenagers. They are assumed to be runaways. I supposed some of them even are."[55] Chief of Police Rademacher refuses to investigate and explains away the disappearances, reflecting and reinforcing the conspiracy of silence. Likewise, Nassar was able to molest at least fifty more girls due to the plodding pace of the FBI investigation. Despite the seriousness of the allegations, there was a lack of urgency to the FBI investigation between July 2015, when he first fell under FBI scrutiny, and September 2016, when he was exposed by an *Indianapolis Star* investigation.[56] Nearly a year passed before agents interviewed two of the three young women who were at the center of the inquiry. The mother of athlete Maggie Nichols was not contacted by the FBI for nearly eleven months after the information she provided sparked the federal inquiry. This in turn has led to an investigation by the Department of Justice of the FBI's failure to investigate.[57] Although much of the focus has been on the relationship between Penny and FBI agent Jay Abbott in an alleged cover-up, most of the emails between Penny and Abbott were copied to several other FBI officials and a lawyer representing USA Gymnastics.[58] Penny not only kept Abbott and other FBI officials updated on the availability of potential victims to be interviewed by the FBI and developments with Nassar, but also asked Abbott and other agents for advice and help in managing Nassar and the media, and in some cases for favors in how the FBI presented and handled the case.[59]

The effect of these organizational failures is horrific. Ultimately they discouraged complainants from coming forward in the first place. In *IT*, Mike's dad sees no point in calling Chief Borton when Mike was viciously bullied by Bowers, as Borton would do nothing. These failures to investigate and enforce meant that even if complainants did come forward, nothing would be done. Calling the authorities was pointless.[60] A classic trope of horror is the portrayal of authorities as ineffective or themselves corrupted—a fictional expression of very real, structural problems. In the cases of both *IT* and Nassar, conventional sources of protection—adults, family, the law—all come up short when confronting crimes.[61] The bystanders to the crimes committed by It and Nassar represent and evoke the intensified fear of feeling that there is no one to turn to and that authorities cannot or will not help.[62]

EXPLANATIONS FOR THE FAILURE TO ACT

A key question to be asked about the bystanders around Nassar is why they did not act. While various explanations for such inaction are given by Nassar's bystanders, the sentiment has its echoes in *IT*, as well. One explanation for those who abstain is that they did not want to know since it was easier and simpler not to know: "They won't see, they won't hear, they won't know."[63] Zerubavel has explained this in terms of rules of irrelevance—sets of social

and collective expectations of what should be ignored.[64] Judith Herman
has explored the dynamic of willful blindness in relation to crime, asserting
"it is very tempting to take the side of the perpetrator. All the perpetrator
asks is that the bystander do nothing. He appeals to the universal desire to
see, hear, and speak no evil. The victim, on the contrary, asks the bystander
to share the burden of pain. The victim demands action, engagement and
remembering."[65] The novel *IT* powerfully portrays a father's decision to do
nothing rather than to see and act. One of the bullies, Patrick Hockstetter,
killed his baby brother when he was five:

> Only Patrick's father came within brushing distance of the truth. [. . .]
> He looked down and saw a pair of tracks on the hardwood floor. They
> had been made by the snow melting off Patrick's yellow rubber boots.
> He looked at them, and a dreadful thought rose briefly in his mind like
> bad gas from a deep mineshaft. His hand went slowly to his mouth
> and his eyes widened. A picture began to form in his mind. Before it
> could come clear he left the room, slamming the door behind him so
> hard that the top of the frame splintered.
>   He never asked Patrick any questions. (813)

On this account, it is easier not to know since accepting knowledge would
require action. But Patrick's father refuses knowledge also because it would
be too horrific to consider. This failure to engage with wrongs is consistent
with Mary Douglas's arguments about dirt: we prefer not to think on it, to
brush it away.[66]

Both *IT* and Nassar's bystanders portray an additional reason for not acting, that is, that it may result in punishment or the loss of benefits: "Derry has
thrived, in an unspectacular, unnewsworthy way . . . it is simply a fairly prosperous small city in a relatively unpopulous state where bad things happen
too often . . . and where ferocious things happen every quarter of a century
or so."[67] These benefits are not necessarily large, but the threat of loss may
militate against action. *Athlete A* strongly suggests that Maggie Nichols lost
her place on the Olympic team despite her performance because her parents
continued to pursue the issue of Nassar's abuse.[68] During the "investigation"
of Nassar, Penny and FBI agent Jay Abbott discussed on multiple occasions
the possibility of Abbott becoming the US Olympic Committee's chief of
security after his retirement from the bureau. Penny recommended Abbott
to USOC officials during this same time period.[69] It is arguable that Abbott
failed in his duty to investigate due to his concern not to jeopardize this
possible job. But this concern extends beyond individual benefits to a form

of communal narcissism, preferring to protect the reputation of the town or organization rather than record, react to, and prevent offending. Penny was a sports marketing expert, and his primary care was the image of the AGA, to protect sponsorship by companies that wanted to be attached to the wholesome image of gymnastics.[70]

An additional justification for not intervening is the assertion that it is none of our business or is outside our expertise. *IT* relays the story of the "queerest mass murder" at the Silver Dollar in 1905, in which Claude Heroux cut off a victim's hand at the bar and buried his axe in another person's head while the other customers in the bar just kept playing poker and talking about the weather. Hanlon asks an elderly local, Edgar Thoroughgood, who was present at the mass murder:

> "How did it happen? Are you saying you didn't know it was going on, or that you knew but you let it go on, or just what?"
> "We knew. But it didn't seem to matter. It was like politics, in a way. Ayuh, like that. Like town business. Best let people who understand politics take care of that and people understand town business take care of that. Such things be best done if working men don't mix in."[71]

Thoroughgood justified the failure to act because it was outside his expertise, something that should be left to "people who understand politics." This idea of not intervening because it was outside of their expertise was also expressed in Nassar's case. Police and FBI accepted claims that Nassar's treatment was medical (and beyond their expertise) despite Nassar recording instructional videos which:

> Show him kneading the legs of girls before his ungloved hands begin to work under a towel, between the girls' legs. "It's not a fun place to dig," Dr Nassar says to the camera. "Do the hand-shaky thing," he adds later, demonstrating how he shakes his hand vigorously when it is deep between a girl's legs.[72]

One of the investigators at the FBI reflects:

> At the time, it was being portrayed as a legitimate medical procedure. But to the layman, like ourselves, we were—"you've got to be kidding me."[73]

Despite concerns about Nassar's actions, his claims that they were legitimate, albeit revolutionary, medical treatments forestalled investigations.[74]

Both *IT* and Nassar's case have examples of upstanders.[75] Minow has explained, "the term upstander gives recognition and approval to people who stand up for their beliefs, even if they are alone; it means not being a bystander."[76] *IT* shows that upstanders are few and far between, and as Pennywise moves towards a gaudy sacrifice, rules of behavior, order, and authority are dismantled. Thus, when Mr. Gredeau steps in to stop Henry from beating Eddie, "Henry made as if to lunge for him, and Mr. Gedreau flinched back. That was the end, Eddie realized. As incredible, as unthinkable as it seemed, there was no protection for him here. It was time to go."[77] Likewise, Henry ran after the old woman who intervened to save Bev, snarling, "Get outta here, you dried-up old bitch!"[78] In *IT*, the few people who did intervene, were unexpectedly threatened with violence. In contrast, no violence was threatened in Nassar's case; the primary threat was loss of benefits. If bystanders had fulfilled their duties, they could have prevented Nassar's offending. Interestingly, a minimal standard applied to bystanders is that they at least call the police. This is of no personal risk for them. However, the horror of Nassar's offending was that even calling the police would have no effect as shown by the plodding FBI investigation. Nassar's case epitomizes the horror and failure of systems that should have protected his victims and did not.

In *IT*, "many adults could be used without knowing they had been used, and It had even fed on a few of the older ones over the years."[79] It is not clear if this overriding of autonomy and individual morality and agency is supernatural. By contrast, in Nassar's case, the explanation is more prosaic, commonplace, and depressing. One explanation is that the bystander effect is a form of "group think." As Gobert and Punch explain:

> Organizations can exert powerful "pressure cooker" forces on individuals within the organization, turning them into group actors responsive to institutional demands. [. . .] In this environment individuals who may be highly moral in their private life may submit to group pressures and concur with amoral or even immoral decisions that they would never have taken with respect to their own affairs. Individual responsibility may give way to an invidious form of "group think" . . . wherein members of a homogenous and cohesive group will defer to views with which they disagree in order not to alienate a valued colleague, undermine what would otherwise be a unanimous decision, or give the appearance of being "difficult."[80]

Elite gymnastics openly expressed and celebrated an organizational culture of sacrifice and cruelty in a quest for medals. Reputation of the organizations (and country) was privileged over the wellbeing of children in care. There were examples of individual bystander inaction, but much of this was situated within an organizational culture that enabled and facilitated the perpetrator. We feel fear and disgust not only at the great harms inflicted by Nassar, but also a kind of deadening, depressing horror at the failure of the organizations supposed to protect children and act in their best interests. If people and the organizations in authority had done the right thing, most of his victims would never have met Nassar.

CONCLUSION

The horror genre is designed to disturb, and to arouse fear and disgust. The bystanders in *IT* and around Nassar show horror is aroused not only in response to the harms caused by Pennywise and Nassar, but for something more banal, insidious, and depressing. We feel horror because Nassar was able to continue offending with impunity for so long due to a bureaucratic, collectivized failure. These kinds of institutional failures are terrifyingly and terribly normal.[81] The novel *IT* offers a cathartic conclusion—Pennywise is resolved and the town center explodes and collapses in upon itself—punishing bystanders by destroying their homes and businesses. In contrast, cases like Nassar's demonstrate the absence of, and need for, an account of collective responsibility. Many of the organizations involved have been sued civilly, resulting in massive fines in compensation,[82] but at the time of this writing, none of these organizations have been charged with criminal offenses for failing to fulfill their legal duty of care. Civil compensation is significant, but it does not have the expressive power of the criminal legal system to communicate right and wrong. Civil compensation may simply be regarded by some organizations as a cost of doing business.

The horror genre is fictional. We know that monsters like Pennywise will not leave the novel or the screen. The genre can be conservative in the reimposition and statement of order (e.g., in the policing of sexual boundaries), but it can also be radical in its critique and challenge of existing boundaries.[83] The affect of horror justifies and requires change. *IT* illuminates important critiques of real systemic failures by powerfully demonstrating that Pennywise flourished because of the complicity by the townspeople and the town of Derry. Nassar's offending has aroused horror in response to the detailing of the harms to his victims. But this fear and disgust has also been felt in relation to the people and organizations in authority that enabled his offending. But what are we to do with these negative emotions? The ongoing institutional failures that enable, facilitate, or fail to prevent harm have a compulsive repetitiveness that continues across time, reminiscent of horror remakes. One of the first victims of Larry Nassar to go public, Rachael Denhollander, said: "If we are ever going to genuinely deal with the problem, we have to go after the community that surrounds the predator—because they are the only people who have the ability to stop sexual assault. And if they fail to do that, there need to be real consequences."[84]

Cases like Larry Nassar's demonstrate the ongoing and urgent need to reform criminal law categories so that they go beyond the responsibility of the perpetrator to include a compelling narrative of organizational failure as culpable and deserving in criminal sanctions. As novels like *IT* show, the monsters are only part of the problem.

Notes

This work was supported by the Australian Research Council (DE18010057).

1. Noël Carroll, "The Nature of Horror," *Journal of Aesthetics and Art Criticism* 46, no. 1 (1987): 51–59.

2. Cilve Bloom, "Horror Fiction: In Search of a Definition," in *A New Companion to the Gothic*, ed. David Punter (Somerset, UK: John Wiley & Sons, 2012), 211–23, http://ebook central.proquest.com/lib/uts/detail.action?docID=843409.

3. Bloom, "Horror Fiction: In Search of a Definition," 6.

4. E.g., Weinstein's behavior was notorious within both Miramax and the Weinstein Company. Ronan Farrow, *Abuses of Power, New Yorker*, October 23, 2017, 42.

5. See for example the Australian Royal Commission into Institutional Responses to Child Sexual Abuse and the UK Independent Inquiry into Child Sexual Abuse.

6. Stephen King, *IT*, eleventh edition (Great Britain: Hodder and Stoughton, 1989).

7. Robin Wood, "The Return of the Repressed," *Film Comment* (1978), 25–32.

8. Bloom, "Horror Fiction: In Search of a Definition," 213.

9. James Grant, *The Curriculum of Horror: Or, the Pedagogies of Monsters, Madmen and the Misanthropic* (Peter Lang Publishing, 2019), 31.

10. Zachary D. Kaufman, "Protectors of Predators or Prey: Bystanders and Upstanders amid Sexual Crimes," *Southern California Law Review* 92, no. 6 (2018): 1317–1406.

11. Kaufman, "Protectors of Predators or Prey," 879.

12. King, *IT*, 165.

13. King, *IT*, 163.

14. Zachary D. Kaufman, "When Sexual Abuse Is Common Knowledge—But Nobody Speaks Up," SSRN Scholarly Paper (Rochester, NY: Social Science Research Network), August 3, 2018, https://papers.ssrn.com/abstract=3225992.

15. Harvey Weinstein likewise offended within an organizational context. The Australian Royal Commission into Institutional Responses to Child Sexual Abuse focused on offending within an organizational context. See Penny Crofts, "Criminalising

Institutional Failures to Prevent, Identify or React to Child Sexual Abuse," *International Journal for Crime, Justice and Social Democracy* 6, no. 3 (2017): 104–22.

16. Katherine Hampel, "Whose Fault Is It Anyway: How Sexual Abuse Has Plagued the United States Olympic Movement and Its Athletes Comments," *Marquette Sports Law Review* 29, no. 2 (2019): 547–70.

17. King, *IT*. 29.

18. King, *IT*, 254.

19. King, *IT*, 43.

20. King, *IT*, 44.

21. Hampel, "Whose Fault Is It Anyway," 549.

22. The number of complainants is unknown due to the use of nondisclosure agreements by the university.

23. E.g., Richard J. McNally, Carel S. Ristuccia, and Carol A. Perlman, "Forgetting of Trauma Cues in Adults Reporting Continuous or Recovered Memories of Childhood Sexual Abuse," *Psychological Science* 16, no. 4 (April 1, 2005): 336–40, https://doi.org/10.1111/j.0956-7976.2005.01536.x.

24. Bill speaking with Audra (King, *IT*, 142).

25. Dan Barry, Serge F. Kovaleski, and Juliet Macur, "As F.B.I. Took a Year to Pursue the Nassar Case, Dozens Say They Were Molested (Published 2018)," *New York Times*, February 3, 2018, https://www.nytimes.com/2018/02/03/sports/nassar-fbi.html.

26. The majority of statutes criminalizing the failure to report a crime exempt victims from the offense, in deference to the victims, to protect the victim's privacy and to promote a culture where victims feel comfortable to confide to others. Kaufman, "Protectors of Predators or Prey." 1384.

27. Eviatar Zerubavel, *The Elephant in the Room* (Oxford: Oxford University Press, 2006).

28. King, *IT*, 32.

29. This silencing also took place at MSU. For example, a student-athlete reported concerns about Nassar to the University in 2000, but according to a lawsuit filed in 2017, the university failed to take any action in response to her complaint. Hampel, "Whose Fault Is It Anyway," 549.

30. For example, McKayla Maroney signed a confidentiality agreement with USA Gymnastics resolving her previous claims of sexual abuse by Nassar. This agreement included both a nondisclosure and non-disparagement provisions, each with a fine attached of more than $100,000 if Maroney violated the terms (Hampel, 552).

31. Barry, Kovaleski, and Macur, "As F.B.I. Took a Year to Pursue the Nassar Case, Dozens Say They Were Molested (Published 2018)."

32. Crofts, "Criminalising Institutional Failures to Prevent, Identify or React to Child Sexual Abuse."

33. King, *IT*. 500.

34. Kaufman, "Protectors of Predators or Prey."

35. King, *IT*, 31.

36. King, *IT*, 29.

37. Penny Crofts, "Monsters and Horror in the Royal Commission into Institutional Responses to Child Sexual Abuse," *Law and Literature.*

38. Donald Palmer, *Normal Organizational Wrongdoing: A Critical Analysis of Theories of Misconduct by and in Organizations* (Oxford: Oxford University Press, 2012).

39. King, *IT*, 26.

40. Eren Orbey, "The Victims of Larry Nassar Who Dared to Come Forward First," *New Yorker*, May 25, 2019, https://www.newyorker.com/culture/culture-desk/the-victims -of-larry-nassar-who-dared-to-come-forward-first.

41. Barry, Kovaleski, and Macur, "As F.B.I. Took a Year to Pursue the Nassar Case, Dozens Say They Were Molested (Published 2018)."

42. USA Gymnastics is not the only elite sport governing body to face allegations of sexual misconduct by officers and employees. Kari Fasting, Celia Brackenridge, and Jorunn Sundgot-Borgen, "Experiences of Sexual Harassment and Abuse among Norwegian Elite Female Athletes and Nonathletes," *Research Quarterly for Exercise and Sport* 74, no. 1 (March 1, 2003): 84–97, https://doi.org/10.1080/02701367.2003.10609067; Ingunn Bjørnseth and Attila Szabo, "Sexual Violence Against Children in Sports and Exercise: A Systematic Literature Review," *Journal of Child Sexual Abuse* 27, no. 4 (May 19, 2018): 365–85, https://doi.org/10.1080/10538712.2018.1477222.

43. King, *IT*, 892.

44. Kaufman, "Protectors of Predators or Prey."

45. Mary Midgley, *Wickedness: A Philosophical Essay* (London New York: Routledge, 1984); Penny Crofts, *Wickedness and Crime: Laws of Homicide and Malice* (London and New York: Routledge, 2013).

46. Hanlon says: "Terrible things that have happened here—the nominally explicable as well as the utterly inexplicable. There was the fire at a Negro nightclub called the Black Spot in 1930. A year before that, a bunch of half-bright Depression outlaws was gunned down on Canal Street in the middle of the afternoon" (King, *IT*, 500).

47. Hauser and Zraick, "Larry Nassar Sexual Abuse Scandal: Dozens of Officials Have Been Ousted or Charged," *New York Times*.

48. Crofts, "Criminalising Institutional Failures to Prevent, Identify or React to Child Sexual Abuse."

49. Augustine, *The Confessions of St Augustine*, trans. Edward Pusey (New York: Collier Books, 1961); Midgley, *Wickedness: A Philosophical Essay*.

50. Scott Veitch, *Law and Irresponsibility: On the Legitimation of Human Suffering* (Oxon: Routledge, 2007).

51. https://www.espn.com.au/college-sports/story/_/id/28703239/former-michigan -state-gymnastics-coach-kathie-klages-found-guilty-lying-police.

52. https://www.espn.com.au/college-sports/story/_/id/28703239/former-michigan -state-gymnastics-coach-kathie-klages-found-guilty-lying-police.

53. James Dator, Former USA Gymnastics CEO Steve Penny Arrested for Tampering with Evidence in Larry Nassar Case, *SB NATION*, October 18, 2018, https://www.sbnation .com/2018/10/18/17994160/steve-penny-usa-gymnastics-arrested-larry-nassar-tampering [https://perma.cc/7KX5-HU2Q].

54. Tim Evans, Mark Alesi, and Marisa Kwiatkowskl, "Former USA Gymnastics Doctor Accused of Abuse," *Indianapolis Star*, accessed October 29, 2020, https://www.indystar .com/story/news/2016/09/12/former-usa-gymnastics-doctor-accused-abuse/89995734/.

55. King, *IT*, 166.

56. Barry, Kovaleski, and Macur, "As F.B.I. Took a Year to Pursue the Nassar Case, Dozens Say They Were Molested (Published 2018)."

57. Scott Reid, "Justice Department Says Investigation of FBI's Handling of Larry Nassar Case Remains Ongoing," *Orange County Register* (blog), July 7, 2020, https://www .ocregister.com/justice-department-says-investigation-of-fbis-handling-of-larry-nassar -case-remains-ongoing.

58. Serge Kovaleski and Juliet Macur, "Steve Penny Asked F.B.I. to Help Protect U.S.A. Gymnastics' Image During Sex Abuse Case," *New York Times*, October 18, 2018, https://www.nytimes.com/2018/10/18/sports/steve-penny-usa-gymnastics-fbi.html?action =click&module=RelatedCoverage&pgtype=Article&region=Footer.

59. This cosy relationship between police and a corporate offender was likewise demonstrated in the UK Gosport Hospital Inquiry, in which hundreds of patients were killed over time. Independent Gosport Panel, "Gosport War Memorial Hospital: The Report of the Gosport Independent Panel" (United Kingdom: House of Commons, June 20, 2018), https://www.gosportpanel.independent.gov.uk/panel-report/.

60. For other examples of the failure of authorities to respond to sexual violence, see Kaufman, "Protectors of Predators or Prey."

61. Jeffrey Andrew Weinstock, "What Is IT? Ambient Dread and Modern Paranoia in It (2017), It Follows (2014) and It Comes at Night (2017)," *Horror Studies* 11, no. 2 (October 2020): 205–20, https://doi.org/10.1386/host_00019_1.

62. Penny Crofts, "Monsters and Horror in the Royal Commission into Institutional Responses to Child Sexual Abuse," *Law and Literature* 30, no. 1 (2018): 123–48.

63. King, *IT*, 588.

64. Zerubvael, *Elephant*.

65. Judith Lewis Herman, *Trauma and Recovery: The Aftermath of Violence—From Domestic Abuse to Political Terror* (Hachette UK, 2015), 2.

66. Mary Douglas, *Purity and Danger: An Analysis of the Concepts of Pollution and Taboo* (London: Routledge and Kegan Paul, 1966).

67. King, *IT*, 501.

68. *Athlete A*, 2020, Bonni Cohen and Jon Shenk, Actual Films.

69. Reid, "Justice Department Says Investigation of FBI's Handling of Larry Nassar Case Remains Ongoing."

70. Since Nassar's offences and the failure of AGA to appropriately respond have become public, some of AGA's biggest sponsors have dropped the organization as a client.

71. King, *IT*, 876.

72. Barry, Kovaleski, and Macur, "As F.B.I. Took a Year to Pursue the Nassar Case, Dozens Say They Were Molested (Published 2018)."

73. Barry, Kovaleski, and Macur.

74. Similar arguments were made by Dr Barton, and accepted by police, in relation to the homicides of patients at Gosport Hospital. Gosport, "Gosport War Memorial Hospital Report."

75. Samantha Power is widely credited with creating the term "upstander" when promoting her book, *A Problem From Hell*, to describe individual acts of courage. Samantha Power, *A Problem from Hell: America and the Age of Genocide* (New York: Basic Books, 2002).

76. Martha Minow, "Upstanders, Whistle-Blowers, and Rescuers," *Utah Law Review* 2017, no. 4 (August 1, 2017), https://dc.law.utah.edu/ulr/vol2017/iss4/9.815.

77. King, *IT*, 769.

78. King, 911.

79. King, 998.

80. James Gobert and Maurice Punch, Rethinking Corporate Crime (LexisNexis Butterworths, 2003), 17–18 (citations omitted).

81. This draws upon Hannah Arendt, *Eichmann in Jerusalem: A Report on the Banality of Evil* (London: Penguin, 1994).

82. Associated Press, 'Larry Nassar survivors offered $125m settlement by USA Gymnastics, *The Guardian*, Januay 31, 2020, https://www.theguardian.com/sport/2020/jan/30/usa-gymnastics-settlement-larry-nassar-survivors.

83. Judith Halberstam, *Skin Shows: Gothic Horror and the Technology of Monsters* (Durham: Duke University Press, 1995).

84. Mark Alesia, Marisa Kwiatkowski, Tim Evnas, "Rachael Denhollander's brave journey: Lone voice to 'army' at Larry Nassar's sentencing." *Indy Star*, January 24, 2018, https://www.indystar.com/story/news/2018/01/24/larry-nassar-usa-gymnastics-sexual-abuse-rachael-denhollander-mckayla-maroney-aly-raisman/1060356001/.

References

Alesia, Mark, Marisa Kwiatkowski, and Tim Evans. "Rachael Denhollander's Brave Journey: Lone Voice to 'Army' at Larry Nassar's Sentencing." *Indy Star*, January 24, 2018. https://www.indystar.com/story/news/2018/01/24/larry-nassar-usa-gymnastics-sexual-abuse-rachael-denhollander-mckayla-maroney-aly-raisman/1060356001/.

Arendt, Hannah. *Eichmann in Jerusalem: A Report on the Banality of Evil.* London: Penguin, 1994.

Associated Press, "Larry Nassar Survivors Offered $125m Settlement by USA Gymnastics." *The Guardian*, January 31 2020. https://www.theguardian.com/sport/2020/jan/30/usa-gymnastics-settlement-larry-nassar-survivors.

Athlete A, 2020, Bonni Cohen and Jon Shenk, Actual Films.

Augustine, *The Confessions of St Augustine*. Translated by Edward Pusey. New York: Collier Books, 1961.

Barry, Dan, Serge F. Kovaleski, and Juliet Macur. "As F.B.I. Took a Year to Pursue the Nassar Case, Dozens Say They Were Molested." *New York Times*, February 3, 2018, sec. Sports. https://www.nytimes.com/2018/02/03/sports/nassar-fbi.html.

Bjørnseth, Ingunn, and Attila Szabo. "Sexual Violence Against Children in Sports and Exercise: A Systematic Literature Review." *Journal of Child Sexual Abuse* 27, no. 4 (May 19, 2018): 365–85. https://doi.org/10.1080/10538712.2018.1477222.

Bloom, Clive. "Horror Fiction: In Search of a Definition." In *A New Companion to the Gothic*, edited by David Punter, 211–23. Somerset, UK: John Wiley & Sons. http://ebookcentral.proquest.com/lib/uts/detail.action?docID=843409.

Carroll, Noel. "The Nature of Horror." *Journal of Aesthetics and Art Criticism* 46, no. 1 (1987): 51–59.

Crofts, Penny. "Criminalising Institutional Failures to Prevent, Identify or React to Child Sexual Abuse." *International Journal for Crime, Justice and Social Democracy* 6, no. 3 (2017): 104–22.

Crofts, Penny. "Monsters and Horror in the Royal Commission into Institutional Responses to Child Sexual Abuse." *Law and Literature* 30, no. 1 (2018): 123–48.

Crofts, Penny. *Wickedness and Crime: Laws of Homicide and Malice.* London and New York: Routledge, 2013.

Dator, James. "Former USA Gymnastics CEO Steve Penny Arrested for Tampering with Evidence in Larry Nassar Case." *SB Nation*, October 18, 2018. https://www.sbnation.com/2018/10/18/17994160/steve-penny-usa-gymnastics-arrested-larry-nassar-tampering [https://perma.cc/7KX5-HU2Q].

Douglas, Mary. *Purity and Danger: An Analysis of the Concepts of Pollution and Taboo.* London: Routledge and Kegan Paul, 1966.

Evans, Tim, Mark Alesi, and Marisa Kwiatkowskl. "Former USA Gymnastics Doctor Accused of Abuse." *Indianapolis Star*, September 12, 2016; updated January 24, 2018. https://www.indystar.com/story/news/2016/09/12/former-usa-gymnastics-doctor-accused-abuse/89995734/.

Farrow, Ronan. "Weinstein's Behaviour was Notorious within Both Miramax and the Weinstein Company." *The New Yorker*, October 23, 2017.

Fasting, Kari, Celia Brackenridge, and Jorunn Sundgot-Borgen. "Experiences of Sexual Harassment and Abuse among Norwegian Elite Female Athletes and Nonathletes," *Research Quarterly for Exercise and Sport* 74, no. 1 (March 1, 2003): 84–97. https://doi.org/10.1080/02701367.2003.10609067.

Gobert, James, and Maurice Punch. *Rethinking Corporate Crime.* Cambridge University Press, 2003.

Grant, James. *The Curriculum of Horror: Or, the Pedagogies of Monsters, Madmen and The Misanthropic.* Peter Lang Publishing, 2019.

Halberstam, Jack. *Skin Shows: Gothic Horror and the Technology of Monsters.* Durham: Duke University Press, 1995.

Hampel, Katherine. "Whose Fault Is It Anyway: How Sexual Abuse Has Plagued the United States Olympic Movement and Its Athletes Comments." *Marquette Sports Law Review* 29, no. 2 (2018–19): 547–70.

Hauser and Zraick. "Larry Nassar Sexual Abuse Scandal: Dozens of Officials Have Been Ousted or Charged." *New York Times*, October 22, 2018. https://www.nytimes.com/2018/10/22/sports/larry-nassar-case-scandal.html.

Herman, Judith Lewis. *Trauma and Recovery: The Aftermath of Violence—From Domestic Abuse to Political Terror.* UK: Hachette, 2015.

Independent Gosport Panel. "Gosport War Memorial Hospital: The Report of the Gosport Independent Panel" (United Kingdom: House of Commons, June 20, 2018). https://www.gosportpanel.independent.gov.uk/panel-report/.

Kaufman, Zachary D. "Protectors of Predators or Prey: Bystanders and Upstanders amid Sexual Crimes," *Southern California Law Review* 92, no. 6 (2019): 1317–1406.

Kaufman, Zachary D. "When Sexual Abuse Is Common Knowledge—But Nobody Speaks Up," *SSRN Scholarly Paper*. Rochester, NY: Social Science Research Network, August 3, 2018. https://papers.ssrn.com/abstract=3225992.

King, Stephen. *IT*. Eleventh edition. Great Britain: Hodder and Stoughton, 1989.

Kovaleski, Serge, and Juliet Macur. "Steve Penny Asked F.B.I. to Help Protect U.S.A. Gymnastics' Image During Sex Abuse Case." *New York Times*, October 18, 2018. https://www.nytimes.com/2018/10/18/sports/steve-penny-usa-gymnastics-fbi.html?action=click&module=RelatedCoverage&pgtype=Article&region=Footer.

Midgley, Mary. *Wickedness: A Philosophical Essay*. London New York: Routledge, 1984.

Minow, Martha. "Upstanders, Whistle-Blowers, and Rescuers," *Utah Law Review*, no. 4 (August 1, 2017). https://dc.law.utah.edu/ulr/vo12017/iss4/9.

Orbey, Eren. "The Victims of Larry Nassar Who Dared to Come Forward First." *New Yorker*, May 25, 2019. https://www.newyorker.com/culture/culture-desk/the-victims-of-larry-nassar-who-dared-to-come-forward-first.

Palmer, Donald. *Normal Organizational Wrongdoing: A Critical Analysis of Theories of Misconduct by and in Organizations*. Oxford: Oxford University Press, 2012.

Power, Samantha. *A Problem from Hell: America and the Age of Genocide*. New York: Basic Books, 2002.

Reid, Scott. "Justice Department Says Investigation of FBI's Handling of Larry Nassar Case Remains Ongoing." *Orange County Register* (blog), July 7, 2020. https://www.ocregister.com/justice-department-says-investigation-of-fbis-handling-of-larry-nassar-case-remains-ongoing.

Richard, E. G., et al. "Forgetting of Trauma Cues in Adults Reporting Continuous or Recovered Memories of Childhood Sexual Abuse." *Psychological Science* 16, no. 4 (April 1, 2005): 336–40. https://doi.org/10.1111/j.0956-7976.2005.01536.x.

Veitch, Scott. *Law and Irresponsibility: On the Legitimation of Human Suffering*. Oxon: Routledge, 2007.

Weinstock, Jeffrey Andrew. "What Is IT? Ambient Dread and Modern Paranoia in It (2017), It Follows (2014) and It Comes at Night (2017)." *Horror Studies* 11, no. 2 (October 2020): 205–20. https://doi.org/10.1386/host_00019_1.

Wood, Robin. "The Return of the Repressed." *Film Comment* (1978), 25–32.

Chapter 8

MEMORY AS MONSTER

Remembering and Forgetting in Stephen King's *IT*

JEFF AMBROSE

The synopsis on the back cover of Stephen King's *IT* teases that "the horror of It was deep-buried, wrapped in forgetfulness" and that the Losers' Club, now adults, must confront "the sullen depths of their memories, reaching up again to make their past nightmares a terrible present reality."[1] In King's novel, the titular It is a physical creature beyond fathoming that came from a crashed meteorite in the time before humans. However, I will argue that the most fearsome monster in the story is memory and what happens when trauma is buried rather than confronted. To show this, I use three sections. The first section examines the townspeople and how they choose to forget and look the other way rather than face trauma themselves. The second section explores the members of the Losers' Club and how each of them is terrorized by their memories stemming from childhood traumas. The final section shows the takeaway of the novel: that it is only through confronting fear and trauma, often with the help of others, that the Losers overcome their own memories and suppressed traumas. I argue that the forgetting performed by the townspeople allows for the violent cycle of It to continue. This cycle passes a poisonous, psychic mindset onto the Losers that is only ultimately broken when they come to break the pattern by facing their traumatic memories. Facing their trauma allows for a cleansing forgetting to occur at the end of the book. Informing this analysis will be the psychological trauma studies of Ron Eyerman, Michael S. Roth, and Jonathan D. Lewis, as well as the horror studies of Noël Carroll, Tony Magistrale, and Stephen King himself.

CHOOSING TO FORGET:
"[H]E JUST DOESN'T WANT TO REMEMBER"[2]

In King's novel, Derry's townspeople have for centuries denied the reality of the traumas they witness or even take part in, creating mass collective guilt and a sweeping suppression of memory. As Mike Hanlon explains in the first interlude, "There is a kind of curtain of quiet which cloaks much of what has happened here,"[3] and in the second interlude, that "in Derry people have a way of looking the other way."[4] Even the opening pages of the novel reveal, in the words of the adult Bill as he reminisces about his father and brother seventeen years later, "The thing was to get through this one, to get the power back on, and then to forget it. In Derry such forgetting of tragedy and disaster was almost an art."[5] This mindset plays out in awful ways, such as when Beverly is chased by her father, who is bent on physical harm: "She ran toward downtown, passing more and more people as she went. They stared—first at her, then at her pursuing father—and they looked surprised, some of them even amazed. They looked and then they went on toward wherever they had been going."[6] The townspeople feign ignorance at the cost of any harm to others. Tony Magistrale, in his book *Landscape of Fear: Stephen King's American Gothic*, writes that in *IT*, "The town has come to accept the loss of its children as a price for conducting daily business."[7] That sacrifice of a child could very well have occurred again in the scene with Beverly escaping her father. In his book studying the cultural traumas suffered in and around the Vietnam War, the Katyn massacre, and Harvey Milk's assassination, Ron Eyerman observes that "collective forgetting is as important to national identity formation as collective remembering."[8] He goes on to posit that such forgetting spawns "perpetrator trauma" which is "moral injury . . . something that can be experienced individually as well as collectively."[9] In King's novel, the people of Derry attain such guilt in their overtly averted eyes or claims of ignorance from incidents. Forgetting and ignoring has become the identity of Derry, the "curtain of quiet" Mike writes about. Another of Mike's interludes in the book addresses the incident of the Bradley Gang massacre in 1929, wherein even the mayor was among those shooting at the criminals. Despite so many people participating in, or at least observing, the event, "[p]eople would lie to you about being in Derry that day because they wish they hadn't been."[10] Moments in the novel such as the Bradley Gang shootout, or the neighbor looking away from Beverly being chased, point to the collective guilt Eyerman observes in studying and interviewing trauma survivors and observers. This guilt creates double the trauma as those affected remember the horrors of the event, and they also recall their inaction or participation in the moment itself.

In the same way that the suppression of memory and trauma is cyclical in the town, so is the lack of moral and social development of its citizens. The reason It endures for so long is that the people participate in its cycle of torture by never fully facing the trauma It inflicts upon or around themselves; instead, they turn away, pretend to forget, or do their best to deny what occurred. Michael S. Roth, in the first chapter of his book *Memory, Trauma, and History* titled "Remembering Forgetting," proclaims: "By examining cultural imaginations of remembering and forgetting we can learn much about cultural investments in questions about continuity and change."[11] The same can be said of the townspeople in King's work. Whether observed in the Bradley Gang shootout, the axe massacre at the Sleepy Silver Dollar in 1905, the Kitchener Ironworks explosion in 1908, the 1930 fire at the Black Spot, or any of the other traumatic moments in Derry's past linked to It, the people continuously try to forget them rather than face what these events mean and try to evolve or change. Mike describes, "As with the fire at the Black Spot, many Derry residents affect not to remember what happened that day. [. . .] Or they will simply look you full in the face and lie to you."[12] Thus, the cultural investments in change, as described by Roth, never occur in Derry, only the continuity of violence and then the subsequent denial of such violence. That is the legacy the Losers are forced to inherit: one of denial, suppression, and repression. Because of this, King devotes much of his novel to exploring the effect of trauma on both the childhood and adult lives of each Loser.

THE TRAUMA OF REMEMBRANCE: "MY GOD, I AM BEING DIGESTED BY MY OWN PAST."[13]

Each of the seven Losers—Ben, Richie, Mike, Bill, Stan, Eddie, and Beverly— find their childhood memories of Derry to be a monster, an entity capable of robbing them of their very sanity. Mike retains most of his memories because he never leaves Derry, but for the other six, their memories return only after being drawn back to Derry by Mike. When Bill's wife, Audra, asks him about George's death and why Bill will not talk about his childhood, Bill explains: "I can sense those memories . . . waiting to be born. They're like clouds filled with rain. Only this rain would be very dirty. The plants that grew after a rain like that would be monsters."[14] For Bill, memories create monsters. He admits his successful horror novels are based on the feelings he remembers of Derry, but that his life is *"like he's been sitting in a darkened theater for twenty-seven years, waiting for something to happen.*"[15] One of the first memories from Bill's childhood to return is wanting to ride his bike so fast he might die and join his brother George, brutally murdered by It—in the form of Pennywise—when George was a small child: "his runs down Kansas Street had become more and more like *banzai* charges."[16] Even more than that, "Bill's feet found the pedals again and he began to pump, wanting to go even faster, wanting to reach some hypothetical speed—not of sound but of memory—and crash through the pain barrier."[17] Here are the two sides of memory in the novel: on the one hand, Bill feels death might be a release as he would no longer have to live with the pain of his brother's death. On the other hand, Bill feels that it is possible to break the "pain barrier" of memories and instead of fearing them, learn to embrace them and learn from them.

However, Bill's parents do not cope as well or believe there is anything else to live for. Though we are given far fewer looks into the adults who have never left Derry, an exception appears in the form of Bill's parents. Both Bill's mother and father have become emotionless zombies following the trauma of losing their youngest son, George, at the cost of ignoring their living one. Bill feels crushed by "the way his parents seemed to ignore him now, so lost in their grief over their younger son that they couldn't see the simple fact that Bill was still alive, and might be hurting himself."[18] The disparity between the Losers' Club, who come to believe memory can be wielded and controlled, and the adults, who shut down or ignore their memories, is startling. This disconnection is typified in the following passage on Bill's parents:

> In those days his mom and dad had also been bookends on the couch, but he and George had been the books. Bill had tried to be a book between while they were watching TV since George's death, but it was cold work. They sent the cold out from both directions and Bill's defroster was simply not big enough to cope with it.[19]

Bill's parents broke with George's death, and thus with It's interference in their lives. They emotionally shut down and cannot even comfort or love their remaining son. The constant memory of George's passing, and their grief for him, destroyed them. George's death became a memory monster, personified as the figurative coldness Bill could never break through. Before he later learns to confront fearful memories directly, Bill thinks the world is like how his father sees it. "Bill saw his father crying and this increased his terror" because he worries "maybe sometimes things don't just go wrong and then stop; maybe sometimes they just keep going wronger and wronger."[20]

This is exactly what has been occurring in Derry for centuries: by acting like Bill's parents, the adults have not come to terms with their grief, their guilt, or their traumatic memories as a whole. As a result, It flourishes. It feeds on the sadness and loss and fear.

The Losers, before their growth, fear that they will be just like their parents and the older generations of Derry, that is, co-conspirators of It:

> And he felt suddenly that *It* was the seventh [loser] . . . that It wore their faces as well as the thousand others with which It had terrified and killed . . . and the idea that *It* might be *them* was somehow the most frightening idea of all. *How much of us was left behind here . . . How much of us never left the drains . . . Is that why we forgot? Because part of each of us never had any future, never grew, never left Derry? Is that why?*[21]

The Losers associate a lack of change with Derry. They have learned about and experienced firsthand the feigned ignorance or suppressed guilt of the townspeople and even their own parents. As a group, the Losers then are not just fighting the physical body of It. They are also fighting the psychological trauma of the memories It has left in its wake. More on that will appear in the third section.

Another Loser experiences this keenly as well: Ben, on a plane following Mike's call to return to Derry and as he begins to remember what happened to them as children, realizes, "My God, I am being digested by my own past."[22] Earlier, he tells a bartender in Oklahoma: "I'm scared almost insane by what else I may remember before tonight's over."[23] This anxiety and fear born out of a lack of true memories is personified similarly throughout the novel. Eddie feels "[h]e has been poisoned by his own memories."[24] For Beverly, remembering is "excavating a mental graveyard."[25] And Richie cannot remember everything all at once because "*the force would have been like a psychological shotgun blast let off an inch from his temple. It would have torn off the whole top of his head.*"[26] These examples demonstrate how the act of remembering trauma has *become* a trauma: memory has become a monster.

Richie, as an adult, is a successful comedic radio host in Los Angeles. His impressions and the silly "voices" that the other losers ridiculed him for as children have become his entire career. Still, right after he gets the call from Mike asking him to come face It again, he is "feeling again how easy it had been to slip through an unexpected fissure in what he had considered a solid life—how easy it was to get over onto the dark side, to sail out of the blue and into the black."[27] Jonathan D. Lewis, in an essay examining modern theories of trauma and treatments, writes about the "psychological disintegration" that Richie worries about and that can occur when confronting repressed trauma or memory.[28] Lewis further explains the reasons trauma gets suppressed in the first place:

> Trauma victims may also be reluctant to speak for fear that they will not be believed and at times may even doubt the reality of their own experiences once they have been liberated from the extreme environment. The destruction of language, the destruction of meaning, and the destruction of confidence that one will be believed, certainly interferes with the possibility of treatment which depends upon language to convey meaning and affect. Yet such a treatment, I believe, retains the possibility of transforming what seems unbearable into something that can be communicated.[29]

Lewis writes based on his experiences with civilians and soldiers from war environments in Africa and the Middle East and suffering from post-traumatic stress disorder. But in the context of King's novel, this passage conjures Richie's remembering, after he has tried to break free from the trauma of his memories and past. Richie's voices are his defense mechanism, a way of avoiding dealing with the trauma head on: "Now he had to go back to being himself, and that was hard—it got harder to do that every year. It was easier to be brave when you were someone else."[30] Richie has long found solace and escape in his voices, and importantly, as will be explored later, his channeling of voices becomes one of his weapons to defeat It.

Lewis's ideas on the destruction of language and meaning can be seen in the very way King structures the novel; the author's unconventional formatting choices allow memories to invade the narrative, the style itself thus demonstrating the characters' experiences of trauma in fragments. Thoughts return to them without context, frightening them, such as Stan's wife remembering when Stan once said, "*The turtle couldn't help us,*" which she recalls "for no reason at all" believing it to be a "fragment of an otherwise forgotten dream."[31] Beverly, in a later scene, shouts, "*The grackles know your real name!*" but "she certainly had no idea why she said such a crazy thing."[32] In these two scenes, characters say lines that mean absolutely nothing without the magical context of fighting It when the Losers were children. Without knowing the full context of the trauma and the meaning of the experience, they cannot overcome or understand the memories. Memory is again a monster. This is not the only narrative technique King uses to show the trauma of memory.

Again and again, King uses fragmentation to show how feelings and memories come flooding back to haunt the Losers. In particular, sections often end mid-sentence and then move from that present moment right into the past memory. This begins in part two of the novel, after Mike has called each of the Losers and they make their way back to Derry. The first instance is with Ben, but it occurs again and again throughout the novel with each of the Losers.[33] Chapter six in part two even contains newspaper snippets about all the missing children, one of which details a teacher suppressing the abuse of a student because the principal told her "to forget it."[34] The final newspaper blurb ends with Eddie Corcoran's mother winning a legal battle to declare her son as dead "so she could enter into possession" of his savings account. The amount: "sixteen dollars."[35] King could have presented Eddie's story entirely as narrative paragraphs. He chose not to because, as news clippings, the details of the teacher's suppression of a student's abuse by their parents and a mother whose child is missing going to court to declare him dead just for his few dollars work differently: they are examples of Derry's systemic suppression of trauma at the cost of children's pain, even your own, recalling Magistrale's assessment of the novel. Yet, these examples are not even the most striking way that King represents memory as monster in the book.

King shows the fragmentation of the Losers' minds with his writing style most clearly with Beverly, who does not want to think about her father and the effects that his abuse have on her day-to-day decisions as an adult. Several times throughout the book, King writes Beverly's recollections in terrifying fragments. Two examples are especially relevant. The first actually comes from Tom, Beverly's emotionally and physically abusive husband and an echo of her father's ongoing trauma in her life. After he has assaulted her again, Tom sees an odd look on Beverly's face:

> Then the
>   (nostalgia)
> look of a memory . . . of some memory.[36]

Beverly knows her husband is a stand-in for her father; she has married into the abuse and violence she has always known. "He had regressed her."[37] Beverly has always feigned obedience to Tom because it was what she had to do in order to avoid even worse harm by her father. Beverly's mother, in a rare moment of clarity before herself regressing to ask Beverly if she took out the trash, confronts her about the abuse she has suffered, ultimately asking if her father has ever sexually abused her. Beverly's response serves as another time King chooses to fragment Beverly's thoughts this way:

> "I won't
> 	(does he ever touch you)
> "forget."[38]

In response to this disturbing question, Beverly quickly replies "*No!*" but then thinks "her father touched her every *day*." Then as her mom asks her about her chores as the follow-up, Beverly's thoughts are captured by King in the above fragment. This fragmentation works on multiple levels: it is indicative of the fact that Beverly of course *will* forget almost everything about her past, and it echoes the way in which she will eventually remember things—in bits and pieces at first—and then the structure of the passage demonstrates the way trauma is inside of, and in between, all that the Losers are. Memories—and specifically memories of their childhood traumas—are always there to influence them, even if they cannot specifically remember what the traumas were. For Beverly, her husband Tom, despite being abusive and awful in other ways, is also strangely comforting for Beverly because his abuse approximates the life she always knew as a kid. Her life has become a cycle of trauma just like those of the other townspeople of Derry. Beverly recalls a fight with Tom, and the dangers of her obedience to a past she cannot remember is terrifying: when commanded by Tom to come over to him, she feels "[t]here was no question of not going. If the two of them had been standing on the edge of a high cliff and he had told her to step off . . . her instinctive obedience would almost certainly have carried her over the edge before her rational mind could intervene."[39] And that is the crux of monster as memory for the Losers: they have been traumatized, and although they cannot remember by what or whom, that trauma still affects all they think and do.

Stan and Eddie are no different. Even immediately after they begin to remember specific moments from their childhoods, they are afraid of thinking of them again. Eddie "could fix upon almost any scene from that summer he wanted to, but he did not want to. *Oh God if I could only forget it all again.*"[40] In a scene from that summer, when the Losers help Beverly clean the remnants of an eruption of blood only they can see from her bathroom, Stan has an extreme reaction to Bill's call to action against It. "I don't want to *do* anything . . . I want to *forget* about it. That's all I want to *do*."[41] While Stan ultimately succumbs to the fear of his memories when he kills himself after receiving Mike's call to return to Derry, Eddie takes a very different path, which will help set up my third and final section.

Eddie's childhood trauma, like all the losers, extends far beyond the physical creature It. Noël Carroll, in his seminal book *The Philosophy of Horror*, addresses why It scares so many readers: "The monster in King's *IT* is a kind of categorically contradictory creature raised to a higher power. For It is a monster that can change into any other monster, those other monsters already being categorically transgressive."[42] But what the Losers fear is not It itself, but the form it takes of *what they already fear*. And for Eddie in particular, that fear is the disease his mom always worries he may have: leprosy, rotting from the inside out. When Mr. Keene, the pharmacist, calls Eddie into his office, he "tapped his head solemnly. 'Most sickness starts in here, that's what I think.'"[43] That is the real "transgressive" nature of It. It could just be its natural, spider-like form and still be terrifying, but it instead chooses to play on trauma and fear that already exists within the Losers' minds. And what scares Eddie about Mr. Keene is that he might be telling the truth—and "there were ramifications in such an idea that he could not face."[44] Eddie does not want to confront the trauma resulting from the fact that his mother is the monster in his life. "She would tell him that sometimes it was better for a child—particularly a delicate child like Eddie—to *think* he was sick than to really *get* sick."[45] So, It takes on the form of a leper, not just because of the transients from the train Eddie once saw under the house on Neibolt Street. Eddie fears leprosy because it is a disease that rots its sufferer from the inside out. And this leper stands as the representation of the mental sickness of Eddie's mother and the damage she has done to him by being traumatically over-protective. Coming full circle, Eddie's adult life is similar to Beverly's. He has married his mother just as Beverly married her father. He takes many medications and uses a respirator, despite not truly needing any of them physically. Yet, unlike Stan who cannot handle his memories, and despite Eddie wanting initially to forget, he chooses to remember. He chooses to return to Derry. And Eddie, like the other remaining Losers, chooses to fight the It of their traumatic memories and finally face them.

When the six remaining Losers have reunited in Derry, their conversation eventually turns to memory and trauma. Mike brings up the deadlights, and though Bill does not remember exactly what that means, he "jerked convulsively"; as in Beverly's traumatic recollections, King gives us "*(the deadlights)*" as its own line between Bill's thoughts.[46] When Mike tells Bill he will remember what the deadlights are, Bill replies "I hope to God I don't."[47] This discussion leads to the ultimate point of their revival of the Losers' Club: agreeing to defeat It for good. Bill asks them all, "[D]o we stay and fight or do we forget the whole thing?"[48] All of them decide to stay and fight because they are finished with their lives being defined by traumas they cannot even recall. And, importantly, Mike had helped convince them to stay and fight earlier in the conversation with a breakdown of all the passive efforts that are being made to find the missing children and solve the child murders. The FBI is even involved, but as has always been the case, the "sincere" townspeople who actually want It stopped simply leave Derry and forget about It. So, it comes down to the Losers. Even if no one else will truly face the trauma of Derry's past, they will. Their past and current fragmentation means that the ultimate confrontation with the traumatic memories of It will help lead to their future mental reintegration.

THE LOSERS WINNING:
"P-PEOPLE GO BACK TO F-F-FIND THEMS-S-SELVES"[49]

Facing trauma through accurately remembering the event is a hallmark of recovery in therapy. As Judith Herman writes in the introduction to the third edition of her foundational work *Trauma and Recovery*, "Remembering and telling the truth about terrible events are prerequisites both for the restoration of the social order and for the healing of individual victims."[50] King draws on this idea in his novel, as Eddie steels his nerves to go back to Derry as he concludes, "*Home is the place where when you go there, you have to finally face the thing in the dark.*"[51] In facing their memories and confronting their traumas, the Losers begin to heal and, thus, win.

Picking up on King's use of fragmented narrative storytelling as an echo of Lewis's theories on the difficulties of confronting trauma, let us also return to the newspaper-snippets section in the novel. The narrative storytelling resumes following the final section on Eddie Corcoran's mother winning her legal battle for her son's sixteen dollars. King explains that the Losers all react the same way at the same time, unknowingly, each in their own homes, when Eddie was killed.[52] This connection between them, along with their shared childhood traumas, paves the road to confrontation, acceptance, and recovery as the Losers return to Derry as adults.

As they have their reunion at the Chinese restaurant, Mike explains, "At some point we were able to exercise some sort of group will. At some point we achieved some special understanding, whether conscious or unconscious."[53] Forming the Losers' Club in the summer of 1958 is ultimately what saved them when so many other children were lost. Yet, Mike instructs the other five remaining Losers to "go back to the place in Derry he or she remembers best" but alone because they must learn to rely on intuition as they and all "[k]ids . . . operate on it about eighty percent of the time."[54] And even though Mike says he expects not all of them will survive the day, everyone readily agrees to the task and sets off alone. They are able to do so confidently because they trust in their "group will" and "special understanding" that has survived the twenty-seven years when all their other memories were lost.

This attempt at group healing through shared trauma is unique, according to Lewis: "Extreme situations destroy the capacity of language to convey meaning and are meant to destroy the selfhood of the victim, especially in relation to others."[55] But for the Losers, their shared bond is the one thing instantly recalled upon receiving Mike's phone call. They all remember the pact to return if It was not truly defeated when they were children. Language also retains its meaning as it is restored in their returning memories once back together. In the end, the Losers defeat the physical embodiment of their traumatic memories, It, by "the force of memory and desire; above all else, it was the force of love and unforgotten childhood like one big wheel."[56] And, perhaps most telling of all, it is no physical violence that defeats It; Bill wins in a battle of the minds. "Bill bit in—not with his teeth, but with teeth in his mind" (1073). Through love, a shared, unforgotten childhood, and memory, the Losers defeat the monster. The cycle of trauma and violence perpetuated by the townspeople in not facing the events head-on has ended by the "one big wheel" of the Losers' love and memory. The new, redemptive cycle the Losers have entered is one of survival and love, not Derry's longstanding one of death and trauma.

The Losers heal in their own ways, but only because they succeed collectively in facing the monster of their traumatic memories. Mike purges himself of the giant bird attack and Derry's dark past by writing them down and ensuring the stories are not kept inside.[57] Richie remembers that his voices are a weapon that can be used for good, justifying his career as a comedic radio host.[58] Ben had become a successful architect as an adult because of the love of the library in Derry. As Tony Magistrale writes, "Hanscom's passageway [in the library] represents the possibility for adult self-renovation that is available in the recollection of adolescent memories."[59] Beverly, in the end, can move on from her husband/father and realizes her own gifts are what allowed her fashion business to succeed. Eddie gains clarity about his marriage and about his limousine service. And Bill literally saves his wife Audra's life with love, turning his suicidal bike rides on Silver into a restorative ride, bringing Audra back from a near-comatose state.[60] In the end, the Losers win because of their community of love and their ability to face their traumatic memories both alone and, when needed, together.

CONCLUSION

So, even though in the end the Losers begin to forget Derry, their memories, and their traumas, they hold onto the love and the light. Bill knows that *"part of your mind will see them forever, live with them forever, love with them forever. They are not necessarily the best part of you, but they were once the repository of all you could become."*[61] Instead of trauma haunting their lives and living just out of reach, the Losers, by confronting, accepting, and dealing with their past traumas, learn to live with them and instead focus on love rather than monsters.

As Stephen King wrote in *Danse Macabre*, his nonfiction analysis of horror: "The work of horror is not interested in the civilized furniture of our lives."[62] Life is not neat; it is messy. King's novel demonstrates that despite the desire one may have to only focus on "civilized furniture," many of us hold onto or hide from our traumas, fears, and painful memories. Through *IT*, one can learn that ignoring or suppressing trauma only leads to more darkness. Finding friends who listen, who understand, and who can help is the key to confronting and living with traumatic memories. They may not simply disappear in the end like they do in the novel, but it can begin a healing process that does not lead to the "collective guilt" or "disintegration of language" observed by Eyerman and Roth. Instead, the path pursued by the Losers, in confronting their traumatic memories, allows them to heal. The Losers healing through communicating their shared trauma affirms Judith Herman's belief that remembering is a key element in recovery from trauma. Ultimately, in simplest terms, King's novel is about facing one's fears and overcoming them. Memory can be a monster, but as seen in the journey of the Losers' Club, that monster can be defeated and a balanced life can emerge on the other side.

Notes

1. Stephen King, *IT* (New York: Scribner, 1986), back cover.

2. King, *IT*, 292.

3. King, *IT*, 156.

4. King, *IT*, 461.

5. King, *IT*, 4.

6. King, *IT*, 924.

7. Tony Magistrale, *Landscape of Fear: Stephen King's American Gothic* (Madison: University of Wisconsin Press, 1988), 111.

8. Ron Eyerman, *Memory, Trauma, and Identity* (New York: Palgrave Macmillan, 2019), 14.

9. Eyerman, *Memory*, 17.

10. King, *IT*, 651.

11. Michael S. Roth, *Memory, Trauma, and History* (New York: Columbia University Press), 3.

12. King, *IT*, 649.

13. King, *IT*, 168.

14. King, *IT*, 143.

15. King, *IT*, 222, emphasis in original.

16. King, *IT*, 233.

17. King, *IT*, 233.

18. King, *IT*, 237

19. King, *IT*, 245.

20. King, *IT*, 247.

21. King, *IT*, 494–95, emphasis in original.

22. King, *IT*, 168.

23. King, *IT*, 83.

24. King, *IT*, 291.

25. King, *IT*, 394.

26. King, *IT*, 745, emphasis in original.

27. King, *IT*, 71.

28. Jonathan D. Lewis, "Towards a Unified Theory of Trauma and its Consequences," *International Journal of Applied Psychoanalytic Studies*, 9, no. 4 (2012): 300.

29. Lewis, 302.

30. King, *IT*, 62.

31. King, *IT*, 48.

32. King, *IT*, 581.

33. King, *IT*, 168–69, 226, 293, 325, 398, 669, 716, 747, 768, 778, 823, 856, 917.

34. King, *IT*, 254.

35. King, *IT*, 258.

36. King, *IT*, 110.

37. King, *IT*, 110.

38. King, *IT*, 409.

39. King, *IT*, 401.

40. King, *IT*, 103.

41. King, *IT*, 434, emphasis in original.

42. Noël Carroll, *The Philosophy of Horror* (Routledge, 1990), 33.

43. King, *IT*, 784.

44. King, *IT*, 800.

45. King, *IT*, 811, emphasis in original.

46. King, *IT*, 522.

47. King, *IT*, 523.

48. King, *IT*, 531.

49. King, *IT*, 944.

50. Judith Herman, Trauma and Recovery (New York: Basic Books, 1992), 1.

51. King, *IT*, 93.

52. King, *IT*, 259.

53. King, *IT*, 523.

54. King, *IT*, 532–33.

55. Lewis, "Towards," 302.

56. King, *IT*, 1109.

57. King, *IT*, 478.

58. King, *IT*, 383.

59. Magistral, *Landscape*, 116.

60. King, *IT*, 1152.

61. King, *IT*, 1150, emphasis in original.

62. Stephen King, *Danse Macabre* (New York: Gallery Books, 1981), 4.

References

Carroll, Noel. *The Philosophy of Horror: or Paradoxes of the Heart*. Abingdon-on-Thames: Routledge, 1990.

Eyerman, Ron. *Memory, Trauma, and Identity*. London: Palgrave Macmillan, 2019.

Herman, Judith. *Trauma and Recovery: The Aftermath of Violence—From Domestic Abuse to Political Terror*. New York: Basic Books, 1992.

King, Stephen. *Danse Macabre*. New York: Gallery Books, 2010.

King, Stephen. *IT*. New York: Scribner, 2001.

Lewis, Jonathan D. 2012. "Towards a Unified Theory of Trauma and its Consequences." *International Journal of Applied Psychoanalytic Studies* 9, no. 4 (2012): 298–317. doi:10.1002/aps.1305

Magistrale, Tony. *Landscape of Fear: Stephen King's American Gothic*. Madison: University of Wisconsin Press, 1988.

Roth, Michael S. *Memory, Trauma, and History*. New York: Columbia University Press, 2012.

Chapter 9

TOXIC NOSTALGIA IN STEPHEN KING'S *IT*

DANIEL P. COMPORA

INTRODUCTION

"It seems he just cannot stop remembering, he thinks the memories will eventually drive him mad. And now he bites down on his lip and puts his hands together palm to palm, tight, as if to keep himself from flying apart."[1] For some people, connecting with the past is a pleasant experience that awakens forgotten memories of a happier, more innocent time. For the members of the self-named Losers' Club in Stephen King's 1986 novel *IT*, however, nostalgia is definitely not that. It is a toxic experience that, like the novel's titular villain, must be confronted. *IT* focuses on seven children in the fictional town of Derry, Maine, and their battle against Pennywise the Dancing Clown. This evil, shapeshifting entity, which is also known as "It," has been preying on the town's children for decades. King's novel moves between two time settings: the children's confrontation with Pennywise in 1957–58, and their return engagement as adults in 1984–85. Despite their childhood self-image as losers, the seven children have become successful adults in the 1980s. Bill Denbrough has achieved success as a writer. Beverley Marsh is a renowned fashion designer. Ben Hanscomb is a famous architect. Richie Tozier has attained celebrity status as a disc jockey. Eddie Kaspbrak owns and runs a successful limousine services. Stanley Uris leads a successful accounting firm. Even Mike Hanlon, who never leaves Derry, serves as the town's head librarian. Yet they still bear the scars of their battle with It.

They all have some form of repressed dysfunction that is reawakened in adulthood when they are called home to face their childhood menace. Noted King scholar/critic Tony Magistrale writes that "[i]n King's fiction, the children are more often than not the outcasts."[2] Psychiatrist Harry Greenberg agrees, reflecting on the otherness of members of the Losers' Club. He writes that "[e]ach is an outsider in some fashion, often denigrated: variously, the tomboy, a stutterer; Jew; brainy nerd; off-putting chatterbox."[3] Rather than functioning as a stereotype, though, each character's otherness as children brings them together, and also illustrates how nostalgia can function in a negative fashion.

Their past traumas are reawakened when a phone call from Mike Hanlon, the "Loser" who still lives in Derry, reawakens their painful memories, making nostalgia a toxin each character must deal with. Noted psychiatrist and author David Viscott, defines toxic nostalgia as "a subtle mixture of feelings, attitudes, perspectives and needs of different ages all showing themselves at once as the unresolved past attempts to define the present."[4] King's novel intertwines the past with the present, creating a narrative in which the characters are deeply affected by toxic nostalgia. The focus is on the earliest introductions to the each of the characters and their responses to Mike's call, since it is these early scenes that establish the basis of their traumas. *IT* is established on the idea that nostalgia can be a destructive force. *IT* explores dark notions of the past and their impact on the characters as adults. Regina Hansen states that *IT*'s "depiction of child protagonists commingles fear, wonder and nostalgia, especially nostalgia for being the odd person (usually man) out, the loser or 'nerd' in its older, less positive sense."[5] The past is a burden the characters carry, and it is as much an obstacle to overcome as is Pennywise. Their defeat of him is a symbolic victory over their toxic nostalgia.

In the opening chapter, ten-year-old Bill Denbrough makes a paper boat for his little brother, Georgie, who floats it down the city's flooded streets, only to have it sail down a sewer drain. Here, Pennywise makes his first appearance in the narrative, luring the six-year-old boy close enough to rip off his arm, killing him instantly. This event is arguably the most iconic scene from *IT* and vividly establishes Bill's childhood trauma. All seven characters are traumatized by their childhood encounters with the clown; each also fights additional burdens, either at home, from local bullies, or from the general attitudes of the citizens of Derry. These include bigotry, homophobia, and seemingly hostile, or at the very least uncaring, parents. As Magistrale puts it, "[I]ndeed, the adults in this novel are most conspicuous by their absences; in the midst of Pennywise's slaughter, children remain unattended and are permitted to play in the secluded Barrens.[6] With such poor adult role models, it is not surprising that the members of the Losers' Club remain childless as adults.

Beverly Marsh, the only female member of the club, is not only bullied by a young girl, Greta Bowie, but is also abused, physically and sexually, by her father Alvin "Al" Marsh. Ben Hanscom is an overweight, shy boy who has a crush on Beverly. Because of his weight and his refusal to allow local bully Henry Bowers to copy his homework, he is tormented by Bowers and members of his gang. Mike Hanlon, the only African American member of the group, must deal with being a Black child in pre-civil rights era America. He also is traumatized by Bowers and his gang, primarily due to his race. Mike is unique in that he is the only character, despite his trauma, to never leave Derry. Stanley Uris, one of the only Jewish kids in school, also experiences the wrath of the Bowers gang. He is the only character who refuses to return to Derry to confront Pennywise, choosing to commit suicide.

Bullying is not the only childhood trauma presented in the novel. Eddie Kaspbrak's mother exhibits characteristics of Munchausen's syndrome by proxy, convincing her healthy child that he is seriously ill. Richie Tozier, the founding member of the group, is the only character who experiences no obvious trauma prior to the showdown with Pennywise, being a straight-A student with what appears to be a stable home life. Despite their varying backgrounds and traumatic experiences, the members of the Losers' Club leave Derry and experience success as adults. And except for Stan Uris, are all drawn back to Derry for a final confrontation with Pennywise. While a sense of duty to finish what they started is partially responsible for bringing some of them back, nostalgia plays a major part in their decision to return to the place where their childhood traumas were born.

NOSTALGIA

Despite carrying generally positive connotations, the term "nostalgia" can also reflect elements of negativity. According to *The Oxford English Dictionary*, nostalgia is the "sentimental longing *for* or regretful memory of a period of the past, especially one in an individual's own lifetime."[7] According to this definition, nostalgia arouses both positive and negative emotions. This is shown in *IT*, in which the ensemble of adolescent protagonists is both blessed and cursed by it. Their childhood traumas unite them against a common enemy—Pennywise—but as adults, nostalgia estranges them from their childhood home and friends. Constantine Sedikides and Tim Wildschut state that "[n]ostalgia helps people find meaning in their lives, and it does so primarily by increasing social connectedness (a sense of belongingness and acceptance), and secondarily by augmenting self-continuity (a sense of connection between one's past and one's present.)"[8] While the sense of belonging applies strongly to the characters in their childhood, the same cannot be said of their adult selves. Aside from Mike, all of the members of the Losers' Club fled Derry, and until their phone calls from Mike, they had separated themselves from their pasts to the point that they had forgotten about the town, their friends, and their confrontations with the clown.

The *OED*'s definition of nostalgia alludes to both positive and negative aspects of the concept, but the term's origins indicate that, "By the beginning of the 20th century, nostalgia was regarded as a psychiatric disorder."[9] In *IT*, King expresses differing sentiments about nostalgia, reflecting both positive and negative elements, signifying the original complexity of the idea. In the novel, the allure of childhood and the positive power of nostalgia is best expressed by Richie Tozier, who reflects:

> The energy you drew on so extravagantly when you were a kid, the energy you thought would never exhaust itself—that slipped away somewhere between eighteen and twenty-four, to be replaced by something much duller. [. . .] It was no big deal; it didn't go all at once, with a bang. And maybe, Richie thought, that's the scary part. How you didn't stop being a kid all at once, with a big explosive bang, like one of that clown's trick balloons. [. . .] The kid in you just leaked out, like the air of a tire.[10]

Despite their childhood being traumatic for members of the Losers' Club, King, through Richie, still offers an idealized view of it. Becoming an adult is not the same as ceasing to be a child. Rather, it is a gradual process that results in disappointment, despite whatever success the characters have achieved. During the epilogue, an adult Bill reinforces this notion with his thoughts as he leaves Derry: "You don't have to look back to see those children; part of your mind will see them forever. They are not necessarily the best part of you, but they were once the repository of all you could become."[11] Adult success does not fulfill childhood potential; rather, it limits it, becoming a known outcome that starkly contrasts with the infinite potential one possessed as a child.

For the members of the Losers' Club to overcome their traumatic pasts, they need to reconcile it with their adult present. Doing so is the only way they can defeat the evil menace of Pennywise, which they were incapable of destroying as children. The complex relationship between childhood trauma and adult recognition and reconciliation with that past is well expressed by scholar Erin Mercer:

The imaginative power of youth is a recurring element in King's fiction, but what critical emphasis on the figure of the child in *IT* tends to overlook is the novel's concomitant exploration of the knowledge of adulthood. As adults, the protagonists have lost the power of innocent belief, but remembering their traumatic pasts and bringing their hometown's history to light allows them to finally destroy the monster that their childish plans to kill "had come to nothing in the end."[12]

King's time-shifting narrative reinforces the connection between childhood and adulthood. This element is not present in Andy Muschietti's *IT* (2017), which focuses entirely on the protagonists as children. Though *IT: Chapter Two* (2019) employs some flashbacks connecting and juxtaposing adolescence and adulthood, King's consistent, pronounced alternation between the past and present draws clearer connections between the two and allows the Losers' Club to use their childhood trauma to defeat Pennywise.

The inability to recall, and therefore deal with, their childhood traumas hinders the member of the Losers' Club as adults. They repress their memories of Derry, their childhood friendship, and the confrontation with Pennywise. But closing themselves off to their childhood pain causes them to become successful, albeit unfulfilled, adults. As Magistrale indicates, "To defeat It once and for all the Losers' Club must reopen their personal and collective conduits to childhood."[13] All the characters experience unique childhood traumas so they are affected differently when forced to confront their pasts. Examining each one individually reveals that, though nostalgia can be a useful force in helping people confront their pasts, it also has the potential to be toxic, destroying meaningful relationships and limiting one's potential.

THE TOXIC EFFECT OF NOSTALGIA ON
MEMBERS OF THE LOSERS' CLUB

"Six Phone Calls (1985)," the third chapter of *IT*, examines the adult members of the Losers' Club. Each character, who has gone on to achieve some measure of success, receives a phone call from Mike, explaining that the killings have begun again and informing them that they must return to Derry to finish what they could not accomplish in 1958. The chapter is subdivided into six numbered sections, each one presenting an adult member of the Losers' Club at the time they receive their call from Mike. The order in which the characters are introduced is significant. Those with arguably less childhood trauma prior to their confrontation with Pennywise are presented first, escalating in order to those whose childhood trauma created more significant lifelong burdens. This is not to diminish any of the characters' traumas. While bullying, ostracization, and overprotective mothering can lead to lifelong psychological distress, Beverly, who is physically and sexually abused, and Bill, whose brother was murdered, are presented last. It is important to look at each character individually to examine how blocking out memories of their pasts has affected them as adults.

Since Mike makes each phone call, this section of the novel does not directly address his emergence into adulthood directly. As the only member of the Losers' Club to remain in Derry, he serves as a unifying presence who reunites the other members of the group. Despite being tormented by Bowers and his gang, Mike remains in Derry through adulthood, using his interest in local history to figure out how long Pennywise has been part of Derry's troubled history. He waits nearly three decades for the right time to call the group back together. In this regard, Mike never leaves his childhood behind; instead, he sacrifices any chance at career success to remain in his hometown, biding his time until Pennywise returns. Mike deals with toxic nostalgia differently than other members of the group in that he has not blocked memories of his past, rather, he has never left it. While other members of the Losers' Club suffer from some form of repressed amnesia once they leave Derry, Mike's phone calls serve as a catalyst that reconnects them with their pasts, allowing them to remember their childhood vow to come back if Pennywise ever returned.

Stanley's call is the first one presented, and it results in the worst possible outcome: Stanley's suicide. Because he is not part of the final confrontation with Pennywise, the only glimpse of his adulthood is presented in chapter 3, which reveals that Stanley had become a successful accountant and was happily married. Most of Stanley's childhood trauma stems from him being one of the only Jewish children in school and being bullied at the hands of Bowers and his gang. Despite Stanley's success, the childhood confrontation with Pennywise casts a shadow over his adult life. Despite a strong desire to become parents, Stanley's wife, Patty, is unable to become pregnant, despite neither of them having any physical problems. Stanley inherently knows that is it his fault, but he does not exactly know why. He muses:

> "Sometimes I have a dream, a bad dream, and I wake up and I think, 'I know now. I know what's wrong.' Not just you not catching pregnant—everything. Everything that's wrong with my life. [. . .] Something

should be over and isn't. I wake up from these dreams and think, 'My whole pleasant life has been nothing but the eye of some storm I don't understand.' I'm afraid. But then it just . . . fades. The way dreams do."[14]

In Stanley's case, the effect of toxic nostalgia is manifested in his inability to be happy despite a loving marriage and a successful career. This glimpse at his adult life reflects how his adolescent trauma has directly affected his adult future, even though he has forgotten most elements of his childhood. His inability to reconcile his childhood past with his adult self ultimately destroys him. As Magistrale indicates, "The passageway from innocence to experience is a crucial one for many of [King's] characters; those who pass through this symbolic corridor to sever completely their connection to childhood are doomed to the isolated sterility of adulthood.[15] Stanley's inability to reconcile his past trauma with his adult self leads him to kill himself. According to Viscott, "In the middle of a toxic nostalgic episode it is common to believe that the past is repeating itself."[16] Stanley chooses death rather than confronting his past. His reaction here seems excessive and irrational, but it is consistent with toxic nostalgia. "Typically, when the emotions of the past are triggered, your reaction to the present seems appropriate."[17] This pattern repeats with each ensuing phone call with the other members of the Losers' Club, though Stanley is the only one who kills himself.

Richie's call occurs next and, like Stanley, he has repressed most of his memories of Derry. Though Richie is not unique in this repression of his childhood, his adult life seems to have been impacted the least by the childhood ordeal with the clown. As an adult, Richie has found success as a popular deejay, famously known as the Man of a Thousand Voices for humorously voicing imaginary characters. However, his ability to slip into other personas, mostly for comedic affect, serves as an escape mechanism for Richie. Rather than suppressing memories of his childhood with alcohol or drugs, Richie drowns himself in artificial identities in order to bury his fear born out of the confrontation against Pennywise. His ability to slip into different identities allows him to distance himself from his childhood trauma. After he receives the phone call from Mike and is booking his trip back home to Maine, Richie calls his travel agent and effortlessly slips into two of his favorite voices to amuse her.[18] Immediately after hanging up, Richie's thoughts reflect the escapist nature of his voices. "Now he had to go back to being himself, and that was hard—it got harder to do that every year. It was easier to be brave when you were someone else."[19] Richie cannot escape his past entirely, and his reconnection with his hometown makes him remember what he has repressed. When he calls the Derry Town House to book his reservation, he realizes that he has not thought of it in more than two decades: "Crazy as it seemed, he guessed it *had* been at least twenty-five years, and if Mike hadn't called, he supposed he might never have thought of it again in his life."[20] When the memories do come back, Richie is indeed frightened. "Did he remember?" he asks himself. "Just enough not to want to remember any more, and you could bet your fur on that."[21] These statements indicate that Richie's feelings of nostalgia are indeed toxic. Despite a lifetime of hiding behind humor, and simply trying to forget, he has been unable to bury these memories forever.

Richie's character is portrayed differently in director Muschietti's films *IT* (2017) and *IT: Chapter Two* (2019), which portray him as homosexual. Though this theory has long been floated by fans, in an interview with *Vanity Fair*, King indicates that, while he liked the change, he did not write the character as gay. "'No, I never did,' King said. 'But again, it's one of those things that's kind of genius, because it echoes the beginning.'"[22] The beginning, which King refers to, occurs in chapter 2 of the novel. Adrian Mellon, an openly gay man, is brutally attacked by a group of teenagers, who dump his body into a canal, where he is subsequently killed by Pennywise. This clear definition of Richie's sexuality is significant in that it adds a layer of trauma to Richie's character, in addition to those presented in the text. This distinction allows for a reexamination of the novel that helps inform Riche's character. Richie is a straight-A student who has the most stable home life among members of the group. Viewing his character through Muschietti's lens, as a child with homosexual tendencies in 1986, the early days of AIDS paranoia and fears, apparently places additional burdens on Richie, especially considering the town's homophobic attitude. Both the novel and the film illustrate this attitude by presenting the attack on Mellon. In the text, more anti-gay sentiments are expressed in local graffiti, which includes phrases such as, "KILL ALL QUEERS" and "AIDS FROM GOD YOU HELLBOUND HOMOS!"[23] Given the cultural attitudes of Derry, Muschietti's portrayal of Richie as gay provides an additional reason for the character to bury his childhood memories, making his nostalgic burden even heavier. However, since Richie's sexuality is never directly addressed in the text, it is possible that he does indeed already possess these burdens. In fact, viewing Richie this way allows readers to consider a possible hidden trauma that Richie carries into adulthood, since his home life appears to be quite stable. Such a reading makes the character more complex and makes his suppression of his childhood potentially more relevant.

Successful, world-renowned architect Ben reacts to Mike's call by scaring Ricky Lee, the owner of his favorite local bar, the Red Wheel, with a shocking attempt at getting drunk, squirting lemon juice up his nostrils, numbing his senses, and distracting himself enough to chug a stein of whisky. This unsettling display contrasts with the usual biweekly appearance of Ben, who quietly drinks just a few beers per visit. During their conversation, Ben shares with Ricky that he has completely forgotten being a kid: "Did you ever hear, Ricky Lee, of having an amnesia so complete you didn't even know you *had* amnesia?"[24] Ben's explanation here illustrates a "toxic nostalgic manifestation of split-off stored pain [that] often takes the form of an altered state of consciousness, such a as a fugue state."[25] Mike's call awakens him from this state, and his memories of his childhood return. He intimates that he was fat and poor and incoherently weaves in elements of his confrontation with Pennywise (including having his life saved by a silver coin) that do little but scare Ricky even more. This visit ends with a slightly inebriated Ben driving away after giving Ricky three valuable silver coins from his childhood. Unfortunately for Ben, giving away the coins does not lessen his emotional burden.

While Richie attempts to shield his pain with false identities, Ben attempts to do the same with a shocking, potentially deadly amount of alcohol. Neither coping method is effective, nor do they prevent their painful memories from returning. Prior to the confrontation with Pennywise, Ben was bullied for being severely overweight, and had the letter "H" carved into his stomach by Henry Bowers. In addition to this physical scar, Ben carries an emotional one as well, stemming from the serious crush he had on Beverly. Though he is successful in his career, perhaps that unrequited love from his childhood is the reason that Ben remains, well into his thirties, a bachelor. Though Ben's childhood traumas may not be as devastating as Beverly's sexual abuse or Bill's loss of his brother Georgie, his pain is still powerful. Through the fog of alcohol, Ben expresses some wisdom that indicates that he understands the connection between one's past and adulthood:

> "Maybe that's why God made us kids first and built us close to the ground, because He knows you got to fall down a lot and bleed a lot before you learn that one simple lesson. You pay for what you get, you own what you pay for . . . and sooner or later whatever you own comes back home to you."[26]

This comment shows that Ben knows that going back home will make him confront the fat, poor version of himself that he has buried. Rather than run from his past, Ben, like Richie, but unlike Stan, overcomes the burdens of toxic nostalgia and returns to Derry for the final confrontation.

If Ben deals with his childhood trauma by becoming the antithesis of his childhood self, Eddie does exactly the opposite, marrying Myra, a woman who bears a striking resemblance to Eddie's severely overweight and over-protective mother. This is no secret to Eddie himself, who "did not need a shrink to tell him that he had, in a sense, married his mother."[27] Not only does Myra possess physical characteristics similar to his mother, she also perpetuates the cycle that enables Eddie's dependence on medications he does not need. Viscott indicates that this "is not a relationship in its own right but a projective opportunity in which to replay the dynamics of the past."[28] Eddie's reaction to Mike's call is to grab on to that which comforts him the most: medicines. King employs five paragraphs to describe Eddie's medications, most of which Eddie packs prior to leaving for Derry. As a child, Eddie's overprotective mother convinced him that he was frail, asthmatic, and seriously ill. The townspeople of Derry, however, recognized that Eddie's illnesses were psychosomatic. In one humiliating experience, Eddie recalls his grade-school coach stating, "Mrs. Kaspbrak, Dr. Baynes confirmed that he could find nothing at all—'physically wrong.'"[29] Despite being embarrassed by his mother's overprotectiveness, Eddie responds as an adult by marry-ing Myra, against his own better judgment. This is evidenced when he asks himself: "The jokes and snide remarks he could take, but did he really want to be a clown in a Freudian circus such as this?[30] Despite his misgivings, he marries Myra and, in his own way, loves her. Unlike the other members of the Losers' Club, most of whom reject their past selves, Eddie deals with his childhood trauma by perpetuating it. Viscott describes actions such as this as a "toxic form of nostalgic behavior."[31] Though Eddie achieves success as an adult, he succumbs to nostalgia to the point of essentially recreating his past.

Beverly Rogan, née Marsh, also fails to escape the horrors of her past—specifically, being sexually abused by her father. Beverly emerges from this adolescent trauma to find success as a clothing designer. Unfortunately, she ends up in another abusive household, marrying Tom Rogan, who, while not possessing the physical characteristics of her father, has the same penchant for abuse. Viscott states that "[s]ometimes a pattern of abusive behavior becomes stablished as a toxic nostalgic response."[32] Mike's call, however, has a different impact on Beverly than it does on the other members of the Losers' Club. It does not simply reawaken painful memories from her childhood, but it emboldens Beverly to fight back against a drunken, rage-driven Tom, who is furious not because she received a phone call from a man in the middle of the night, but because she was smoking, despite his beating her previously for the same offense. Beverly, like Eddie, has dealt with her painful past by perpetuating it, choosing a spouse who bears frightening similarities to her domineering parent. However, a reading of toxic nostalgia in the novel reveals a significant difference in their respective outcomes.

Beverly is the only character whose memories of the past allow her to escape from a bad situation. While she is in the process of leaving Tom, he notices a change in Beverly after she receives the call from Mike. After smacking her across the face, he gets a reaction he is not expecting:

> He replayed what had just happened. Her face. What had that third expression been, there for a bare instant and then gone? First the surprise. Then the pain. Then the
> *(nostalgia)*
> look of a memory . . . of some memory. It had only been for a moment.[33]

Here, nostalgia, and remembering the past, provide Beverly the strength to fight back against Tom, galvanizing her to hurl projectiles at him as she makes her escape from her home and terrible relationship. Reawakening her past traumas—both the abuse by her father and the confrontation with Pennywise—enables her to escape from her badly dysfunctional marriage. "Frightened but free,"[34] Beverly finds herself laughing as this portion of the chapter ends, despite the physical and emotional pain she has just endured. Both Eddie and Beverly flee from a present that strongly resembles their pasts. But in Beverly's case, the nostalgic reuniting with her past produces both positive and negative consequences. On the one hand, it establishes a pattern of her being on the receiving end of abuse in her interpersonal relationships, a point noted by Magistrale, who states that Beverly's father "has done permanent psychological damage to her, as her eventual choice of marriage to Tom is simply a continuation of the violent pattern that originated with her father and extends to Pennywise the clown."[35] On the other hand, the phone call from Mike allows her to remember the meaningful friendships she had as an adolescent, allowing her to end the cycle of violence.

Bill Denbrough's phone call is presented last and, like many protagonists in King novels,[36] Bill is a successful writer. And, like the other members of the Losers' Club, he has repressed memories of his childhood, even the murder of his brother Georgie. When his wife Audra tries to understand how Bill has forgotten his childhood despite remembering that he had a brother, he tries to explain:

> "What I am trying to tell you Audra, is that I haven't even thought of George in twenty years or more."
> "But you told me you had a brother named—"
> "I repeated a *fact*," he said. "That was all. His name was a word. It cast no shadow at all in my mind."[37]

Though Bill can remember facts about his childhood, he is unable to recall the trauma he experienced while growing up. For Bill, nostalgia not only reawakens painful memories of his past, but it also brings back his stuttering problem which he had overcome as a child. In a sense, Bill returns to his childhood more fully than other members of the group because his trauma was the most severe.

Bill's repressed trauma manifests itself physically as well as psychologically. A cluster of faded scars on his palm resurface after Mike's phone call. The cuts were made by Stanley with the jagged edge of a Coke bottle during an impromptu ceremony in which the members of the Losers' Club cut their palms, formed a circle, joined hands, and swore a blood oath to come back home if Pennywise ever returned. When Audra tries to convince Bill that the call from Mike triggered a hallucination, Bill points out that the scars prove what he is saying is true. "*But the scars, Audra—how do you explain the scars? He's right. They weren't there . . . and now they are.*"[38] Even though every member of the club bears these scars, Bill is the only character the novel describes as having both physical and mental scars reappearing. This suggests both that Bill's trauma was the most severe, and that his repression of it was the most thorough. And even though he has put geographic distance between himself and Derry, he has not been able to outrun his past. Bill's ability to reconcile his childhood trauma, defeat Pennywise, and avenge his brother's death allows him to overcome the toxic nostalgia that has haunted him for twenty-seven years.

CONCLUSION

The seven children in *IT* must overcome their childhood traumas in order to defeat Pennywise. They all are burdened by the past, which has hindered them as adults. King scholar Sharon Russel states, "Adults need their connection to the world of childhood to survive, and children cannot conquer evil alone. The group of children in *IT* must return to Derry as adults to really destroy the monster."[39] Their detachment from their childhood hinders each of them. Mike is unable to leave Derry, haunted by the promise made when he was a child. Stanley is unable to start a family, resulting in an underlying dissatisfaction with his life. Richie employs shifting personas to hide from his childhood trauma. Ben chooses a path of loneliness and isolation. Eddie recreates his childhood codependent relationship with his mother by marrying her doppelgänger. Beverly fails to escape the abusive relationships that were part of her formative years, marrying a man with a penchant for spousal abuse. And Bill has both mental and physical scars resurface before he returns home to confront his childhood menace. Only by remembering and accepting their pasts can the members of the Losers' Club defeat Pennywise.

In *IT*, nostalgia is presented somewhat positively as a powerful force that not only allows the characters to overcome their childhood traumas but also to defeat a powerful evil that has cast a shadow over their lives. Though the outcome of their fight with Pennywise is positive, nostalgia also serves as a toxin that causes pain. For Stanley, confronting his past results in his suicide. For Eddie, the final confrontation with the clown costs him his life. For the others, years of repressed memories have led them to live somewhat unfulfilling lives despite attaining a great deal of career success. Anthony Sacramone addresses the idea of toxic nostalgia directly, pointing out that "[o]ne of the functions of nostalgia is to be very selective. It keeps the good stuff and buries the bad—or buries the bad in a pit of hope that the worst is not yet to come.[40] Though Sacramone makes this statement regarding the film *Ready Player One*, another nostalgic adolescent tale, it also applies to *IT*. Unfortunately for the members of the Losers' Club, the worst does eventually come. The bad is indeed buried in a pit of hope for twenty-seven years, but when the day of reckoning arrives, each of them is forced to deal with the fact that they have lived nearly three decades hiding from the pain and fear of their childhoods. In that regard, nostalgia is indeed toxic, resulting in more trauma and pain that can only be remedied by remembering, reliving, and confronting the evils from their pasts.

Notes

1. Stephen King, *IT* (New York: Viking, 1986), 320.

2. Tony Magistrale, *Landscape of Fear: Stephen King's American Gothic*, 111.

3. Harvey Greenberg, "*IT*: On the *Unheimlich* Maneuvers of Stephen King," *Psychiatric Times*, November 2017, 28E–28F.

4. David Viscott, *Emotional Resilience: Simple Truths for Dealing with the Unfinished Business of Your Past* (New York: Harmony, 1996), 279.

5. Regina Hansen, Stephen King's *IT* and *Dreamcatcher* on Screen: Hegemonic White Masculinity and Nostalgia for Underdog Boyhood," *Science Fiction Film and Television* 10, no. 2 (2017): 161–76.

6. Magistrale, 111.

7. "Nostalgia." *OED Online*, Oxford University Press, December 2020, https://oed.com /view/Entry/128472?redirectedFrom=nostalgia. Emphasis in original.

8. Constantine Sedikides and Tim Wildschut, "Finding Meaning in Nostalgia," *Review of General Psychology* 22, no. 1 (2018): 48.

9. Constantine Sedikides, Tim Wildschut, Jamie Arndt, and Clay Routledge, "Nostalgia Past, Present, and Future," *Current Directions in Psychological Science* 17, no. 5 (2008): 304.

10. Stephen King, *IT* (New York: Viking, 1986), 734–35.

11. King, 1135.

12. Erin Mercer, "The Difference Between World and Want: Adulthood and the Horrors of History in Stephen King's *IT*," *Journal of Popular Culture* 52, no. 2 (2019): 317.

13. Magistrale, 117.

14. King, 51.

15. Magistrale, 116.

16. Viscott, 299.

17. Viscott, 299.

18. Among these voices were a fictional character, Kinky Briefcase, Sexual Accountant, and the famous comedian W. C. Fields.

19. King, 61.

20. King, 62.

21. King, 69.

22. Anthony Breznican, "Stephen King Loved Insulting *IT: Chapter Two*'s Stephen King Stand-In," *Vanity Fair*, September 9, 2019, https://www.vanityfair.com/hollywood/2019/09/it-chapter-two-stephen-king-cameo-interview.

23. King, 19.

24. King, 80.

25. Viscott, 217.

26. King, 82.

27. King, 85.

28. Viscott, 323.

29. King, 89–90.

30. King, 90.

31. Viscott, 323

32. Viscott, 304.

33. King, 106.

34. King, 122.

35. Magistrale, 114.

36. Ben Mears in *'Salem's Lot*, Jack Torrance in *The Shining*, and Paul Sheldon in *Misery* are prominent examples.

37. King, 134.

38. King, 140, emphasis in original.

39. Sharon Russell, *Stephen King: A Critical Companion* (Westport, CT: Greenwood Press, 1996), 38.

40. Anthony Sacramone, "The Toxic Nostalgia of *Ready Player One*," *Intercollegiate Review Online*, November 9, 2018, 2.

References

Breznican, Anthony. "Stephen King Loved Insulting *IT*: *Chapter Two's* Stephen King Stand-In." *Vanity Fair*, September 9, 2019. https://www.vanityfair.com/hollywood /2019/09/it-chapter-two-stephen-king-cameo-interview.

Greenberg, Harvey. "*IT*: On the *Unheimlich* Maneuvers of Stephen King." *Psychiatric Times*, November 2017, 28E–28F.

Hansen, Regina. "Stephen King's *IT* and *Dreamcatcher* on Screen: Hegemonic White Masculinity and Nostalgia for Underdog Boyhood." *Science Fiction Film & Television* 10, no. 2 (2017): 161–76.

King, Stephen. *IT*. New York: Viking, 1986.

Magistrale, Tony. *Landscape of Fear: Stephen King's American Gothic*. Bowling Green, OH: Bowling Green State University Popular Press, 1988.

Mercer, Erin. "The Difference Between World and Want: Adulthood and the Horrors of History in Stephen King's *IT*." *Journal of Popular Culture*, 52, no. 2 (2019): 315–29.

"nostalgia." *OED Online*. Oxford University Press, December 2020. https://oed.com/view /Entry/128472?redirectedFrom=nostalgia.

Russell, Sharon. *Stephen King: A Critical Companion*. Westport: Greenwood Press. 1996.

Sacramone, Anthony. "The Toxic Nostalgia of *Ready Player One*." *Intercollegiate Review Online*, November 9, 2018, 1–4. https://isi.org/intercollegiate-review/the-toxic -nostalgia-of-ready-player-one/#:~:text=The%20Toxic%20Nostalgia%20of%20Ready %20Player%20one%20April,by%20a%20massive%20online%20simulation%20called %20The%20oasis.

Sedikides, Constance, and Tim Wildschut. "Finding Meaning in Nostalgia." *Review of General Psychology* 22, no. 1 (2018): 48–61.

Sedikides, Constantine, Tim Wildschut, Jamie Arndt, and Clay Routledge. "Nostalgia Past, Present, and Future." *Current Directions in Psychological Science* 17, no. 5 (2008): 304–7.

Viscott, David. *Emotional Resilience: Simple Truths for Dealing with the Unfinished Business of Your Past*. New York: Three Rivers Press, 1996.

Counterfeits

Chapter 10

GOODBYE POGO

Pennywise and the Serial Murder of the American Dream

HANNAH LINA SCHNEEBERGER AND MARIA WIEGEL

On May 10, 2018, the Los Angeles-based art gallery Lethal Amounts opened its exhibition *Goodbye Pogo: The Art of John Wayne Gacy*. The exhibition contained "33 original oil canvas paintings by America's most prolific serial killer."[1] Most of them were painted while Gacy was on death row and depicting clowns. One of these, called "Pennywise the Clown," was, of course, the well-known killer of Stephen King's It. Gacy, who, in the 1970s killed at least thirty-three young men before painting those thirty-three original oil canvas paintings, is also known as the "Killer Clown," due to his regular performances as a party clown in his neighborhood. Despite the exhibition's controversial character—or maybe precisely because of its controversy—visitors lined up around the block to see the serial killer's artwork, drawn by the intrigue of a killer clown painting a killer clown. King, on the other hand, does not mention Gacy as inspiration for the villain of his 1986 novel.[2] We, however, will argue in the following chapter that Gacy and It do have much in common: most intriguingly, that they are both products of the same parameters, and at once reflect and shape the American ethos of the 1980s. In this chapter, we examine Pennywise's function as a fictional character mirroring society by comparing and contrasting it with the real-life serial killer John Wayne Gacy. On the one hand, we reveal in this connection how closely King's character reflects its historical moment. On the other hand, we demonstrate how American culture is rooted in both its dreams and its nightmares. We argue that the interconnectedness of the fictional character It, John Wayne Gacy, and the white middle-class suburbs serves as a part of a symbolic machine that is the American society. A machine that, like a perpetuum mobile, keeps on spinning and working without the addition of outside energy.

When on December 22, 1978, the police in Des Plaines, Illinois, arrested John Wayne Gacy, the nation was shocked, since Gacy was perceived, as his own sister reported to the *New York Times*, as a "normal person."[3] Born in Chicago in 1942, Gacy was a respected entrepreneur and family man, who was twice married, had two children, and was living in the small suburban town of Des Plaines. This side of Gacy pursuing prosperity for posterity seems to embody the American Dream.[4] This can also be seen as something Slavoj Žižek might call the sublime object of ideology. In his book of the same title (1989), he claims that ideologies are built around a "sublime object." The subject that believes in an ideology cannot grasp the true meaning of the sublime object the ideology thrives on. Rather, the subject only has a limited notion of this sublime object. Žižek, therefore, defines the ideological as:

> a social reality whose very existence implies the non-knowledge of its participants as to its essence—that is, the social effectivity, the very reproduction of which implies that the individuals "do not know what they are doing." "Ideological" is not the "false consciousness" of a (social) being but this being itself in so far as it is supported by "false consciousness."[5]

Hence, ideology functions as the subject's social reality. It determines the subject's way of life and way of thinking, without the subject's ability to grasp its meaning. The subject's decision to subject themselves to the "symbolic machine" ultimately causes their belief in that ideology "unconsciously."[6] The symbolic machine, therefore, is both external and internal.[7] Žižek further argues that ideological structure consists of the very "leftover" created by the subject's inability to fully succeed in the internalizing of the ideology.[8] Therefore, ideology is not something believed and lived in consciously. However, it is also not something to be reduced to a "dreamlike illusion that we build to escape in supportable reality,"[9] says Žižek. Instead, ideology should be considered "a fantasy-construction which serves as a support for our reality itself: an illusion which structures our effective, real social relations and thereby masks some insupportable, real, impossible kernel."[10] According to this line of argument, the subject of American ideology,[11] or any national ideology, does not consciously believe in the ideology in order to escape "reality"—an unstructured realm consisting of coincidences and chances. Rather, they unconsciously live in and with the ideology that simultaneously structures their reality. With respect to the structures and layers of reality, on the following pages we will show how King's It and John Wayne Gacy are created and create reality by subjecting themselves to the symbolic machine.

As Paul A. Cantor observes in *Pop Culture and the Dark Side of the American Dream—Con Men, Gangsters, Drug Lords, and Zombies* (2019), the American Dream, which "was very much embodied in material terms,"[12] has the American Nightmare as its byproduct. This byproduct is similar to what Žižek defines as a symptom, which "subverts its very own foundation."[13] Jacques Lacan's early definition of a symptom as being "[s]tructured like a language" suggests that it is a "sign of the unconscious" which "is hidden in plain view, like the purloined letter in Poe's story."[14] The symptom, therefore, is the consequence of the notion of the sublime object and its ungraspable truth. By pointing at the void, the sublime object creates by being unreachable for the subject, a symptom, as Žižek argues, is a necessary function to "avoid madness."[15] It "represents the return of truth as such into the gap of a certain knowledge."[16] It is, in other words, a graspable and readable representation of an ungraspable and unreadable void and thereby points at the very same void. Accordingly, this is displayed by Gacy's other, murderous, side. Gacy and his nightmarish traits can be considered a symptom of the American ideology, since his failing in being a functioning part of American society points at the volatility of the subject's notion of its sublime object, such as the pursuit of prosperity and the establishment of a nuclear family. We can even go further than that and argue that the American Nightmare, here embodied by Gacy, is not only subverting the American Dream. Instead of being a symptom, it is part of the American ideology itself. A similar argument is made by James A. Sparks in his chapter on "Serial Killers," in which he states that serial murder is part of the American experience.[17] By being its symptom and byproduct, it is also the negative of the ideal picture. Like the negative is needed for a photograph for the process of materialization, the ideal also needs the undesirable apocalyptic worst-case scenario in order for it to achieve manifestation.

The crimes of John Wayne Gacy, as mentioned above, shook up American society because, in addition to being horrifying, they were especially surprising to come from one of the local community's respected members. Gacy is known to have targeted young men by offering them lucrative job opportunities and drugs to lure them into his house where he raped, tortured, and killed them, and finally deposited their bodies in a crawl space underneath his house.[18] Twenty-eight of his victim's corpses were found in and around his home. Five bodies were disposed of in a river, as Gacy himself stated, and could not be located, much less retrieved during the investigations.[19] Despite his media designation as the "Killer Clown," which is based on his public act as Pogo the Clown during parades and community events,[20] Gacy never wore his clown costume or persona while committing crimes. Yet, his persona makes it evident that reality is more horrifying than fiction.

Nevertheless, Gacy's double life is most famously reflected by his personification of Pogo, behind whose makeup hid, as Sparks notes, "the most prolific serial killer of the twentieth century."[21] This embodiment characterizes another subversion of common beliefs and expectations. Both Gacy and King use the figure of the clown to hide something horrific and dark under a layer of fun and family entertainment marked by the clown's makeup and characteristics and, at the same time to reveal the easy subversion of those beliefs and expectations. However, neither Gacy nor King's Pennywise represent the first appearances of the clown as a figure of horror. Andrew McConnell Stott argues that the shift in the depiction of the clown goes back to the decline of the circus industry originating in the Great Depression and the emerging "dark carnivals."[22] As early as the 1940s, the Joker made his appearance as Batman's antagonist, subverting common expectations of the clown as a funny fellow.[23] This shift in the depiction of clowns goes hand in hand with a concurrent shift in their reception.[24] Coulrophobia, as the fear of clowns is called in psychoanalytical terms, may not be a fear exclusive to modern times, but it is a phobia with a rather young name, only having been discussed as such since the 1980s, and mostly due to a heightened discussion of clowns and their unsettling nature.[25] This contributes to the clown's frequent monstrous depictions in popular culture: the subversion of the well-known idea of the clown as a naïve and friendly entity imbues it with dark humor, potential violence, and the unknowability of the person behind the makeup or mask of the clown.

This subversion of known and ordinary entities into something uncanny,[26] in a Freudian sense, is what makes Pennywise a fitting appearance for the monstrous antagonist of Stephen King's *IT*—an entity that represents absolute evil.[27] The suburban setting in the town of Derry, by being a homogenous space, repressing everything that is undesirable, further reflects the anxieties Erin Mercer mentions in connection to It's shape-shifting ability to appear as its victims' greatest fears.[28] Meanwhile, McConnell Stott argues that "a key theme of coulrophobia is the sufferer's suspicion that clowning provides cover for sexual predators and child abductors,"[29] which he links to reports of clowns harassing Boston children in 1981."[30] Pennywise's own introduction to Georgie Denbrough as a middle-aged man in the form of "Bob Gray"—as Karina Paola Meyrer observes in her article, wherein she connects Pennywise to Carl Gustav Jung's archetype of the trickster[31]—links It, as we argue, to Gacy and, thereby, reflects the horrors of suburbia. Although Gacy had a criminal record and was sentenced to time in jail prior to moving to Chicago's suburbs,[32] as mentioned above, he embodied the image of the everyday man through his connections with his neighbors and his seemingly charitable acts. The first encounter with It described in the novel even includes the lines "I . . . am Mr. Bob Gray, also known as Pennywise the Dancing Clown. [. . .] And now we know each other. I'm not a stranger to you, and you're not a stranger to me,"[33] something that not only links It to its most prominent embodiment as Pennywise, but also to the behavioral patterns related to small towns and suburbia by conducting something that could be considered a "proper introduction," playing with the belief that people who live in small towns or suburbs not only know each other from afar but more intimately by name and occupation. At the same time, this makes a stranger in either of those locations stand out as a possible source of suspicion. Thereby, It mimics a surface level of respectability that labels it as no threat to the community, but instead, as with Gacy's public persona, makes him trustworthy for that community.

Being both Gacy's and Pennywise's preferred hunting grounds, the suburbs expose their nightmarish character. As Sparks argues, Gacy's motivation for committing the murders was one of his personality's aim to purge queer men and boys from society, since "Jack [one of Gacy's personalities] did not like homosexuals."[34] Being a bisexual man himself, Gacy subjected himself to the ideology of heteronormativity and "engaged in what he perceived to be a desirable social ritual, eliminating 'punks' and 'fags,' especially young street hustlers who sold their bodies for money."[35] A similar ideology and rhetoric can be seen in *IT* as well, when Adrian Mellon is murdered during a hate crime. The perpetrators of the crime are homophobes whose "civic pride had been wounded by seeing a fucking faggot wearing a hat which said I ♥ Derry."[36] The murderers situate their homophobia and hatred against homosexuals as a marker of their "belonging" to and love for Derry, so that this scene reflects suburban ideals of homogeneity and heteronormativity, which are exacerbated by their reproducibility. This also shows that horror in *IT* does not solely stem from a supernatural source but lies in everyday hatred as well. This makes this crime, in comparison to the horrifying supernatural crimes of the absolute evil, even more horrifying.

Beyond just taking advantage of the social rules inscribed in Derry, It *embodies* Derry and each of its communities and neighborhoods. This is evidenced by Derry's history and development, and further, is visible in the way the town has been both stalked and influenced by It. As Bill Denbrough muses during his return flight to his hometown, "Derryfolk had lived with Pennywise in all his guise for a long time . . . and maybe, in some mad way, they had even come to understand him. To like him, need him. *Love* him?

Maybe. Yes, maybe that too."[37] In the same way that Gacy as a serial killer represents the American Nightmare in American society, It displays the nightmarish character of the American Dream of 1950s suburbia. As a small town, Derry and its citizens represent an American ideal of a white middle class, which became manifested by its mass production during the late 1940s and early 1950s.[38] This American ideal can be noticed in Gacy's case, too. He was a self-made man; as an employer, Gacy gained respectability in a sub-urban setting. This possibility for social mobility connects Gacy once more to the notion of the American Dream turning into an American Nightmare when his murders come to light. The same interconnectedness between dream and nightmare can be traced in King's *IT*. The Losers' success as adults seems to be strongly linked to their past and future encounters with It. Mike Hanlon's "conclusion is that [their] success stems from what happened here twenty-seven years ago. If [they] had all been exposed to asbestos at that time and had all developed lung cancer by now, the correlative would be no less clear or persuasive."[39] At the same time, their success is portrayed as distinctly American when "[t]hey glanced around at each other almost fur-tively, embarrassed, as Americans always seem to be, by the raw fact of their own success."[40] However, only the Losers who *left* Derry became success-ful "by the standards of the American upper-middle class."[41] Mike, who stayed in Derry, seems to be an exception to his own explanation. However, Mike's logic suggests that his lack of economic success can be traced back to his staying in Derry, while everyone else moved away when they were children. Mike also being the only Loser of color might further show the exclusion of minority groups from the rights stated in the American consti-tution.[42] The notion of economic success being an expression of American-ness is manifested in the American Dream, which is an ideal James Truslow Adams formulated in his book *The Epic of America* (first published in 1931, and in which he coined the term). However, even before Adams's defini-tion of the American Dream as an economical potentiality, the notion of the American Dream as a dream of improving one's social and economic status was strongly connected to American history and culture, as can be seen in Max Weber's book *The Protestant Ethic and the Spirit of Capital-ism*, which was published in 1904 (and was first translated into English in 1930).

King's Derry seems to be a microcosm of the United States. This is already reflected on the novel's first page: "The terror, which would not end for another twenty-eight years—if it ever did end—began, so far as I know or can tell, with a boat."[43] The above-mentioned ideal of profitability can be traced back to the very beginnings of the American nation. When, in 1630, John

Winthrop, the second governor of the Massachusetts Bay Colony, delivered his sermon addressing "A Model of Christian Charity" on board of the *Arabella*, he coined the term "City upon a Hill," which stands as a symbol for the Puritan dream for what would become the United States and which has helped shape the American identity throughout the centuries. In the sermon, he stated that humans are divided by God "into two sortes, riche and poore; vnder the first are comprehended all such as are able to liue comfortably by theire owne meanes duely improued; and all others are poore according to the former distribution."[44] The Losers' focus on success is overshadowed by an underlying predestination, which, for instance, can be seen in the context of the school, where the cheerleaders' "fathers help to buy the sports equipment and uniforms" (360). This suggests a socioeconomic structure where winners and losers are not so much predestined by God's grace to belong to the elect. Rather, economic success becomes something one inherits, since certain possibilities are only accessible to certain demographics in American society. Even when taking God out of the equation, there exists a dichotomy between rich and poor. This also stresses Winthrop's claimed Puritan aim to provide prosperity for their own and their children's posterity.[45] Likewise, Gacy's personality disorder is linked to his father's "Jekyll-Hyde" personality.[46] Similar to his father's different personalities, depending on him being sober or drunk, Gacy's multiple-personality disorder is often explained as inherited from his father. More than an explanation of Gacy's personality and crimes, this reveals society's structures, where social mobility is limited by inheritance and financial and social preconditions. Furthermore, accessibility of mental health issues institutions is strongly tied to gender, race, and social status.

More than a microcosm, Derry can even be seen as an American heterotopia, as defined by Michel Foucault. Heterotopias are spaces that create layers of meaning by placing the undesirable in a position of the Other to create the possibility of a utopia. They, thereby, reflect society like a mirror.[47] King's novel constantly raises the question of how far reality can be separated from dreams and memories, or rather in how far those layers of meaning are intertwined. An excellent example of this disruption appears in Derry's new mall, which the Losers see for the first time when they return to Derry in the 1980s. By presenting a break with the Losers' memories of Derry from the 1950s, the mall becomes a symbol for reality, while at the same time reflecting American fixations on prosperity and economy. However, dreams and reality are not entirely separable. They influence one another, which animates the horrors It embodies. Considering the scope of Pennywise's powers, Ben contemplates:

> These things were . . . well . . . they were dreams-made-real. And once
> dreams became real, they escaped the power of the dreamer and
> became their own deadly things, capable of independent action. The
> silver slugs had worked because the seven of them had been unified
> in their belief that they would.[48]

Dreams and belief, as American traits, similar to It, can be seen as shape-
shifting entities, as well. Dream and reality, like ideology and reality in Žižek's
sense, form a "symbolic machine." The Losers subject themselves to this
"symbolic machine," while at the same time, by contributing their dreams,
beliefs, and nightmares, they are producing an ideology and therewith a
reality. Though not being successful in an economic sense, Mike becomes
the author of Derry's history and is the only Loser to remember It well
enough to bring the Losers back together upon Pennywise's return in the
1980s. This provides agency to him in writing Derry's history and, at the
same time, creating Derry's reality. However, as subjects of their dreams,
nightmares, and beliefs, the Losers are not able to tell where the symbolic
machine ends and reality begins, the same way one could not separate Gacy
as the "Killer Clown" from Gacy as a family man and entrepreneur. Richie,
therefore, "believed he would never think of it as exactly 'real' again; he would
see it as a clever canvas scene underlaid with a crisscrossing of support-
cables . . . cables like strands of a spiderweb."[49] In a Matrix-like description
of the desert of the Real, a poststructuralist notion of the Real is portrayed,
and depicted as something that is ungraspable.[50]

Moreover, Derry is not only separated into layers of reality, but clearly
into levels that portray Derry's surface and underground, with its surface
showing a perceived ideal and its underground a place of abjection.[51] Early
in the novel, Bill's father explains the intricate system of pipes and maintenance facilities built upon by generations of townspeople and forgotten
by the population inhabiting them now. This system runs under Derry's
surface and mirrors life over the ground. Further, it is supplemented by
pumping stations acting as connecting points between surface and underground and protruding as cylinders into the Losers' safe place, the Barrens.
Similarly, the underground is It's dwelling, which can be accessed through
a path by entering the pumping stations. Throughout *IT*, the Losers' Club
travels into Derry's underground once as children and then again as adults,
in order to descend into It's lair. Thereby, they not only traverse Derry's
history, but its excrement and waste as well, and face the abject, which is
described by Julia Kristeva in *The Powers of Horror* (1982) as that which

"disturbs identity, system, order" and as "death infecting life."[52] Furthermore, the abject is something that connects the self to life through bodily waste and death as a lived border and thereby provokes a physical reaction. The Losers' Club is quite aware of the fluids and waste, which they repeatedly call "grey water," as well as the human corpses they stumble upon during their chase of It.[53]

It repeatedly uses multiple openings to the drains to haunt and prey on the population of Derry; this begins with Georgie in the narrative and continues with Betty Ripsom's parents hearing their dead daughter's voice coming from the sink to taunt them. This culminates in multiple voices speaking to Beverly Marsh through *her* bathroom sink and causing it to erupt in blood that covers the whole room.[54] Not only does this reveal something that should stay underground coming (violently) to the surface, but it functions as an abject reminder of life and death as well with only the Losers being able to see and clean the blood in the bathroom. It has hollowed Derry out and infiltrated the town through that which the townspeople consider waste and filth, revealing that the things they consider dirty and banished through the drain system are still present within the town despite Derry's veneer of concrete and white, middle-class pretenses. When this underside of Derry collapses with the demise of It in 1985, the surface must collapse as well, proving that there was never a clear separation between the two levels.

Gacy in his active years as a serial murderer also used the separating levels of surface and underground to hide his victims' remains. He placed the abject within his own home and lived upon the unmanageable reality of his own crimes. "Any crime, because it draws attention to the fragility of law, is abject, but premediated crime, cunning murder, hypocritical revenge are even more so because they heighten the display of such fragility," writes Kristeva, who explains this as the "immoral, sinister, scheming and shady" nature of abjection.[55] Gacy himself created a place of abjection to live in that contrasted the performed self he showed on an outside and surface level.[56] Just as Derry's abject self and filth could not stay hidden under a town's ideals, Gacy's murders had to come to the surface. Furthermore, Gacy used the suburban dream of the white middle class and its learned and expected behaviors to create its nightmare counterpart and to emulate its exploitation of people's pursuits of economic success and security. Gacy could commit crimes and still be perceived as an ideal and integral part of his neighborhood because his neighborhood was willing to partake in the reality Gacy created on the surface. This reflects Winthrop's Puritan ideal of economic success as an indicator for being a valuable part of American society.

While It, as mentioned in the beginning of this chapter, is considered the absolute evil, the Turtle, by contrast, represents the absolute good. Gacy cannot be organized into one or the other. As a human being, after all, he has to be considered diverse and complex in his characterization, which makes it impossible to categorize him within such limiting and absolute categories as good and evil. Here we have to face a limit to the comparison between It in the shape of Pennywise and Gacy. While neither It nor the Turtle have a scope of action, since they are barred from diversion and complexity by only being able to act in an absolutely good or absolutely bad way, Gacy, though caught in the symbolic machine of American ideology, as a human being is capable of making diverse and complex decisions. However, considering both as products of their milieu, Derry's draining system can be compared to the American system.[57] Similar to Derry's draining system, in the American system,

> nobody knows where all the damned sewers and drains go, or why. When they work, nobody cares. When they don't, there's three or four sad sacks from Derry Water who have to try and find out which pump went flooey or where the plug-up is. [. . .] It's dark and smelly and there are rats. Those are all good reasons to stay out, but the best reason is that you could get lost. It's happened before.[58]

In a sense, Gacy, as a believer in the righteousness of his actions, might be considered as lost in the American draining system. Moreover, he is one of the pumps that "went flooey." Pointing at the volatility of American ideology, Gacy shows how much of an American Nightmare can be experienced and created while pursuing the American Dream.

As criminology professor Scott A. Bonn argues, "[T]he serial killer identity is a mirror reflection of society itself."[59] As a symptom, it points at society's "fears, lust and anger."[60] This is also noticeable in Americans' obsession with serial killers, which can be traced by the recently increased production of documentaries and movies on serial killers, such as those on Ted Bundy and Charles Manson.[61] In a narcissistic way, society loves to see and reassemble itself in its mirror image. In this mirror image, as a symptom of society's longing and striving for its sublime object of ideology, that object's reversal becomes part of the very same ideology. This might also be a reason for society's melancholia for serial killers, such as that expressed in Sufjan Steven's 2005 song "John Wayne Gacy, Jr.," which represents Gacy's childhood as deserving of sympathy and which seeks explanations for his crimes. For example, the song first refers to his father as "a drinker," and then states in the end that in the lyrical I's "best behavior / I am really just like him / Look beneath the floor boards / For the secrets I have hid." These lyrics attempt to show Gacy as a symptom of society living inside the symbolic machine structuring reality. More than that it even suggests that everyone can be or become Gacy.

Gacy and It, in the form of Pennywise, point to the volatility of American ideals by breaking with expectations and showing how closely related the American Dream is to the American Nightmare. The reproduction of the American Dream as a form of belonging to the suburbs does not work on a deeper level than the surface level. Only the façades look perfectly similar. The basement, however, provides a shelter for the horrors of the suburban unconscious. One of those horrors is the figure of the clown. The fear of clowns did not decline or stay in the fictional sphere. This is evidenced by the popularization of clown sightings as a topic on the internet in 2016,[62] with clowns lurking in the dark to scare passersby, not only in the US, but also worldwide; mass hysteria soon followed, proving once again, and as McConnell Stott argues by tracing the history of coulrophobia back to the Great Depression, that the fear of clowns is deeply rooted in the Western unconscious.[63] This shows that the image of the terrifying clown, shaped by, among others, Gacy's Pogo and King's Pennywise, takes part in the creation of reality. Both Gacy and It share many characteristics, not the least of which is their function as society's symptom. As society's undesirables, they show the other side of the American Dream. Embodying society's biggest fears, they mirror the wrongdoings of the symbolic machine. Next to the ideal of posterity for prosperity, there are all of those who did not succeed. There are homicides, homophobia, psychological disorders, addictions, and racism, just to mention a few. However, Gacy and Pennywise have to be distinguished, since they do not share the characteristic of factuality or, respectively, fictionality. However, a comparison shows that "after all, there is more to the story than six boys and one girl, none of them happy, none of them accepted by their peers, who stumbled into a nightmare during one hot summer when Eisenhower was still President."[64] This nightmare is created by a subversion of predominant ideals of the American Dream as embodied by social and financial status, ultimately highlighting that the abject cannot be separated from reality. Instead, it takes part in the creation of reality by disrupting the prevalent image of an "ideal" American society. Nothing shows this disruption better than It in its desire to prey on children in their suburban homes, undermining the institutional security Americans rely on and their trust in the American Dream.

Notes

1. Lethal Amounts, @lethalamounts, Twitter, April 10, 2018, https://twitter.com/lethal amounts/status/983737554326446080.https://twitter.com/lethalamounts/status/98373755 4326446080

2. *Stephen King—The Official Website*, https://stephenking.com/library/novel/it _inspiration.html.

3. Douglas E. Kneeland, "Suspect in Mass Deaths Is Puzzle to All," *New York Times*, January 10, 1979, https://www.nytimes.com/1979/01/10/archives/suspect-in-mass-deaths -is-puzzle-to-all-affable-driven-businessman.html. "Normal" as a descriptive term is connected to a heteronormative white middle-class background. The interviewee themself was located in the same suburban milieu as Gacy.

4. Paul A. Cantor defines the American Dream as something that "was very much embodied in material terms—a family happily ensconced in a spacious house, preferably in the suburbs, with the most up-to-date appliances and two or three cars in the garage" (Cantor, *Popular Culture and the Dark Side of the American Dream* [Lexington: University Press of Kentucky, 2019], 133f). This is encased by a notion of security provided by an institutional framework.

5. Slavoj Žižek, *The Sublime Object of Ideology* (London and New York: Verso, 1989), 15f.

6. Žižek, *The Sublime Object of Ideology*, 42.

7. Žižek, *The Sublime Object of Ideology*, 42.

8. Žižek, *The Sublime Object of Ideology*, 42.

9. Žižek, *The Sublime Object of Ideology*, 45.

10. Žižek, *The Sublime Obect of Ideology*, 45.

11. In his book *The American Ideology—A Critique* (New York and London: Routledge, 2004, 7), Andrew Levine provides the commonly used definition of the American ideology as a complex construct consisting of "two constituent parts." First, the notion of efficiency through practical reason "that is most often enlisted in defense of market arrangements, private property and, lately, globalization" (Levine, *The American Ideology*, 7). Second, the American political practice which is the notion of a "political liberalism" that is run by reason and "modern understandings of justice" (Levine, *The American Ideology*, 7) plays a role in its ideology.

12. Cantor, *Popular Culture and the Dark Side of the American Dream*, 133.

13. Žižek, *The Sublime Object of Ideology*, 16.

14. Tim Dean, "Art as Symptom. Žižek and the Ethics of Psychoanalytic Criticism," *Diacritics* 32, no. 2 (Summer 2002): 27.

15. Žižek, *The Sublime Object of Ideology*, 81.

16. Jacques Lacan, *Écrits*, trans. Bruce Fink (New York and London: W. W. Norton & Company, 2007), 194. According to the "late" Lacan who redefines the symptom as sinthome, the symptom "binds the subject to his or her jouissance" (Dean, "Art as Symptom," 27).

17. James A. Sparks, "Serial Killers," in *Extraordinary Behaviour: A Case Study Approach to Understanding Social Problems*, eds. Dennis L. Peck and Norman A. Dolch (London: Praeger, 2001), 252.

18. Peter Vronsky, *Serial Killers: The Method and Madness of Monsters* (New York: Berkley Books, 2004), 199.

19. Vronsky, *Serial Killers*, 198.

20. Vronsky, *Serial Killers*, 197.

21. Sparks, "Serial Killers," 253.

22. Andrew McConnell Stott, "Clowns on the Verge of a Nervous Breakdown: Dickens, Coulrophobia, and the Memoirs of Joseph Grimaldi," *Journal for Early Modern Cultural Studies* 12, no. 4 (Fall 2012): 5.

23. Stott, "Clowns on the Verge of a Nervous Breakdown," 3f.

24. Stott, "Clowns on the Verge of a Nervous Breakdown," 5.

25. According to the *Online Etymology Dictionary*, the term was first used in the 1980s the earliest (https://www.etymonline.com/word/coulrophobia). Consequently, defining and explaining coulrophobia, American writer and investigator, Benjamin Radford's examples of terrifying clowns date back to the 1980s (and newer). See Benjamin Radford, *Bad Clowns* (Albuquerque: University of New Mexico Press, 2016).

26. Freud defines the uncanny (Das Unheimliche) as something frightening that is familiar at the same time, existing somewhere between *heimisch* (homely) and *heimlich* (secret) and that which has been repressed returning to the surface. See Sigmund Freud, *The Uncanny* (London: Penguin Classics, 2003).

27. Chiara Tozzi, "From Horror to Ethical Responsibility: Carl Gustav Jung and Stephen King Encounter the Dark Half Within Us, Between Us and In the World," *Journal of Analytical Psychology* 65, no. 1 (2020): 223.

28. Erin Mercer, "The Difference Between World and Want: Adulthood and the Horrors of History in Stephen King's IT," *Journal of Popular Culture*, 52, no. 2 (2019): 315.

29. Stott, "Clowns on the Verge of a Nervous Breakdown," 5.

30. Stott.

31. Paola Karina Meyrer, "Would You Like a Balloon? An Analysis of the Clown in Stephen King's 'It,'" *Macapá* 8, no. 3 (2018): 247.

32. Vronsky, *Serial Killers*, 197.

33. Stephen King, *IT* (London: Hodder & Stoughton, 2017), 14.

34. Sparks, "Serial Killers," 263.

35. Sparks, 265.

36. King, *IT*, 21–22.

37. King, *IT*, 489, emphasis by SK.

38. See, for instance, Jan Nijman "Introduction: Elusive Suburbia," in *The Life of North American Suburbs: Imagined Utopias and Transitional Spaces*, ed. Jan Nijman (Toronto: University of Toronto Press, 2020), 7f.

39. King, *IT*, 525.

40. King, *IT*, 523.

41. King, *IT*, 523.

42. See, for instance, Jill Lepore, *These Truths: A History of the United States* (New York: W. W. Norton & Company, 2019).

43. King, *IT*, 3.

44. John Winthrop, "A Model of Christian Charity," in *Winthrop Papers*, volume II, 1623–1630, The Massachusetts Historical Society (Norwood: Plimpton Press, 1931 [1630]), 283.

45. Winthrop, "A Model of Christian Charity," 285.

46. Sparks, "Serial Killers," 257.

47. See Michel Foucault, "Of Other Spaces: Utopias and Heterotopias," *Architecture / Mouvement/ Continuité*, October 1984.

48. King, *IT*, 899.

49. King, *IT*, 1094.

50. For more on poststructuralist's views on the Real, see Jean Baudrillard's *Simulation* (1983) (esp. "The Hyperreal and the Imaginary") and Slavoj Žižek's *Welcome to the Desert of the Real* (2002).

51. See Julia Kristeva, *Powers of Horror: An Essay on Abjection* (New York: Columbia University Press, 1982).

52. Kristeva, *Powers of Horror*, 2f.

53. King, *IT*, 1039.

54. King, *IT*, 403–5.

55. Kristeva, *Powers of Horror*, 4.

56. Performed self is used in accordance to the definition of performativity by Erika Fischer-Lichte from the 2004 published book *The Transformative Power of Performance: A New Aesthetics*. Fischer-Lichte describes performativity as an act the creates that which it portrays but needs a willing audience that partakes in acts of performance and grants substance through co-presence.

57. We use the term "American system" as an umbrella term for political, economic, social and cultural structures, containing economic, academic, governmental and medical institutions.

58. King, *IT*, 1102.

59. Scott A. Bonn, "What Drives Our Curious Fascination with Serial Killers? Why We are Captivated by 'Celebrity Monsters' in Fact and Fiction," *Psychology Today*, October 2017, https://www.psychologytoday.com/us/blog/wicked-deeds/201710/what-drives-our-curious-fascination-serial-killers.

60. Bonn, "What Drives Our Curious Fascination with Serial Killers?"

61. Such as, for instance, *Extremely Wicked, Shockingly Evil and Vile* (2019), *Charlie Says* (2018), *Once Upon a Time . . . in Hollywood* (2019), and *Mindhunter* (2017).

62. In 2014, Clown sightings have been reported, which have seemed to be a reaction to the fourth season of *American Horror Story* (2011–), which is set in a circus (Sophie Gilbert, "How Clowns Became Terrifying: American Horror Story: Freak Show Caps Off Centuries of Suspicion towards Bozo & Co.," *The Atlantic*, October 9, 2014, https://www.theatlantic.com/entertainment/archive/2014/10/how-clowns-became-terrifying/381306/).

63. See Steven Poole, "The Great Clown Panic of 2016: 'A Volatile Mix of Fear and Contagion,'" *The Guardian*, October 31, 2016, https://www.theguardian.com/culture/2016/oct/31/the-great-clown-panic-of-2016-a-volatile-mix-of-fear-and-contagion.

64. King, *IT*, 154.

References

Bonn, Scott A. "What Drives Our Curious Fascination with Serial Killers? Why We are Captivated by 'Celebrity Monsters' in Fact and Fiction." *Psychology Today*, October 2017. https://www.psychologytoday.com/us/blog/wicked-deeds/201710/what-drives -our-curious-fascination-serial-killers.

Cantor, Paul A. *Popular Culture and the Dark Side of the American Dream: Con Men, Gangsters, Drug Lords, and Zombies*. Lexington: University Press of Kentucky, 2019.

Dean, Tim. "Art as Symptom. Žižek and the Ethics of Psychoanalytic Criticism," *Diacritics* 32, no. 2 (Summer 2002): 20–41.

Fischer-Lichte, Erika. *The Transformative Power of Performance: A New Aesthetics*. New York: Routledge, 2008.

Foucault, Michel. "Of Other Spaces: Utopias and Heterotopias." *Architecture/Mouvement/ Continuité*, October 1984.

Freud, Sigmund. *The Uncanny*. London: Penguin Classics, 2003.

King, Stephen. *IT*. London: Hodder & Stoughton, 1986.

Kneeland, Douglas E. "Suspect in Mass Deaths Is Puzzle to All." *New York Times*, January 10, 1979. https://www.nytimes.com/1979/01/10/archives/suspect-in-mass-deaths-is -puzzle-to-all-affable-driven-businessman.html.

Kristeva, Julia. *Powers of Horror: An Essay on Abjection*. New York: Columbia University Press, 1982.

Lacan, Jacques. *Écrits*. Translated by Bruce Fink. New York and London: W. W. Norton & Company, 2007.

Levine, Andrew. *The American Ideology: A Critique*. New York and London: Routledge, 2004.

Mercer, Erin, "The Difference Between World and Want: Adulthood and the Horrors of History in Stephen King's IT." *Journal of Popular Culture*, 52, no. 2 (2019): 315–29.

Meyrer, Karina Paola, "Would You Like a Balloon? An Analysis of the Clown in Stephen King's 'It.'" *Macapá* 8, no.3 (2018): 239–52.

Nijman, Jan. "Introduction: Elusive Suburbia." *The Life of North American Suburbs. Imagined Utopias and Transitional Spaces*, edited by Jan Nijman, 3–20. Toronto: University of Toronto Press, 2020.

Poole, Steven, "The Great Clown Panic of 2016: 'A Volatile Mix of Fear and Contagion.'" *The Guardian*, October 31, 2016. https://www.theguardian.com/culture/2016/oct/31 /the-great-clown-panic-of-2016-a-volatile-mix-of-fear-and-contagion.

Radford, Benjamin. *Bad Clowns*. Albuquerque: University of New Mexico Press, 2016.

Schechter, Harold. *The Serial Killer Files. The Who, What, Where, How, and Why of the World's Most Terrifying Murders*. New York: Ballantine Books, 2004.

Sparks, James A., "Serial Killers." In *Extraordinary Behaviour: A Case Study Approach to Understanding Social Problems*, edited by Dennis L. Peck and Norman A. Dolch, 252–67. London: Praeger, 2001.

Stephen King—The Official Website. https://stephenking.com/library/novel/it_inspiration .html.

Stott, Andrew McConnell, "Clowns on the Verge of a Nervous Breakdown: Dickens, Coulrophobia, and the *Memoirs of Joseph Grimaldi.*" *Journal for Early Modern Cultural Studies* 12, no. 4 (Fall 2012): 3–25.

Tozzi, Chiara. "From Horror to Ethical Responsibility: Carl Gustav Jung and Stephen King Encounter the Dark Half Within Us, Between Us and In the World," *Journal of Analytical Psychology* 65, no. 1 (2020): 219–34.

Vronsky, Peter. *Serial Killers: The Method and Madness of Monsters*. New York: Berkley Books, 2004.

Winthrop, John. "A Model of Christian Charity." In *Winthrop Papers*, Volume II, 1623–1630, The Massachusetts Historical Society, 282–95. Norwood: Plimpton Press, 1931 [1630].

Žižek, Slavoj. *Enjoy Your Symptom! Jacques Lacan in Hollywood and Out*. Second edition. New York and London: Routledge, 2008.

Žižek, Slavoj. *How to Read Lacan*. London: Granta Books, 2006.

Žižek, Slavoj. *The Sublime Object of Ideology*. London and New York: Verso, 1989.

Žižek, Slavoj. *Welcome to the Desert of the Real*. London and New York: Verso, 2002.

Chapter 11

SEND IN THE CLOWNS

Pennywise and the Monstrousness of Colonialism

SHANNON S. SHAW

In the newest movie adaptation of Stephen King's, *IT*, the adult voice of one of the seven members of the Losers' Club, Mike Hanlon (Isaiah Mustafa), concedes that "people want to believe that they are what they choose to remember: the good stuff, the moments, the places, the people we all hold on to." He continues, ominously, "but, sometimes . . . sometimes . . . we are what we wish we could forget."[1] This sentiment is fitting in a narrative based on the King novel, because as Regina Hansen writes, Stephen King's narratives "are well known for their depiction of the terror and wonder of childhood."[2] In this particular story, King uses a quaint, all-American town as a backdrop for murderous horror and absurdity as a group of seven preteens fight off a shape-shifting killer clown—six of them to return years later to defeat it once again. Undeniably, as adults they realize that the nostalgia for the past that comes with adulthood isn't always summer sleepovers and carnival rides. In the case of the Losers, as memories of their childhood flood back upon their return to Derry, they realize the extent of the horror they experienced as children and that the monster clown has a long history of terrorizing people in their town. Just as Derry is romanticized as a quintessential representation of harmony, the common zeitgeist of American exceptionalism, specifically during the mid-to-late twentieth century, created a mirage of peace and prosperity. Despite occasional upsets such as the unrest during the civil rights movement and the Vietnam War, this exceptionalism has been branded and rebranded using revisionist history and nostalgia tropes. Furthermore, it was in the twentieth century that the nickname for the United States became simply "America." Disregarding the fact that the Americas encompasses the entire landmass of North, Central, and South America, the United States—once it began colonizing lands beyond its own shores—claimed the name America.[3]

Given the national habit of usurping land designations and nomenclature, using imperialistic tactics of claiming territories outside of the Union, and revising history to hide such practices, Mike's words have a much broader implication and hint at a deeper darkness than that of the terror the Losers' Club experiences. The larger significance of the monster that is Pennywise lies in the darkness embedded in the horror of colonialism and the clowning spectacle of the American Dream: ultimately, underneath the candy apples, cotton candy, and capitalism, America is "what we wish we could forget."

DESTRUCTION OF COLONIALISM: THE TERROR BEGAN WITH A BOAT

Much like the true origin stories of the United States, King begins the journey of the Losers—Mike, as well as Bill Denbrough, Ben Hanscom, Beverly Marsh, Richie Tozier, Eddie Kaspbrak, and Stan Uris—with an apropos introduction: "The terror . . . began . . . with a boat."[4] It is fitting that King begins the novel with a parallel of the birth of the "New World." Indeed, the genocide of the original inhabitants of North America began with a boat. As first-contact narratives—stories of Europeans' first encounters with the Indigenous people of the "New World"—circulated in Europe and Great Britain, diseases such as smallpox, measles, and influenza followed suit among the approximately 60.5 million Indigenous people in the Americas at the time.[5] Additionally, these epidemics that initiated the reign of colonial terror was not simply an act of ignorance on the part of the European colonizers. Evidence suggests it was used by some as a form of biological warfare against the unsuspecting natives.[6] As Tricia E. Logan outlines, the monstrosity of colonization is one that would see the utter decimation of entire cultural and ecological systems— the "total destruction of biological, physical, and cultural spheres of life, destruction of the religious order, obliteration of language, the mass murder of all people, and destruction of the land."[7] Furthermore, the terror of slavery began with a boat when slavers' ships docked off the coast of West Africa to kidnap men, women, and children and sell them to white landowners in North America in 1619. These boats carried over 12 million Africans to the New World—a period of time in the slave trade known as the Middle Passage— constituting a transit of unimaginable horror, as approximately two million people died during the span of these cross-Atlantic journeys. The public reckoning of this horrendous history and the collective trauma of the past, particularly in the United States, has been bubbling to the surface since the passing of the Thirteenth Amendment. Indeed, colonial terror did not end with slavery, nor did it end after Indigenous tribes were given land on which to settle. The collective trauma of these acts perpetrated in the name of control, expansion, prosperity, and ironically, freedom weren't just horrors of the past best left *in* the past. Rather, they have had far reaching consequences that, if left unresolved, fester beneath the surface, only to reemerge and begin the cycle of violence all over again. As Erin Mercer writes, "King's novel suggests that the past is an inescapable force within that present that the sins of the father are to be forever revisited upon their children."[8] The story of It, then, becomes a metaphor for this cycle: horrible violence, revising the past (nostalgia), forgetting, and finally the recurrence of violence. Mercer's argument, undoubtedly, is a micro-examination of the novel and the characters' journeys through the town's and their personal history. However, a macro-examination is inescapable—and, in fact, necessary—when considering the scope of the damage colonialism has had in the United States.

In the case of the terror inflicted upon the town of Derry, that boat was a paper vessel made to journey "bravely through the treacherous whirlpools" and storm waters flowing down the sidewalk-lined neighborhood in 1957.[9] As the boat drifts into a storm drain, George—the little brother of Bill Denbrough—encounters Pennywise the Dancing Clown in a situation incongruous to what George knows about clowns even at the age of six: they do not generally inhabit storm drains. This incongruity contributes to George's reluctance to retrieve his boat from Pennywise. After all, he expresses, he is "not supposed to take stuff from strangers."[10] Yet, after Pennywise introduces himself with "the kind of smile you just had to answer," and offers to return the boat along with a shiny red balloon, George's fears are appeased, and he proceeds to reach into the storm drain to retrieve his boat and booty.[11] George's initial fears, of course, come to fruition when Pennywise, the killer clown, rips little George's arm off, killing him within minutes. George's apprehension and subsequent death foreshadows the horror the clown inflicts on the town as much as it represents the gullibility of the masses to believe in the ideal of American exceptionalism and ignore the truth of the past as long as it means mass consumption remains intact. Ultimately, It's concealment as Pennywise the clown and his promise to George of more booty to consume distracts from the horrible truth of the clown intent on inflicting pain, torment, and death. In this instance, little George's arm is what is ultimately consumed.

When looking at the monstrous violence that It inflicts on the town and the parallels to colonial violence inflicted on the Indigenous populations of the Americas, it may be easy to interpret Pennywise as a curse set upon Derry by the victims of the atrocities inflicted by white European colonizers upon arrival. Indeed, as increasing numbers of early settlers flooded into North America in the sixteenth century, they experienced a similar tactic to the one Pennywise uses on George. The promise of trade and protection turned to betrayal, murder, and genocide. It would be fitting to interpret Pennywise as a manifestation of a man-eating monster come to seek revenge for the horrors inflicted upon the original inhabitants of the land. As Mercer argues, "The monstrousness of the entity that haunts Derry is inextricably linked to the monstrousness of Derry itself, which is racist, homophobic, misogynistic, and defined by violence."[12] Pulling the focus out, one cannot deny that the monstrousness of this fictional town follows the template for the monstrousness of the colonial endeavor: to eradicate or assimilate those who stand in the way of the advancement of colonization.

Subsequently, when trying to disassemble the colonial effects, the connections King makes to Native lore take on a somewhat appropriative tone when he deliberately includes a conversation between the members of the Losers' Club discussing a figure from Native lore that Bill calls a "Glamour": "other races and cultures at other times had different words for it, but they all meant the same thing."[13] However, the premise that Pennywise is a Native boogieman terrorizing this all-American town as punishment for the ultimate sin of the United States—no matter how justified it feels—still places the blame on Indigenous cultures and leaves room to interpret Native Americans as "savages," perpetuating the connection between Indigenous people and monstrosity. This interpretation has a long history when it comes to the subordination of Indigenous culture, rendering this literary interpretation of a fictional novel rooted inescapably in history. For example, as Gregory Smithers explains, "Europeans and Euroamericans accused Native Americans of cannibalistic practices to justify colonial attempts to extinguish Indigenous communities and to objectify Native people."[14] Furthermore, these tropes were used as justification of the systematic extermination of the people and their customs: "the only effective way to deal with Indigenous cannibals was to annihilate the problem."[15] When examining the conversation between the Losers' Club using this perspective, it's implied that the monster terrorizing the town has been there all along and that most cultures have their own representations of the evil entity, thereby removing the onus of the terror from the shoulders of the true perpetrators of the terror: white European settlers—evil, thy name is colonialism. Perhaps the resurgence of It every twenty-seven years, rather than being a curse, is in actuality a self-inflicted manifestation of the main function of colonialism and humanity's deprivation, which ironically, is to consume.

THE LOSERS' CLUB: MISFITS AND MARGINALIZED

It is only after Georgie's death that the Losers' Club is formed. Each of the characters, dealing with their own traumas and oddities, bond over their sense of otherness and their awareness of the violence that lurks beneath the surface of their picturesque town. While traversing the landscape of teenage-hood and Derry, the Losers' Club discovers the disturbing history of their quaint all-American town. Upon the settlement of the area that would become Derry, a group of inhabitants vanish, much like the settlers of Roanoke, Virginia, in 1590. From that point on, tragedy after tragedy befalls the town in a cyclical pattern. Each one of these tragedies, the children discover, is orchestrated by an entity of evil that manifests itself in many different ways throughout many generations who become, "haunted by [their] own violent history that returns" every twenty-seven years.[16] In the case of the children of Derry, the evil they call "It" presents itself visually as the archetypal symbol of tomfoolery in the figure of the clown, all the while simultaneously, by way of its brutality, forcing the protagonists to confront the absurdity of this juxtaposition of happiness and monstrosity.

This juxtaposition that lies at the heart of the American mythos is the result of decades of revisionist history, the inception of which can be traced from the myth of the first Thanksgiving to the little-discussed Japanese internment camps during World War II and the "Lost Cause"[17] narratives that gained traction during the civil rights movements of the 1950s and 1960s when the last of the aging former Confederate soldiers began to die. In an attempt to maintain white supremacy—as immigrants were pouring into the growing nation during the late nineteenth and early twentieth centuries—these myths proliferated American dogma.

In parallel to a national reconciliation between the American mythos and the truth of the horrors of American history, each of the Losers, bringing their own fears to their encounters with Pennywise, have to reconcile the juxtaposition of their picturesque town with the evil that lies under the surface. One of the first stories young Mike ("Mikey") Hanlon learns of the horror in Derry, and that is emblematic of true American history, is that of the burning of the Black Spot, a warehouse-turned-bar and hangout established by Black soldiers stationed on a base in town in the 1930s. Lying in a hospital bed, Mikey's father describes the incident: "they came in their white sheets early that November and cooked themselves a barbecue."[18] With this line, there is, undoubtedly, no need for further description. The monstrousness of the burning of the Black Spot is as common to American history as apple pie.

With the story of the Black Spot, King invokes the racist horrors inflicted upon minority communities throughout the nineteenth and twentieth centuries: the 1868 massacre in Opelousas, Louisiana, for example; the Elain massacre of 1919 in Arkansas; the Tulsa massacre of 1921 in Oklahoma; and the many more incidents of terror and murder inflicted on Black communities throughout our nation's history. However, in his telling, Mikey's father admits to seeing something inexplicable to the situation at hand: Although the fire was started by members of the local Derry KKK—the Maine Legion of White Decency—Mikey's father describes seeing a giant bird in the sky above the men fleeing in their white sheets: "It was big . . . maybe sixty feet from wingtip to wingtip. It was the size of a Japanese Zero. [. . .] It swooped down and grabbed the last man up. Got him right by the sheet, it did."[19]

For Mikey, hearing the story about the giant bird snatching up one of the Legion members at the burning of the Black Spot brought back a memory he had all but forgotten. In the spring of 1958, Mikey's dad had instructed him to explore the remains of an old ironworks building that had exploded in 1908. In Mikey's exploration, he discovers a giant bird, with "the *spirit* of Rodan," nesting in the collapsed cellarhold. The reference to Rodan is one of the many pop-culture references in the novel. In their encounters with It, the monster often manifests as the popular creatures from the horror flicks of the 1950s—Boris Karloff's mummy, the creature from the Black Lagoon, and Godzilla's giant flying foe, to name a few—each of which is a representation of a young American teen's fears. After a tense standoff with the bird, in which Mikey gets trapped in a collapsed smokestack, the young teen finally makes his escape "like Roy Rodgers showing off for Dale Evans on his way back from the corral with Pat Brady and the rest of the buckaroos."[20] By 1986 standards, these references would elicit nostalgia for readers. Although these particular horror references might have produced a fright with 1950s audiences, King's 1980s reader might have described those monsters as campy, especially when measured against his other horror stories. However, while It initially manifests as a creature from classic horror flicks that 1980s, cynical moviegoers might scoff at, he ultimately morphs into something that few would mock—for example, a teen's dead brother who was murdered by his abusive stepfather.[21] For Mikey, the giant bird he sees at the ironworks rubble is terrifying, to be sure, but to know the monster was present at such a horrific massacre as the Black Spot arson only amplifies his terror. Just as the youth of Derry have to reconcile the juxtaposition of the campy creature from the Black Lagoon morphing into the young victim of filicide, Mikey has to reconcile his encounter with a B-movie creature and the horror of racism in his quaint little town. Yet, the impulse to know the full truth is ever-present for him, as he recounts, "I didn't want to hear [the truth], but I *had* to hear. [. . .] As I suppose Lot's wife had to turn back and look at the destruction of Sodom."[22] In this moment, as his father tells him the story, Mikey realizes he has to face Derry's racist past in order to fight the monster that's been plaguing the town for centuries. Similarly, mitigating the damage caused by colonialism can only be accomplished—the monster defeated—when the horrors of colonialism are confronted.

Racism against the Black community and Native peoples and the systematic obliteration of their cultures and identities aren't the only sins committed by colonialism. Just as white hegemonic power is pervasive in colonized lands, so too is male supremacy. As Suzanne Spencer-Wood explains, colonizers brought their "patriarchal gender and sexual colonization" with them to the new world: "Women who deviated from the sexually modest domestic ideal were considered wanton, lascivious, or dangerous witches threatening the patriarchal social order."[23] Given that the "social institution of patriarchy was intrinsic to all aspects of European colonialism," the evolution of this patriarchal power is evident in Beverly's father Al Marsh. The relationship between Beverly and her father illustrates what Spencer-Wood describes as the "hegemonic Western gender ideology of subordinate women dominated by superior, public men."[24] During a scene in which Al thinks someone has been spying on Beverly in the bathroom after hearing her scream—"There was concern in his face but it was a predatory concern"—his possessiveness is so conditioned into Beverly that she capitulates to his demand to come closer and receive her punishment regardless of her innocence: "if the two of them had been standing on the edge of a high cliff and he had told her to step off—right *now*, girl—her instinctive obedience would almost certainly have carried her over the edge before her rational mind could have intervened."[25] Additionally, much of the abuse her father doles out is masked as concern for her future domestic skills: "I worry about you . . . I don't think you're ever going to grow up, Beverly. You go out running around, you don't do hardly any of the housework around here, you can't cook, you can't sew . . . I worry."[26] His words of worry are followed by a slap to the buttocks, a hit on her arm, and a punch in the stomach. In this moment, Al Marsh justifies his abuse by espousing his disappointment in Beverly's domestic skills. The most troubling aspect of Al Marsh's control, however, is when his domination over his daughter goes farther than his expectations of domesticity, morphing into an obsession with Beverly becoming a woman. Already prone to abusing Beverly, her father exhibits "sexual possessiveness over his daughter" as she begins puberty.[27] In the aforementioned scene, Al chastises Beverly while standing in a blood-covered bathroom in which the red stains are invisible to him. Indeed, the reason for Beverly's scream in the first place wasn't a peeping Tom but a balloon ascending from the sink drain and popping, covering the bathroom in blood that is only visible to her. This is Beverly's first encounter with the terror that It can bring, and the incident leaves her with an even more disturbing fear: "that when her menstrual blood arrives there will be a new form of threat to face from her father."[28] In Beverly's encounter with It as an adult, her fears are compounded when they finally take on a sexual tone. It, in the guise of her father, says, "*I beat you because I wanted to FUCK you, Bevvie, that's all I wanted to do, I wanted to FUCK you.*"[29]

Pennywise manifests as not only the witch from the childhood folktale that scared her the most, "Hansel and Gretel," but also as her father in a clown costume donning the coonskin cap of the iconic American frontiersman, Davy Crockett, conqueror of the Wild West. While Crockett is remembered by the epithet "King of the Wild Frontier," and by having died single-handedly fighting off a dozen Mexican soldiers while defending the Alamo, analysis of evidence suggests that this is another American myth.[30] Instead, it has been reported that Crockett surrendered and was subsequently executed by Santa Anna's men. King's nod to Crockett's coonskin cap isn't necessarily a reference to the myth itself; rather, it is an illustration of the mythologizing that takes place in the retelling of the history of the United States, revising narratives to obfuscate behaviors that could be construed as unexceptional and, in many cases, horrific. For Beverly, the significance of seeing her father years after his death is the real terror of the situation. Indeed, outfitting Beverly's abusive father with Crockett's famous coonskin cap conflates the American icon with the monstrousness of her childhood horror and abusive sexual possession. Consequently, by subtly gesturing towards another pop-culture figure from the 1950s, as well as an icon of American expansion, King subverts the myth of American exceptionalism.

One of the most significant features of colonialism—in addition to the destruction of Indigenous people and culture—is the destruction of the land that is being colonized. From Puritan notions of the prosperity gospel and Puritans' beliefs that they were chosen by God to possess the "new" land, to the notion of manifest destiny, American ideology has largely centered around the entitlement to land at any cost. These sentiments are evidenced in *IT* by the circumstances surrounding Derry's formation. Founded as a logging community, and thus as an extension of an industry responsible for massive deforestation as a means toward economic development, the pictur-esque town of Derry certainly illustrates this notion of colonial destruction of the land. An adult Mike describes this in terms of sexual assault, remark-ing that the lumber barons "raped the woods . . . it was their [townspeople's] grandfathers and great-grand fathers who actually spread the legs of the forests north of Derry and Bangor and raped those green-gowned virgins with their axes and peaveys."[31] Consequently, Derry's legacy of destruction manifests when Pennywise transforms into the iconic pop-culture character that represents this ideal: Paul Bunyan, a figure who becomes the stuff of nightmares for Richie. This American and Canadian "fakelore"[32] character is a famous lumberjack first utilized by an advertising agent for a campaign for the Red River Logging Company and has become as much a part of the myths of American history as the Pocahontas and John Smith marriage.[33] What's more, he's also an apropos representation of capitalism run amok: the devastation of land and ecosystems for the sake of expansion and profit.[34] Of course, deforestation wasn't (and isn't) the only destructive land practice the colonizers brought with them to the new world. Settlers also introduced new plants and animals to the Americas that, in many instances, caused exponential destruction to native landscapes and ecologies. For example, Andrew C. Isenberg and Lawrence H. Kessler explain, "insect blights crippled settlers' attempts to develop agricultural economies in Hawai'i based on introduced coffee, citrus, and mulberry trees, as well as wheat, cotton, and tobacco."[35] Furthermore, settlers eliminated crop diversity by "[plowing] up native grasses and [planting] wheat, unintentionally transforming the landscape to facilitate the spread of an indigenous pest, the Rocky Mountain locust."[36] As a consequence of this practice of agrarian monoculture geared toward maximizing profit, several environmental catastrophes can be traced back to the ecological disruptions of settler-colonialism, including a plague of locusts in the late 1800s and the Dust Bowl phenomenon of the 1930s.

In *IT*, King emphasizes the noxious effects on the land caused by settlement, development, and growth as the Losers' Club becomes more familiar with the Barrens and the history of the town. After successfully building a dam in a tributary stream connected to the main river that runs through the town, the Losers' Club gets chastised by the local deputy, Mr. Nell, for "paddlin around in Derry's pee an [sic] old wash-water" and backing up the Derry drainage system.[37] He explains one part of the system "carries solid human waste—shit" and gets dumped into the Kenduskeag river, while the other "carries grey water—water flushed from toilets or run down drains" gets dumped in the streams in which the Losers were spending much of their time.[38] Later, Ben feels "a dull sort of helpless anger" while thinking about the drainage system and the damage it has caused: "Someone takes a crap uptown and here's where it comes out. [. . .] Once there had probably been fish in this river. [. . .] Your chances of catching a used wad of toilet paper would be better" than catching a trout.[39] Later, as an adult Bill is standing—for the first time in twenty-seven years—on the edge of the Kenduskeag he remembers how the town of Derry exemplifies the destruction of the land: "the smell was the same, even with the dump gone. The heavy perfume of growing things at the height of their spring strut did not mask the smell of waste and human offal. It was faint but unmistakable. A smell of corruption; a whiff of the underside."[40]

DEFEATING THE MONSTER OF COLONIALISM

It is in this guise of the clown that the horrors of the colonial reign of terror are embodied and the trauma of colonial destruction seeks payback, slaughtering the town's most vulnerable members. King situates this revenge in the nostalgic Noman Rockwell-esque setting of Derry and uses a classic emblem of childhood fancy to represent the ruse that was the Rockwellian image. Meanwhile, under the surface of this picturesque Americana, the truths of colonialism boil and Pennywise consumes the archetype of American idealism: willful innocence. Ultimately, the performativity of the ideal that is the American Dream functions as a veil under which to hide the real terror. It is altogether fitting that the curse of the town of Derry manifests itself as a clown, representing the absurdity of the farce of the American zeitgeist.

This farce, it seems, is perpetuated by a compulsory need to forget—to forget the transgressions of the past or deny their significance. Indeed, the main culprit that allows It to terrorize the town of Derry for so long is not only the townspeople's willful innocence but their willful ignorance. As King writes, "In Derry such forgetting of tragedy and disaster was almost an art."[41] Beverly experiences this when local bully/sadist Henry Bowers attacks her in the middle of town with the intent to kill her. Neighbors who witness the attack either drive away in fright or quietly go inside their house, leaving Beverly at the mercy of a man intent on harming her. Furthermore, the long list of tragedies and missing children is generally unknown to the townspeople—aside from the occasional curfew—or goes unspoken, as Mike notes, "even if you load them up with booze."[42] This denial of the monstrousness that terrorizes the town, along with forgetting past horrors, parallels the same denial and lack of acknowledgment of the atrocities that colonization has inflicted and, according to Logan, allows these atrocities to continue. Furthermore, it is through this ignorance and refusal to acknowledge the horrors of the town—and more broadly, the country—that the people of Derry give power to the monster, allowing It to kill over and over again:

They let it happen, they always do, and things quiet down, things go on,
It . . . It . . .
(sleeps)
sleeps . . . or hibernates like a bear . . . and then it starts again, and
they know . . . people know . . . they know it has to be so It can be.[43]

At last, the Losers realize the truth, as Bill stutters, "*Duh-Duh-Derry is It.*"[44] As with the country in which it is situated, the monstrousness that has been haunting Derry is not a curse, nor is it some foreign entity from outer space come to wreak havoc on unsuspecting humans. Instead, the monster that lives to torment and consume the people of Derry is the people themselves: Derry is the monster—in other words, the call is coming from inside the house.

In the end, aided by their belief in the story of It, it is Bill, the intrepid writer, who slays the beast by crushing It's heart in his hands. Earlier in the novel, a much younger and more naïve Bill questions the power of stories: "Why does a story have to be socio-anything? Politics . . . culture . . . history . . . aren't those natural ingredients in any story, if it's told well? I mean . . . I mean . . . can't you guys let a story be a *story?*"[45] Ultimately, however, the story of It illustrates that a story is never just a story. It's a living creature that can be deadly as much as it can give life to words. Ignoring or forgetting the power of stories, as the Losers discover, can have dire and long-lasting consequences. Similarly, ignoring or forgetting the power and destruction of colonialism will allow the destruction to continue.

Notes

1. *IT: Chapter Two*, directed by Andy Muschietti (2019; Toronto, Ontario: Warner Bros Pictures, 2019), video.

2. Regina Hanson, "Stephen King's IT and Dreamcatcher on Screen: Hegemonic White Masculinity and Nostalgia for Underdog Boyhood," *Science Fiction Film and Television* (2017): 161.

3. Daniel Immerwahr speaks to the name change in his book, *How to Hide an Empire: A History of the Greater United States* (New York: Farrar, Straus, and Giroux, 2019), but he explains it more succinctly in a 2019 *Mother Jones* article entitled "When Did the U.S. Start Calling Itself 'America,' Anyway?"

4. King, 3.

5. Alexander Koch, Chris Brierley, Mark Maslin, Simon L. Lewis, "Earth System Impacts of the European Arrival and Great Dying in the Americas after 1492," *Quaternary Science Reviews*, no. 207 (2019): 13–36.

6. Author Peter d'Errico compiled an index of microfilm images of letters written by Lord Jefferey Amherst, a British general fighting native tribes in Pontiac's Rebellion. In postscripts from the letters, both to and from his officers, Amherst discusses using small-pox infested blankets to infect the natives and diminish their populations.

7. Tricia E Logan, "Memory, Erasure, and National Myth." In *Colonial Genocide in Indigenous North America*, eds. Alexander Laban Hinton, Andrew Woolford, and Jeff Benvenuto (Durham, NC: Duke University Press, 2014), 154.

8. Erin Mercer, "The Difference Between World and Want: Adulthood and the Horrors of History in Stephen King's *IT*," *Journal of Popular Culture* 52, no. 2 (2019): 319.

9. King, 3.

10. King, 14.

11. King, 14.

12. Mercer, 324

13. King, 683.

14. Gregory D Smithers, "Rituals of Consumption: Cannibalism and Native American Oral Traditions in Southeastern North America," in *To Feast on Us as Their Prey: Cannibalism and the Early Modern Atlantic*, ed. Rachel B. Herrmann (Fayetteville: University of Arkansas Press, 2019), 23–24.

15. Smithers, 24.

16. Mercer, 319.

17. The "Lost Cause" is a movement that attempted (and, for the most part, succeeded) to whitewash the history of the South's intentions in the Civil War, portraying their fight to maintain the practice of slavery as a just cause and the actions of the confederate army as heroic. A resurgence of this narrative occurred in the 1950s and 60s and contributes to the current continuation of the myth.

18. King, 469.

19. King, 477.

20. King, 287.

21. King, 263, 259, respectively.

22. King, 477.

23. Suzanne Spencer-Wood, "Feminist Theorizing of Patriarchal Colonialism, Power Dynamics, and Social Agency Materialized in Colonial Institutions," *International Journal of Historical Archaeology* 20, no. 3 (September 1, 2016): 478.

24. Spencer-Wood, 479

25. King, 401.

26. King, 402.

27. Mercer, 323.

28. Mercer, 323.

29. King, 580.

30. Michael Lind, "The Death of David Crockett," *Wilson Quarterly* 22, no. 1 (1998) 50–57, search.ebscohost.com/login.aspx?direct=true&db=edsjsr&AN=edsjsr.40260491 &site=eds-live&scope=site.

31. King, 896.

32. Richard M. Dorson coined the term "fakelore" in his 1950 essay titled "Folklore and Fake Lore" and cited Paul Bunyan stories as a prime example of the sort of tales that present themselves as genuine folklore.

33. Pocahontas never married John Smith, as the Disney movie would have audiences believe. Instead, she married John Rolfe around the age of seventeen or eighteen.

34. For more on this, one only has to look at the systematic eradication of the mountain lion population of North America in the early twentieth century. While the logging industry destroyed their habitat, many states, and eventually the federal government, put bounties on mountain lions in an effort to protect livestock. This led to the near extinction of the mountain lion within a one hundred-year period.

35. Andrew C. Isenberg and Lawrence H. Kessler, "Settler Colonialism and the Environmental History of the North American West," *Journal of the West* 56, no. 4 (2017): 59.

36. Isenberg, Kessler, 59. The Rocky Mountain locust is one of two species found in North America and typically spanned the western portion of the United States; however, states such as Main, Vermont, Minnesota, and Missouri all experienced plagues.

37. King, 328.

38. King, 327.

39. King, 365.

40. King, 607.

41. King, 4–5.

42. King, 158.

43. King, 987.

44. King, 987.

45. King, 128.

References

d'Errico, Peter. "Jeffery Amherst and Smallpox Blankets: Lord Jeffery Amherst's Letters Discussing Germ Warfare against American Indians." University of Massachusetts, December 30, 2020. http://people.umass.edu/derrico/amherst/lord_jeff.html.

Hanson, Regina. "Stephen King's IT and Dreamcatcher on Screen: Hegemonic White Masculinity and Nostalgia for Underdog Boyhood." *Science Fiction Film and Television* (2017): 161–76.

Isenberg, Andrew C., and Lawrence H. Kessler. "Settler Colonialism and the Environmental History of the North American West." *Journal of the West* 56, no. 4 (2017): 57–66.

IT: Chapter Two. Directed by Andy Muschietti, performances by Jessica Chastain, James McAvoy, Bill Hader, Isaiah Mustafa, Jay Ryan, James Ransone, Andy Bean, and Bill Skarsgård. Warner Brothers, 2019.

King, Stephen. *IT*. New York: Scribner, 2019.

Koch, Alexander; Brierley, Chris; Maslin, Mark M.; Lewis, Simon L. "Earth System Impacts of the European Arrival and Great Dying in the Americas after 1492." *Quaternary Science Reviews*, no. 207 (2019): 13–36.

Logan, Tricia E. "Memory, Erasure, and National Myth." In *Colonial Genocide in Indigenous North America*, edited by Alexander Laban Hinton, Andrew Woolford, and Jeff Benvenuto, 149–65. North Carolina: Duke University Press, 2014.

Mercer, Erin. "The Difference Between World and Want: Adulthood and the Horrors of History in Stephen King's IT." *Journal of Popular Culture* 52, no. 2 (2019): 315–29. doi:10.1111/jpcu.12786.

Silko, Leslie Marmon. *Storyteller*. New York: Arcade Publishing, 1981.

Smithers, Gregory D. "Rituals of Consumption: Cannibalism and Native American Oral Traditions in Southeastern North America." In *To Feast on Us as Their Prey: Cannibalism and the Early Modern Atlantic*, edited by Rachel B. Herrmann, 19–35. Fayetteville: University of Arkansas Press, 2019.

Spencer-Wood, Suzanne. "Feminist Theorizing of Patriarchal Colonialism, Power Dynamics, and Social Agency Materialized in Colonial Institutions." *International Journal of Historical Archaeology* 20, no. 3 (September 1, 2016): 477–91. doi: 10.1007/s10761-016-0356-3.

ABOUT THE CONTRIBUTORS

Amylou Ahava is a PhD student at Texas Tech University who is studying American horror literature and film with an emphasis on disability studies. Since 2009, she has taught English to all ages and levels, but in 2015 she switched primarily to educating undergraduates. Recent conference/publications include a conference paper for *ICFA* entitled "Wheelchairs and Horror Films: Breaking Disability Tropes in *The Texas Chainsaw Massacre* (1974)." Future publications will focus on the use of twins and enfreakment in the film *Basket Case* (1982) and another paper will look at the connection between vampirism and chronic illnesses in the film *My Heart Can't Beat Unless You Tell It To* (2020). Aside from teaching, Amylou also currently writes for a horror-focused website called *Nightmarish Conjurings* in which she creates original reviews or analysis on films and books.

Jeff Ambrose is a PhD candidate in literature and criticism at the Indiana University of Pennsylvania. He holds an MA in literature from the University of Vermont and a BA in literature from Chestnut Hill College. His scholarly interests include the Harry Potter series, works of horror across all media in the last one hundred years, and video game narratives. Before pursuing his PhD, Jeff taught for eight years at Delaware County Community College, including creating a course on the Harry Potter novels. He has presented for years at Chestnut Hill College's academic Harry Potter conference, and he gave a panel on horror in Harry Potter at the Zenkaikon pop culture convention in 2016. As for Stephen King, Jeff is proud to have helped in teaching a course on the films of Stephen King's works while a graduate student at the University of Vermont with noted King scholar Tony Magistrale.

Fernando Gabriel Pagnoni Berns (PhD in arts, PhD candidate in history) works as professor at the Universidad de Buenos Aires (UBA)—Facultad de Filosofía y Letras (Argentina). He teaches courses on international horror film. He is the director of a research group on horror cinema, Grite. He has authored a book about Spanish horror TV series *Historias para no Dormir* (Universidad de Cádiz, 2020) and has edited books on Frankenstein bicentennial (Universidad de Buenos Aires), director James Wan (McFarland & Company, 2021), and the Italian *giallo* film (University Press of Mississippi, forthcoming). He is currently editing a book on horror comics.

Daniel P. Compora, PhD, is an associate professor who teaches a number of literature courses, including folklore, science fiction and fantasy literature, and detective stories. He has published in the areas of folklore, popular culture, and distance learning. He is regarded as an expert on Dog Lady Island, a local urban legend from his hometown of Monroe, Michigan, which he has researched since 1987. His most recent publications include "Undead America: The Emergence of the Modern Zombie in American Culture" and "Ghostly Attractions: The Ghostlore of Television, College Campuses, and Tourism." His forthcoming works include an extensive history of Ohio literature in the *Dictionary of Midwest Literature*, volume II, and a book chapter on the mythicizing of Clark Kent in the television series *Smallville*.

Penny Crofts, PhD, is an associate professor in the Faculty of Law, University of Technology Sydney. She is an international expert on criminal law, models of culpability, and the legal regulation of the sex industry. Her research is cross-disciplinary, drawing upon a range of historical, philosophical, empirical, and literary materials to enrich her analysis of the law. Her research is in the area of socio-legal studies coalescing around issues of justice in criminal law in practice and theory, and makes a distinctive contribution to critical evaluations of criminal legal models of culpability and enforcement. Her analysis of criminal legal models of wickedness has contributed to a jurisprudence of blameworthiness. Penny has published extensively on representations of wickedness and responsibility in law and horror. Penny is currently researching a major project entitled *Rethinking Institutional Culpability: Criminal Law, Philosophy, and Horror*.

Keith Currie is a writer, poet, and freelance academic based in Birmingham, UK. Between 2003 and 2013, he studied at Essex University, gaining a BA in philosophy and literature, an MA in literature, specializing in modernism and postmodernism, and a PhD in literature. His thesis examined critiques of the acts of writing and reading in the works of the twentieth-century French writer Georges Bataille. Keith has a diverse array of interests, encompassing philosophy, critical theory, ethnography, transgressive fiction, literatures of the fantastic, and the conventions and tropes of the fantasy and horror genres. Accordingly, his textual critiques are multi-disciplinary in nature, and endeavor to situate the text(s) in question within wider cultural and discursive contexts. During the course of his PhD studies, Keith presented papers at two interdisciplinary conferences, both of which resulted in publication.

Erin Giannini, PhD, is an independent scholar. She has served as an editor and contributor at PopMatters, and her recent work has focused on portrayals of and industrial contexts around corporate culture on television, including a monograph on corporatism in the works of Joss Whedon (McFarland & Company, 2017). She has also published and presented work on religion, socioeconomics, production culture, and technology in series such as *Supernatural, Dollhouse, iZombie,* and *Angel,* and is currently co-editing a collection on the novel (and series) *Good Omens.*

Whitney S. May is a doctoral student in the American Studies program at the University of Texas and a lecturer for the Department of English at Texas State University. Her primary research interests include the Gothic and nineteenth-century horror literature, as well as the history of capitalism and its carnivalesque representations in horror fiction and popular culture. Her related work appears in *Gothic Studies, Supernatural Studies,* and *The Edgar Allan Poe Review,* as well as in *Religion, Culture, and the Monstrous: Of Gods and Monsters* (2021) and *Circus Space: The Big Top on the Big Screen* (2020), both from Lexington Books.

Diganta Roy is an assistant professor in the Department of English in Falakata College in West Bengal. He has completed his post-graduation in English from Jadavpur University Kolkata. His areas of academic interest include horror literature, popular fiction and Gothic Romanticism. He has written an anthology of poems titled *Pen at the Pollen,* which has been published by Writer's Workshop in Kolkata. His upcoming publication includes a chapter in an edited anthology titled "Retelling the Holocaust with Children: A Pedagogic Study of Stephen King's *Apt Pupil* and Jane Yolen's *The Devil's Arithmetic,*" to be published as part of Routledge's *Popular Culture and World Politics* series.

Hannah Lina Schneeberger holds a degree in German literature and Media Studies from the University of Cologne. Her academic work focuses on the hauntings of digital worlds, the construction of queer time in space in media, and early twentieth-century German literature and film.

Shannon S. Shaw teaches early American literature and composition at Texas State University where she received her MA in literature and is pursuing a second MA in sustainability studies. Her research focuses on postcolonialism and reexamining early texts from before and after the colonization of the Americas. Additionally, she focuses on feminist rebellions in nineteenth- and twentieth-century American literature and how they have influenced current feminist culture. She has given several presentations on such subjects, including presentations on the feminist Transcendentalism of Margaret Fuller, the Beat rebellion of Diane de Prima, the nature of cat-calling culture, the Transcendentalist rebellion of serial killer Aileen Wuornos, and the need to revise the early American literary canon.

Maria Wiegel holds a master's degree in North American Studies from the University of Cologne where she also works as a research assistant. Her current research focuses on the depiction of the 1960s in American literature published after 9/11. She is especially interested in paranoia and surveillance, a topic explored in her article "'Tea first. Then war!'—Alan Ayckbourn's *Neighbourhood Watch* (2011): A Reflection on Great Britain's 21st Century Internal Security Policy and its Citizens' Need for Safety?" (*Cultural Intertexts*, 2017), and in her forthcoming contribution to the blog *Food, Fatness, and Fitness—Critical Perspectives!*, "The Shape of Feminism."

Margaret J. Yankovich is a graduate of Rutgers University School of Communication and Information, where she received an MI in Library Science. Previously she attended Chatham College for Women in Pittsburgh, Pennsylvania, where she earned a BA in English and Cultural Studies. A public librarian, she is employed as the head of information at the Dorchester County Public Library in Cambridge, Maryland. In addition to her work as a librarian serving her small community on the Eastern Shore, Margaret also works as an independent scholar of horror media. Her interests span a range of topics within horror film and literature, including body horror, monstrosity, queer theory, disability studies, and fat studies. In recent years, she has presented her work at the Southwest Popular/American Culture Association and the Popular Culture Association annual conferences. Her first peer-reviewed article, "'Let Me Rip You, Let Me Tear You, Let Me Kill You': Reading *Harry Potter and the Chamber of Secrets* as a Horror Text" was published in the inaugural issue of Southern Illinois University's *Journal of Fantasy and Fan Cultures* in the winter of 2020.

INDEX

CPSIA information can be obtained
at www.ICGtesting.com
Printed in the USA
BVHW040037200822
644981BV00003B/11

9 781496 842237